ORGANIZATIONAL PERCEPTION MANAGEMENT

LEA'S ORGANIZATION AND MANAGEMENT SERIES

Series Editors
Arthur P. Brief
Tulane University

James P. Walsh
University of Michigan

Associate Series Editor
Sara L. Rynes
University of Iowa

Ashforth (Au.): *Role Transitions in Organizational Life: An Identity-Based Perspective.*

Bartunek (Au): *Organizational and Educational Change: The Life and Role of a Change Agent Group.*

Beach (Ed.): *Image Theory: Theoretical and Empirical Foundations.*

Brett/Drasgow (Eds.): *The Psychology of Work: Theoretically Based Empirical Research.*

Darley/Messick/Tyler (Eds.): *Social Influences on Ethical Behavior in Organizations.*

Denison (Ed.): *Managing Organizational Change in Transition Economies.*

Earley/Gibson (Aus.): *Multinational Work Teams: A New Perspective.*

Elsbach (Au): *Organizational Perception Management*

Garud/Karnoe (Eds.): *Path Dependence and Creation.*

Jacoby (Au.): *Employing Bureaucracy: Managers, Unions, and the Transformation of Work in the 20th Century, Second Edition.*

Kossek/Lambert (Eds.): *Work and Life Integration: Organizational, Cultural and Individual Perspectives.*

Lampel/Shamsie/Lant (Eds.): *The Business of Culture: Strategic Perspectives on Entertainment and Media.*

Lant/Shapira (Eds.): *Organizational Cognition: Computation and Interpretation.*

Lord/Brown (Aus.): *Leadership Processes and Follower Self-Identity.*

Margolis/Walsh (Aus.): *People and Profits? The Search Between a Company's Social and Financial Performance.*

Messick/Kramer (Aus.): *The Psychology of Leadership: Some New Approaches.*

Pearce (Au.): *Organization and Management in the Embrace of the Government.*

Peterson/Mannix (Eds.): *Leading and Managing People in the Dynamic Organization.*

Rafaeli/Pratt (Eds.): *Artifacts and Organizations: Beyond Mere Symbolism*

Riggio/Murphy/Pirozzolo (Eds.): *Multiple Intelligences and Leadership.*

Schneider/Smith (Eds.): *Personality and Organizations.*

Thompson/Choi (Eds.): *Creativity and Innovation in Organizational Teams.*

Thompson/Levine/Messick (Eds.): *Shared Cognition in Organizations: The Management of Knowledge.*

For more information about books in this series, please contact LEA at www.erlbaum.com

ORGANIZATIONAL PERCEPTION MANAGEMENT

Kimberly D. Elsbach

University of California, Davis

 LAWRENCE ERLBAUM ASSOCIATES, PUBLISHERS
2006   Mahwah, New Jersey   London

MW

Lawrence Erlbaum Associates, Inc., Publishers
10 Industrial Avenue
Mahwah, New Jersey 07430
www.erlbaum.com

Cover design by Tomai Maridou

Library of Congress Cataloging-in-Publication Data

Elsbach, Kimberly D.
Organizational perception management / Kimberly D. Elsbach
        p. cm.

Includes bibliographical references and index.
ISBN 0-8058-4795-2 (cloth : alk. paper)
ISBN 0-8058-4796-0 (pbk. : alk. paper)
1. Corporate image.   2. Organizational behavior.   I. Title.
HD59.2.E38 2006
659.2—dc22   2005049472
                                                       CIP

Books published by Lawrence Erlbaum Associates are printed on
acid-free paper, and their bindings are chosen for strength and durability.
Printed in the United States of America
10 9 8 7 6 5 4 3 2 1

12/4/06

For Jan Kees and Racha

Contents

Series Foreword

An organization's image, identity, and reputation are very important stuff. Scholars and practitioners alike have paid increasing attention to how organizations are perceived. Despite this attention, the scholarly literature has yet to be brought together in any comprehensive way, much less interpreted sensitively. Kim Elsbach has done this and more. We are most impressed with the research agenda she identifies. It will command our attention for years to come. We are proud to have Kim's book in the Series. Indeed, we are confident that it will become "the book" on the perception of organizations.

—*Arthur P. Brief*
Tulane University

—*James P. Walsh*
University of Michigan

About the Author

 **Kimberly D. Elsbach** is Professor of Management and Chancellor's Fellow at the Graduate School of Management (GSM) at the University of California, Davis. She is also the Director of Executive Education at the GSM. Kim's current research focuses on the perception and management of individual and organizational images, identities, and reputations. She has studied these symbolic processes in variety of contexts ranging from the California cattle industry and the National Rifle Association to radical environmentalist groups and toy designers. Her recent work on assessing creativity images during Hollywood pitch meetings earned the Outstanding Publication in Organizational Behavior Award (2004) and the Best Paper Award (2004) from the *Academy of Management Journal*. Kim is currently the program director for the Organization and Management Theory Division of the Academy of Management and co-organizes the Annual Davis Conference on Qualitative Research.

BS University of Iowa, 1985; MS University of Iowa, 1987; PhD Stanford University, 1993.

Preface

This book summarizes the research findings from a relatively new domain of study called *organizational perception management* (OPM). Although perception management has been studied at the individual level since the 1960s, organization-level perception management (i.e., tactics designed to affect perceptions of the image, identity, or reputation of an organization) was first examined in the 1980s through the study of corporate annual reports and their effects on organizational reputations. In the subsequent decades, empirical studies have expanded the domain of organizational perception management to include the management of organizational identities (e.g., what it means to be a "green" organization), as well as the strategic management of specialized organizational images for specific audiences (e.g., what images to present to stockholders vs. consumers).

The goals of this book are to summarize and organize this evolving literature to provide a complete and comprehensive definition of OPM events and tactics, illustrate OPM events and tactics in specific, real-world contexts, and identify a set of research themes that may stimulate further research on OPM. The book is grounded, primarily, in empirical research on OPM, including qualitative field research. It uses current case studies to illustrate the application and effectiveness of OPM in context. As such, this book is intended for students, scholars, and practitioners of organizational management.

1

Overview

In 1997, the United States Internal Revenue Service (IRS) announced that it was changing. In a series of advertisements, broadcast through TV, radio, and newspapers, the organization that Americans loved to hate—the one that *Newsweek* once dubbed "The Infernal Revenue Service" (Sloan, 1998, p. 12)—claimed that it was becoming a new, kinder, gentler organization that aimed to serve the public in a more user-friendly manner. The impetus for the change was the passage of the IRS reform bill, signed by President Bill Clinton, which shifted the burden of proof in tax disputes from the taxpayer to the IRS and outlined 28 new taxpayer rights including the right of taxpayers to sue the IRS for negligence (Brazaitis, 1997). Journalists speculated that Clinton was influenced by an opinion poll that showed 81% of Americans believed that the IRS had "too much power" (Brazaitis, 1997, p. 16A) and 69% believed that the IRS "frequently abuses its power" (Haga, 1998, p. 1B).

One of the first moves made by the IRS to change its image was to sponsor "problem-solving days" in 33 cities across the United States (Lakamp, 1997). Wearing buttons that read "We Work for You," IRS employees helped taxpayers to sort out problems with tax returns from the current year and from years past. Understanding the image the IRS had with most taxpayers, one IRS worker noted, "We want people not to be afraid of us" (Brelis, 1997, p. B1). Another said, "I don't think we can ever get people to love us. Hopefully we can get them to respect us.... You're going to see a kinder and gentler IRS" (Wiseman et al., 1997, p. 3A).

Reaction from taxpayers was generally positive. Although not everybody had their problems solved, most admitted that they felt better after their encounters with the IRS. Some even expressed surprise at how "nice" the IRS folks could be. "It was wonderful," one said, and another noted, "I've never seen so many polite IRS people" (Brelis, 1997, p. B1). In one instance, a taxpayer who ended up having to pay more than he thought said he was, nevertheless, happy and noted, "They were fair. They didn't say pay it all now or you're dead. That's why I'm smiling" (Wiseman et al., 1997, p. 3A).

In the months to come, the IRS continued to implement changes, including a media campaign, in attempts to counter its bad-guy image. Although some of the reforms may have been window dressing, most observers believed that the IRS was really changing and believed its image management slogans, which emphasized "service, integrity, and fairness" as its missions (Crenshaw, 2001, p. H2). In fact, the campaign worked so well that by 2001 the IRS reported that it had a new problem—catching all the new tax cheats that were attempting to prey on the new, historically low audit rates. It seems that the new perception taxpayers had of the IRS was not only that of a nicer organization but also that of a more vulnerable one. In the end, the lesson for organizations may be that, when it comes to perception management, nothing is simple or straightforward.

EXTANT RESEARCH ON ORGANIZATIONAL PERCEPTION MANAGEMENT

The phenomenon of organizational perception management is hardly new. The efforts of organizational spokespersons to protect and manage positive images, identities, or reputations of their organizations can be found in historical accounts of the Roman Catholic Church and of the universities of ancient Greece. The same perception management problems that plagued these early organizations (e.g., threats of illegitimacy due to changes in social norms, face-saving following scandals or accidents) continue to plague organizations today. During the past 25 years, as the study of social science has evolved, these types of issues have been studied by organizational scholars in attempts to understand how perception management tactics affect the views and support of organizations by critical audiences (i.e., those audiences on which the organization depends for support). This volume provides an overview of this research and presents a framework that defines the primary components of organizational perception management as well as the effective use of organizational perception management in several common contexts. In this chapter, I provide an overview of the study of organizational perception management and an outline of the chapters to follow.

DOMINANT THEMES IN CURRENT RESEARCH

Over the last two decades, research on organizational perception management has focused on three dominant themes: timing, goals, and tactics. An examination of progress in these three areas suggests that effective organizational perception management is contextually defined and may be best understood through examinations of perception management case studies in situ.

First, for example, organizational perception management includes an exploration of timing in dealing with organizational images, identities, and reputations. Typically coming to mind when we think of organizational perception management are news releases and media campaigns immediately following crises like the Exxon Valdez oil spill or the Union Carbide poisoning in Bhopal, India. Yet in recent years organizational researchers have begun to explore long-term perception management issues as well as perception management before and during focal events. Research on the symbolic use of annual reports (Bettman & Weitz, 1983; Staw, McKechnie, & Puffer, 1983), for example, demonstrates how organizations routinely manage perceptions of managerial competence and organizational legitimacy through strategic attributions of corporate successes or failures, despite the absence of any crisis event or emergency. Such attributions may be effective, in part, because of the seemingly official nature of annual reports. In other research, recent studies of anticipatory perception management (Elsbach, Sutton, & Principe, 1998) describe how organizations may pre-empt threats to organizational images by portraying the organizations in ways that motivate audiences to accept organizational actions without question prior to an expected controversy (e.g., an anticipated plant closing or voluntary recall of a defective product). In these cases, the prior track record of legitimate behavior by the organization is often critical to audiences' acceptance of pre-emptive perception management.

Second, organizational researchers have begun to focus broadly on a number of different goals of perception management. In the Exxon and Union Carbide examples, the primary goal appears to be to repair temporarily damaged organizational images (e.g., images of legitimacy or competency). More recently, however, organizational researchers have focused on the management of more enduring organizational reputations (e.g., reputations for social responsibility) and identities (e.g., identities centered on style and design vs. efficiency and economy). For instance, research on business school members' responses to the *Business Week* rankings

(Elsbach & Kramer, 1996) shows the importance of central and distinctive organizational identity traits to members (e.g., being defined as a "research institute"). In other cases (Elsbach, 2001a), researchers have shown the value of general organizational reputations, such as organizational trustworthiness (e.g., consumer loyalty to a trusted automotive repair center that is part of a large department store chain), and the damage that can result from reputational threats (e.g., consumer distrust of the entire department store chain). The distinctive dimensions of organizational images, identities, and reputations suggests that managing these diverse perceptions requires equally distinctive goals.

Third, organizational research during the past several decades has focused on the tactics organizational spokespersons use to influence audiences' perceptions of organizations. In recent years this research has looked beyond the use of official public relations communications, such as press releases and advertising campaigns, to a broader range of tactics for managing images, reputations, and identities. For example, research on the display of physical markers, such as the design of corporate buildings and public reception areas (Ornstein, 1986, 1992), reveals how these physical artifacts are often central means of communicating the organizations' enduring reputations. In other cases, specific types of organizational actions (e.g., contributions to charity or accounting reports) have been shown to be useful in managing the reputation of a firm for social responsibility and financial soundness (Fombrun & Shanley, 1990). Finally, statements by CEOs and other leaders in response to public criticisms of organizations are now seen as a part of a longer term, negotiated perception management process that involves a dialogue between the press, institutional critics, the general public, and the organization (Sutton & Kramer, 1990). This form of perception management involves negotiation tactics as well as influence tactics to convince audiences to back the version of the story given by the organization.

Together, these three themes in organizational perception management research suggest that the task of managing perceptions of organizations is larger than merely responding to the rare organizational crisis. It involves managing day-to-day communications and organizational displays as well as preparing for future controversies or the return of old ones. Further, this research suggests that understanding the subtleties of organizational perception management requires a examination of perception management in context. The social and institutional environments in which organizations operate play critical roles in the processes and outcomes of organizational perception management actions.

OUTLINE OF THE BOOK

In this volume, my goals are to bring together these more recent and broad conceptions of timing, goals, and tactics of organizational perception management in an integrating framework, to illustrate that framework in the context of recent, real-world perception management events, and to use the framework as a starting point for extending our understanding of organizational perception management. To these ends, I divide the book into three parts: defining organizational perception management, illustrating organizational perception management in context, and exploring emerging issues in organizational perception management.

In Chapter 2, I define the construct of organizational perception management. This chapter serves to develop organizational perception management as an umbrella term that encompasses organizational image management, reputation management, and identity management. In defining organizational perception management, I focus on four dimensions of the construct: the specific perceptions of organizations that are managed, the symbolic actions that are used to manage perceptions, the spokespersons who carry out most of these symbolic acts, and the audiences that are the targets of organizational perception management. Further, I differentiate organizational perception management from individual-level perception management by explicating the strategic nature of organization-level perception management. I illustrate the construct of organizational perception management with a case study of the National Rifle Association.

In the next five chapters of the book, I illustrate the practice of organizational perception management in context. Chapter 3 provides an overview of these contexts based on two factors: when perception management takes place and why it is needed. Using these two factors, I describe six different contexts in which organizational perception management may occur. These include before, during, and after organizational controversies and before, during, and after organizational acclaim events (i.e., events that reflect positively on the organization). In Chapters 4 through 7, I examine these six contexts in detail and describe and illustrate effective organizational perception management for each.

In Chapter 4, I describe perception management following organizational crisis events. I describe common organizational crisis events, such as accidents, scandals, and product failures, as well as the effective use of verbal accounts and categorizations in responding to these crises. In addition, I outline three pitfalls of using perception management following organizational crisis, including threat rigidity, self-deception, and protesting too much. I illustrate these pitfalls through a case study of Sears Auto Centers and its response to the 1992 investigation of its Auto Centers

In Chapter 5, I describe organizational perception management during evolving controversies. These types of controversies are characterized by drawn-out change events or negotiations in which one or more organizational audiences disagrees with the direction of change. This chapter also includes descriptions of some of the effective perception management tactics that have been used in these contexts, including verbal accounts that demonstrate consideration and rationality and organizational categorizations that signal status and distinctiveness. I also present pitfalls of organizational perception during evolving controversies such as escalation behaviors and inconsistent behaviors. I conclude the chapter with an illustration of ineffective perception management by the Augusta National Golf Club and its evolving controversy over admitting women as members.

In Chapter 6, I describe how organizations may manage identities and reputations prior to anticipated controversies. Such anticipated controversies include upcoming performance reviews and the planned introduction of new identity statements or new core businesses. In response to these anticipated controversies, I describe how organizations may effectively protect their identities and reputations through anticipatory accounts and strategic renaming. I also describe some pitfalls of these tactics, such as defensive overcompensation and overweighting of low probability events. I illustrate the effective use of anticipatory perception management through the case of the automaker Porsche and its introduction of its sport utility vehicle, the Cayenne.

In Chapter 7, I focus on organizational perception management following acclaim events, such as being positively recognized by an industry analyst or evaluator or achieving a sought-after organizational goal. Following such positive events, I describe how organizations may make the most of their good fortune through perception management tactics such as exclusive self-categorizations, entitlings (i.e., claims of responsibility for the positive event), and the display of prominent physical markers. I also draw attention to some potential pitfalls of perception management following organizational acclaim events, including producing unrealistically high expectations of future performance and engaging in self-aggrandizement by organizational leaders. I illustrate the effective use of organizational perception management following an acclaim event with a case study of the pharmaceutical company Pfizer Inc. and its introduction of the impotence drug Viagra.

Finally, in the last section of the book, I explore some emerging issues in organizational perception management that may benefit from the application of the current framework of organizational perception management. Thus, in chapter 8, I focus on the increasingly discussed topic of corporate ethics by describing two emerging contexts in which organizational perception management is relevant: leadership behavior following organizational scandals and organizational identity issues concurrent with the launch of a non-normative social responsibility campaign. In discussing the issue of leadership following scandals, I use the recent case of the Catholic Church sex abuse scandal to illustrate some of the traps organizations can fall into if they attempt to project strong leadership images following scandals. I follow this case study with a discussion of some more effective uses of perception management for leaders who find themselves embroiled in organizational scandals. Next, in discussing the issue of social responsibility campaigns, I use the case of British Petroleum and its groundbreaking efforts to reduce greenhouse gas emissions during energy production to illustrate how organizations need to be mindful of their historic identities when undertaking a non-normative but ideological campaign. I describe how British Petroleum successfully managed its identity by using the strategy of optimal distinctiveness (Brewer, 1991) in its categorization tactics.

Overall, this volume presents the first comprehensive examination of perception management issues, tactics, and effects at the organizational level of analysis. Further, it incorporates scholarly research with real-world business cases to illustrate both the effective and the ineffective application of perception management in a variety of specific contexts. As such, the book is intended to promote the area of organizational perception management as a field of study in its own right, worthy of much future research.

I

Defining Organizational
Perception Management

2

Defining Organizational Perception Management

In the waning months of 1996 the National Rifle Association (NRA) found itself at a low-point in terms of public perceptions and support. Over the previous 2 years, the nonprofit organization—incorporated in 1871 to provide firearms training and promote shooting sports—had been forced to end its high-profile assignment as the governing body for the Olympic sport of shooting (Longman, 1994), had lost almost 1 million dues-paying members (Broder, 1996), and had run up a debt of more than $40 million in its attempts to promote pro-gun legislation (Zremski, 1996). These events reflected growing criticism of the organization by mainstream gun owners.

Beginning in the early 1980s, the NRA began to shift its focus, almost completely, from its traditions of supporting sportsmen and hunters to supporting political battles over gun control (Zremski, 1996). The organization's extreme political stance on gun control was embodied by NRA president, Wayne LaPierre. In late 1996, LaPierre claimed that the government agents who stormed the Waco, Texas compound of the Branch Davidian cult (whose members were protecting themselves with an arsenal of personally owned firearms) were no more than "jack-booted thugs" (Zremski, 1996, p. 1A). This remark led former president George H. W. Bush to tear up his NRA membership card publicly and eventually led LaPierre to step down from his position in the organization.

In light of these events, the activist group Handgun Control Inc., through its legislative director, suggested, in late 1996, that the NRA was in "very severe difficulty," adding that "its political clout is diminished, and its very future is in doubt" (Broder, 1996, p. A14). In short, it appeared that perceptions of the NRA, among both members and potential members, were increasingly negative. The organization was clearly in need of perception management.

DIMENSIONS OF ORGANIZATIONAL PERCEPTION MANAGEMENT

Organizational perception management involves actions that are designed and carried out by organizational spokespersons to influence audiences' perceptions of the organization. This definition is grounded in psychological research on individual perception management (Leary, 1996; Schlenker, 1980; Tedeschi, 1981), as well as in empirical studies of perception management strategies used by organizations (Elsbach, 2001b; Marcus & Goodman, 1991; Staw et al., 1983). The definition contains four components that are important to understanding the unique nature of organizational perception management: (1) perceptions of the organization, (2) actions or tactics, (3) organizational spokespersons, and (4) organizational audiences. The purpose of this chapter is to explicate and illustrate these four components, which are summarized in Fig. 2.1.

1. Perceptions of the Organization

Organizational perception management is designed to influence audience perceptions of the organization as an entity or whole. Such perceptions include organizational images (e.g., organizational legitimacy or trustworthiness), reputations (e.g., being known as a tough competitor), and identities (e.g., organizational categorizations, such as being top tier). In many cases, perceptions of specific organizational actions (e.g., perceptions of organizational fairness in implementing a downsizing or the quality of organizational decision making that affected economic performance) may motivate organizational spokespersons to engage in perception management of the organization as a whole.[1]

Although prior research on organizational perception management has tended to treat these three perceptions (i.e., images, reputations, or identities) as interchangeable, recently, organizational scholars have made at-

---

[1]Interestingly, although perceptions of fair business practices by organizations are the focus of much of the research in organizational justice and organizational support (Cropanzano, 1993; Folger & Cropanzano, 1998), there is almost no research in these areas that examines intentional attempts to manage images of the fairness of the organization as a whole. This gap is discussed in terms of areas for future research later in this volume.

Perceptions	**Actions**

1. Organizational Images:
- organizational legitimacy
- organizational correctness
  and consistency
- organizational trustworthiness
 	
2.Organizational Reputations:
- status categorizations
- overall "quality"
 	
3. Organizational Identities:
- distinctive identities
- status identities
	1. Verbal Accounts
	- defensive accounts
	- accommodating accounts
	- accounts referring to norms
	- accounts including imagery
	- anticipatory accounts
	
	2. Categorizations/Labels
	- inclusive categorizations/labels
	- exclusive categorizations/labels
	
	3. Symbolic Business Behaviors
	- primary business activities
	- treatment of employees
	- affiliation with other groups
	- escalating commitment to a
	  chosen course of action
	
	4. Physical Markers
	- Permanent buildings/artifacts
	- Logos, letterhead, signs
	- office decor and layout

Spokespersons	**Audiences**	
1. Leaders and officials 2. Employees	1. Internal audiences 2. External audiences	FIG. 2.1. Components of Organizational Perception Management.

tempts to distinguish these three types of organizational perceptions from one another (Schultz, Hatch, & Larsen, 2000). This research suggests that organizational images, reputations, and identities may be compared and contrasted along four dimensions: their primary perceivers, their defining categorizations, their typical endurance, and their specificity. In the following sections and Table 2.1, I describe how organizational images, reputations, and identities are defined by these four dimensions. I also illustrate the most common forms of these three types of organizational perceptions.

Organizational Images

Research on organizational perception management suggests that organizational images are relatively current and temporary perceptions of an organization, held by internal or external audiences, regarding the fit of an

TABLE 2.1

Comparing Organizational Images, Reputations, and Identities

	Organizational Image	Organizational Reputation	Organizational Identity
Primary perceivers	Insiders and outsiders	Outsiders	Insiders
Defining categorizations	Distinctiveness	Status	Distinctiveness and status
Typical endurance	Short-lived	Long-lived	Long-lived
Specificity	Specific	General	General and specific
Common impression management context	Organizational crises: -Industrial accidents -Product recall	Organizational competition: -Performance Reports -Quality Ranking	Organizational change: -Leadership change -Product/service change

organization with particular distinctiveness categories (e.g., organizational legitimacy, organizational correctness and consistency, organizational trustworthiness; Elsbach & Sutton, 1992; Hatch & Schultz, 2000; Mayer, Davis, & Schoorman, 1995; Ross & Staw, 1993). This definition suggests that organizational images are relatively short-lived, specific perceptions of an organization and that organizations may possess several distinct images at the same time. Organizational researchers define what insiders think outsiders think of the organization as construed external image (i.e., they suggest that insiders can have an image of the organization; Dutton, Dukerich, & Harquail, 1994; Gioia & Thomas, 1996). By contrast, organizational reputation and perception management researchers commonly refer to organizational images as specific attributions of an organization by external audiences (Fombrun, 1996; Sutton & Callahan, 1987). Thus, it appears that there is evidence that both insiders and outsiders have images of organization. This finding distinguishes organizational images from organizational identities and reputations (defined later), which tend to be more enduring, are more likely to be defined by status-oriented categorizations of the organization, and are defined by either internal or external audiences but not both.

Organizational Legitimacy. The most commonly studied organizational image is organizational legitimacy (see Elsbach, 2001b, for a review). Organizational legitimacy is defined as "a generalized perception or assumption that the actions of an entity are desirable, proper, or appropriate within some socially constructed system of norms, values, beliefs, and definitions" (Suchman, 1995, p. 574). Organizations may acquire pragmatic legitimacy (i.e., perceived as legitimate because they serve some practical interest, such as increasing shareholder wealth) or moral legitimacy (i.e., perceived as legitimate because their actions are in line with social norms; Suchman, 1995). Legitimate organizations and their leaders are perceived as "more worthy ... more meaningful, more predictable, and more trustworthy" (p. 575) than illegitimate organizations. As a result, organizations perceived as legitimate are likely to receive unquestioned support and resources from constituents (Ashforth & Gibbs, 1990; Tyler, 1990). Legitimate organizations are also more likely to gain the commitment, attachment, and identification of members (Lind & Tyler, 1988; Mueller, Boyer, Price, & Iverson, 1994).

Organizational researchers studying legitimacy have typically been concerned with how firms use their legitimacy as a resource to attract and maintain valued stakeholders (i.e., employees, customers, favorable media representatives, industry analysts, concerned public citizens; Suchman, 1995). The opinions of these stakeholders can influence the bottom line for the organization. For example, organizational strategy researchers have shown that corporate legitimacy allows firms to command premium prices from loyal customers and helps firms to gain recommendations from industry experts without excessive advertising or promotional expenditures (Weigelt & Camerer, 1988). This focus on legitimacy as a resource for improving firm performance differs from the approach of much psychological research, which tends to view individual legitimacy as an attribute that is valued in and of itself (Darley & Zelditch, 2001).

A growing body of research suggests that the value of legitimacy for organizations and their spokespersons is most evident in times of crisis or controversy when legitimacy is challenged or threatened (Chen & Meindl, 1991; Elsbach & Sutton, 1992). When organizational legitimacy is called into question, public support and the positive portrayal of the organization by the media may diminish (Marcus & Goodman, 1991). For example, following the consumer fraud investigation of its auto repair shops in 1992, retail giant Sears, Roebuck & Co. suffered its first quarterly loss in profits since the Great Depression. Sears attributed much of this loss to a 10 to 15 percent decline in automotive repair sales and the $27 million settlement in its consumer fraud case (see Chapter 4 in this volume for more on this case).

Organizational Correctness and Consistency.   A second kind of organizational image that has been an increasing focus of research is organizational correctness and consistency (Staw & Ross, 1987). Much of the work on images of correctness and consistency has focused on the escalation behaviors of top managers who are responsible for decisions regarding ongoing organizational projects (e.g., a negotiation, a merger, a new product launch). This research suggests that when decision makers are known to have been individually responsible for past decisions to support a project or course of action, they will make future decisions in line with that past support (i.e., they will escalate their commitment to the past decision). They reason that such behavior will lead others to view them as correct in their past decisions and consistent in their thinking (see Brockner, 1992, for a review).

Similarly, a few studies have examined escalation behaviors by top management teams (McNamara, Moon, & Bromiley, 2002; Ross & Staw, 1986, 1993). Research on escalation in such group situations suggests that the need to manage images of correctness and consistency are increased in group situations because groups tend to polarize the initial attitudes of groups members (Brockner, 1992). For example, Ross and Staw (1993) described the organizational escalations that occurred during building of the Shoreham nuclear power plant. They describe how decisions by the Long Island Lighting Company (LILCO) to continue to support the nuclear power plant project—despite growing evidence that the costs were severely underestimated—were influenced, in part, by the desire for the company to maintain images of correctness and consistency (Ross & Staw, 1993). The top management of LILCO perceived a threat to the organization's images of correctness and consistency when stockholders and the public utilities commission challenged them to defend their investment decisions. In response to these image threats, top management attempted to justify its past decisions and maintain its images of correctness and consistency by continuing to back its original plan to build and run the plant.

Organizational Trustworthiness.   A third type of organizational image that has become a popular topic is organizational trustworthiness (Elsbach, 2004b). Recent work has defined the image of organizational trustworthiness as the perception that an organization displays competence, benevolence, and integrity in its behaviors and beliefs (Mayer et al., 1995). In this definition, competence refers to the abilities and skills that allow an organization to achieve desired goals, benevolence refers to the apparent willingness of an organization to do good, and integrity refers to adherence to principles or ideals that conform to social norms (Mayer, Schoorman, & Davis, 1995).

Research on perceptions of organizational trustworthiness among employees have shown that equity in compensation practices may be a focal point for determining the integrity and trustworthiness of the actions of an organization (Pearce, 1993; Pearce, Branyiczki, & Bakacsi, 1994). By contrast, when external audiences (e.g., stockholders, potential business partners) gauge the trustworthiness of organizations, they appear to look to the culture and control systems of the organization (Barney & Hansen, 1994). According to strategy theorists, if an organization is viewed by external audiences as having a culture and a set of control systems that are consistent with normative values, standards, and principles of behavior, then it will be perceived as trustworthy. In both cases of internal and external perceptions, organizational trustworthiness appears to be dependent on the presence of industry or organizational structures and procedures that delimit organizational action. By contrast, research suggests that compliance to broad societal norms are more likely to influence images of individual trustworthiness (Elsbach, 2003a).

Organizational Reputations

Organizational reputations involve enduring status categorizations of the quality of an organization as perceived by external audiences and stakeholders. Organizational reputations differ from organizational images by their general nature and endurance, their focus on status, and their importance to outsiders primarily. First, reputations are more general than are images. As Cowden and Sellnow (2002) noted, "image reflects a set of specific associations, whereas reputation denotes an overall judgment regarding the extent to which a firm is held [over time] in high esteem or regard" (p. 199). Similarly, Fombrun (199) defined organizational reputation as "the overall estimation in which a company is held by its constituents" (p. 37). Fombrun's (1996) framework of organizational reputations suggests that this overall reputation is based on perceptions of the reliability, credibility, social responsibility, and trustworthiness of the organization, and further, Theus' (1993) study of the broad attributes that make up perceptions of organizational reputations among American universities showed that "quality" is largely viewed as synonymous with the notion of "good reputation" (although the researchers noted that quality itself can refer to a variety of organizational dimensions).

Another characteristic of reputations is that they often denote relative status or ranking (but may include status based on a distinct trait, such as "best small school" or "most admired large company"). Organizational reputations have, thus, been defined as external audiences' enduring perceptions of how a "firm's products, jobs, strategies, and prospects compare to those of competing firms" (Fombrun & Shanley, 1990, p. 37). In support of this notion, Rindova, Williamson, & Petkova, (2005) showed that the reputations of U.S. business schools can be defined by both the perceived quality of their products and their perceived prominence among peer schools. Further, they found that both prominence and quality of products arose from endorsements from influential external parties (e.g., faculty publications in high-status journals or attendance by applicants with high test scores). As such, Rindova et al. provided evidence that organizational reputation is centrally defined by relative status categorizations and comparisons. By contrast, organizational images are defined primarily by distinctiveness categorizations (i.e., being legitimate, rather than being the "most" legitimate).

Finally, organizational researchers have commonly agreed that reputation is both perceived and legitimated by external audiences (vs. internal audiences; Dukerich & Carter, 2000; Dutton et al., 1994; Fombrun & Rindova, 2000). Thus, external audiences such as consumers or potential members who are searching for the best organization to meet their needs may routinely use the reputation of an organization to gauge its overall quality.

Reputations and Strategy. Theory and research on organizational reputations has come primarily from the domain of strategy. In particular, strategy researchers have identified two perspectives on the use and management of organization reputations: resource-based views (Wernerfelt, 1984) and market-based views (Milgrom & Roberts, 1982). Resource-based views of organizations focus on the capabilities, attributes, and resources of a firm that are distinctive, rare, durable, and generally inimitable. One key resource is the reputation of the firm: "Intangible resources such as reputation significantly contribute to performance differences among organizations because they are rare, socially complex, and difficult to trade and imitate" (Rao, 1994, p. 29). In contrast, market-based views of organizations focus on reputations as strategic attributes that firms use to gain a competitive advantage in incomplete information settings (Milgrom & Roberts, 1982, 1986). In these cases, outsiders are forced, by their lack of information, to predict the future decisions of a firm based solely on its past behavior (Camerer

& Vepsalainen, 1988). A significant amount of research in both para-digms has shown that attractive or distinctive reputations favorably in-fluence organizational customers and competitors when making these predictions. Researchers have also shown that positive corporate repu-tations improve inter-organizational bargaining outcomes, allow firms to command premium prices, and help firms to gain support and re-sources from primary constituents (D'Aveni & O'Neill, 1992; Tsui, 1990; Weigelt & Camerer, 1988).

Cognitive Antecedents of Reputations. In recent years, organiza-tions scholars have built on this strategy work and have focused on the cognitive and social antecedents of organizational reputation (Fombrun, 1996; Mohamed, Orife, & Slack, 2001). These studies suggest that the stability and positiveness of the performance of an organization will help its audiences form enduring perceptions of the firm. In particular, these studies suggest that stability or consistency in behavior and performance is important in reputation building because it helps increase audiences' confidence that they can predict future performance based on the past (Weigelt & Camerer, 1988). In addition, researchers have shown that pos-itive performance is important to reputation building because it helps au-diences to categorize individual organizations on status-relevant traits (Shrum & Wuthnow, 1988). In this vein, Staw and Epstein (2000) found that companies that routinely adopted new management techniques (e.g., total quality management programs) gained a reputation for being more innovative than peer organizations that did not adopt these techniques. Ultimately, the techniques were shown to have no effect on organizational performance, and the researchers suggested that they were adopted, pri-marily because they provided a salient and consistent signal about the rep-utation of the organization for innovation.

Organizational Identities

An organization's identity is the answer to members' question: "Who are we?" (Dutton et al., 1994; Elsbach, 1999). The answer may be relatively complex and may include both status (e.g., top tier) and distinctiveness (e.g., creative) categorizations, as well as specific (e.g., the most family-friendly company in Sacramento, California) and general (e.g., one of the most admired companies in America) foci that define the organization (Hatch & Schultz, 2000). By contrast, organizational images or organiza-tional reputations typically answer questions about the organization's fit with one type of distinctiveness or status categorization at a time. Similar to organizational reputations, organizational identities are commonly perceived as enduring (Dutton et al., 1994), yet researchers have suggested that they are not immutable (Gioia & Thomas, 1996) and that identity management can successfully change an organization's identity (Elsbach & Bhattacharya, 2001). Based on these findings, organizational identities may be conceptualized as insiders' relatively enduring perceptions of the fit of their organization with distinctiveness categorizations and status categorizations along both general and specific dimensions (Dutton & Penner, 1993; Dutton et al., 1994; Hatch & Schultz, 2000; Kramer, 1993).

Relating Individual and Organizational Identities. Individual members who identify with their organization (i.e., who define their own self-concepts, in part, by their memberships in the organization and who perceive their identities to overlap with the identity of the organization) are likely to perceive that their own identities are threatened by events that threaten the identity of the organization (Dutton et al., 1994). As a result, organizational identity management may be motivated as much by members' desires to maintain positive perceptions of their own individual identities as by desires to maintain positive perceptions of the identity of the organization (Elsbach & Kramer, 1996). This link between individual and organizational identities also makes the management of organizational identities more complex because individual members often vary in terms of their level and focus of identification with the organization. For example, individuals who strongly identify with the identity of an organization as top-tier may engage in symbolic actions to affirm that status categorization (e.g., stating the organization's ranking in news interviews), whereas other individuals who weakly identify with the status categorization of top-tier may opt out of such identity affirmation or even disidentify with that aspect of identity by refuting the validity of status categorizations (Elsbach & Bhattacharya, 2001).

Multiple Organizational Identities. Further complicating the management of organizational identities is the fact that organizations may be defined by more than one identity (e.g., a hospital may have both humanitarian and business identities). In some cases, these multiple identities may appear to be in conflict with one another. That is, organizations may have hybrid identities that are "composed of two or more [identities] that would not normally be expected to go together" (Albert

& Whetten, 1985, p. 270). For example, Elsbach (2001a) described the California State Legislature as defined both by an often-derided political identity and by a more noble and contrasting policy-making identity. In other cases, these multiple identities may define distinct yet compatible aspects of the organization (e.g., a university that prides itself on both excellent teaching and research). Such dual identities may support each other (e.g., research informs teaching, and teaching provides a context for research), and, because these distinct identities are often not vulnerable to the same types of threats, may provide a good offense against overall identity damage (e.g., a university that loses a top researcher to a rival institution can still tout its excellent teaching faculty; Elsbach & Kramer, 1996).

2. Symbolic Actions

Symbolic actions include any activities by organizational spokespersons that are used, at least in part, to affect audience perceptions of the organization. Such actions may be primarily symbolic (e.g., changing the name *Kentucky Fried Chicken* to *KFC*—to minimize unhealthy images associated with the word *fried*—without actually changing the menu) or may be primarily practical (e.g., adopting, without fanfare or publicity, a total quality management program based on a desire to improve product quality), or they may be somewhere in between. In most cases, researchers have not been able to separate the symbolic from the practical aspects of such actions completely, and they suggest that most cases of organizational perception management involve both (Russ, 1991).

Research in this area suggests four specific types of symbolic actions used to manage organizational impressions: (a) verbal accounts (e.g., justifications for a corporate downsizing included in an annual report), (b) distinctiveness and status-oriented categorizations or labeling of organizations (e.g., defining a business school as top tier in promotional materials), (c) symbolic business behaviors (e.g., contribution to charitable foundations and causes), and (d) the display of physical markers (e.g., American flags hung in retail stores following the September 11, 2001 terrorist acts).

Verbal Accounts

Psychological frameworks of individual and organizational perception management define verbal accounts as explanations that are designed to influence perceptions of an organization's or person's responsibility for an event, or for the valence of an event (i.e., whether it is seen as positive or negative; Schlenker, 1980; Tedeschi, 1981). Verbal accounts, which have been studied more than any other type of organizational perception management tactic, are used primarily to manage external organizational images and reputations (vs. internal identities). Organizational research on the use of verbal accounts has defined three primary features of accounts: form, content, and communication medium.

Account Forms. A number of common account forms are used following negatively perceived events. *Excuses* are account forms that are designed to minimize perceptions of responsibility for a negative event (e.g., "it wasn't our fault"), whereas *justifications* are accounts that are designed to minimize the perceived negativity of an event when responsibility is not in question (e.g., "it wasn't as bad as you think" or "we had a good reason for doing it"). Similarly, *denials* are account forms that attempt to refute any responsibility for an event (e.g., "we didn't do it") or that claim that an event was not at all negative (e.g., "it didn't happen"), and *apologies* are accounts that accept full responsibility for a negative event but claim regret (e.g., "we did it, but we're sorry").

Other account forms are designed to follow positively perceived events. *Entitlings* are designed to increase perceptions of responsibility for a positive event (e.g., "we did it" or "we were more responsible than you think"), and *enhancements* are account forms designed to increase the perceived positiveness of an event when responsibility is admitted (e.g., "it was positive" or "it was better than you think").

Finally, some account forms are designed as responses to anticipated controversies, such as an impending announcement that may make an organization appear illegitimate to some audiences (e.g., the introduction of new nutritional guidelines that reveal that many processed foods have more fat than consumers were aware of; Hewitt & Stokes, 1975; Snyder, Higgins, & Stucky, 1983). Such anticipatory account forms include anticipatory excuses (e.g., "we weren't allowed to introduce our new low-fat line of foods before the guidelines came out") or anticipatory justifications (e.g., "the increased fat levels reported by the new guidelines reflect the high levels of *healthy fats* in our foods").

Rather than use these specific account form labels, many organizational studies characterize accounts that organizational spokespersons use fol-

"I've taken to working in my shirtsleeves. We might mention that in our annual report."

lowing negative events in more general terms, as *accommodative* or *defensive* accounts (Elsbach, 1994; Marcus & Goodman, 1991), and those that follow positive events as simply *acclaims* (Benoit, 1999). These same terms can be used to describe anticipatory accounts (i.e., anticipatory acclaims are used before potential positive events, whereas anticipatory defensive or accommodative accounts are used before potential negative events). These more general terms may have been used to describe the form of organizational accounts because such explanations tend to include more than one form of account (e.g., excuses and denials may be combined in defensive accounts, whereas justifications and enhancements may be combined in accommodative accounts) and because organizational accounts tend to be designed to meet more general goals than individual accounts such as defending organizational reputations for quality or appearing legitimate to broad audiences (Conlon & Murray, 1996).

In this vein, Sutton and Callahan (1987) studied an illustrative case of the use of defensive organizational accounts. In a study of firms who had filed for Chapter 11 bankruptcy protection, they found that organizational spokespersons commonly managed their images of legitimacy by combining the excuse that the bankruptcy was due to a national recession with the denial that a Chapter 11 filing was in fact a failure (i.e., they claimed that it was a normal and rational business procedure for an organization in certain circumstances). These defensive accounts suggested that the organization was attempting to pursue reasonable and logical goals but was thwarted by extenuating circumstances and was mistakenly attributed with a negative outcome.

In another example, Allen and Caillouet (1994) found that spokespersons for a recycling facility routinely responded to challenges to their organization's legitimacy (e.g., challenges from environmental groups like Greenpeace regarding its licensing status and disposal methods for hazardous waste by offering verbal accounts that combined denials of wrongdoing (e.g., "we're not an incinerator"; "we never put one drop of anything in the river") with denouncements of the challengers (e.g., "the Department of Environmental Quality is acting unlawfully, illegally, and totally outside their constitutional authority in making the latest hearing and other information requests of the organization"). By way of contrast, Allen and Caillouet (1994) found that the recycling facility also used a combination of enhancements (e.g., "The ... U.S. Patent office recognized (our) technology as the first and only process in the country with the ability to substitute large quantities of contaminated soils and other materials for feedstocks and still economically manufacture products that exhibit no hazardous characteristics") and flattery (e.g., "I want to applaud the efforts of the EPA ... for putting together a very fine and excellent draft permit") in acclaims that suggested that the evaluation of the facility was, in fact, a positive event.

In a third example, Elsbach's (1994) study of perception management in the California cattle industry revealed that spokespersons often combined justifications and enhancements in accommodative accounts they gave in response to public concerns about the potentially harmful effects of treating beef cattle with hormones. Some justified the use of hormones, arguing that the drugs helped to keep cattle healthy (i.e., a common concern of consumers), and added that the reduction in costs achieved by producing larger beef cattle was passed on to consumers as reduced prices (i.e., an enhancement). Finally, Zbaracki's (1998) discussion of the rhetoric and conversations used to justify and support the implementation of total quality management (TQM) practices showed how organizational leaders also spread success stories about TQM as a means of enhancing the overall image of legitimacy and efficiency of the organization.

Account Content. The content of accounts includes the arguments, evidence, and illustrations that back up the basic account form. Research on organizational accounts has shown that, in general, "accounts are seen as more adequate to the extent that they are detailed (e.g., Shapiro, Buttner, & Barry, 1994), based on sound reasoning (e.g., Bies, Shapiro, & Cummings, 1988), [and] sensitive (e.g., Greenberg, 1994)" (Folger & Cropanzano, 1998, p. 155). More specifically, a small number of studies suggest that adequate accounts often contain references to social or industry norms as a means of indicating sound reasoning and sensitivity to audience needs (Elsbach, 1994; Zbaracki, 1998). Elsbach and Sutton (1992), for example, found that spokespersons from radical social movement organizations often used references to normative and widely endorsed procedures (i.e., conducting press conferences or nonviolence workshops) in their accounts of illegitimate protest actions. Similarly, Taylor and Bogdan (1980) described how accounts used to manage the legitimacy of mental health institutions often referred to new, widely endorsed organizational goals (e.g., habilitation vs. custodial care) and organizational structures (e.g., team approaches, formal policies, and unitization). Finally, Dutton and Dukerich (1991) found that police officers in the New York City Port Authority Bus Terminal backed up their justifications for removing homeless persons from the terminal by noting that they were enforcing an antiloitering law (i.e., a normative procedure). Later, Port Authority spokespersons backed up their enhancements of the organization by highlighting their use of new, socially endorsed structures, including a paid consultant and a human resource administration to provide sensitivity training for police.

In many cases, references to social norms are contained in a *legitimating label* of the organization (Hearit, 1994). For example, when Chrysler was charged with committing fraud by selling used vehicles as new (i.e., the vehicles had been driven by Chrysler executives with the odometers disconnected prior to sale), CEO Lee Iacocca attempted to manage Chrysler's reputation for trustworthiness by denying that the company had done anything wrong and labeling the actions in question as a "test program" rather than a fraudulent executive perk (Hearit, 1994). In a similar case, the automaker Volvo came under attack after it was demonstrated that the car showcased in an advertisement as withstanding repeated overruns by a Monster Truck, while other vehicles were crushed, had been reinforced with steel and wood. In response, Volvo spokespersons engaged in image repair by claiming that the advertisement was not a hoax or sham as it had been described in the media, but a "re-enactment" of an actual event that had been witnessed by hundreds of people at a Vermont truck rally (Hearit, 1994). In these cases the labels of "test program" or "re-enactment" carry the legitimacy of assumed standards and procedures that guide such actions.

A second, specific type of content used to bolster accounts is *ideological imagery* or *illustration*, which adds to detail and sensitivity (Benoit, 1995). In a case study of the Apollo 13 space mission, for example, Kauffman (2001) described how NASA spokespersons used a "frontier" narrative and imagery to portray the space agency in a positive light in enhancements following the failure of the mission. At post-mission press conferences, NASA administrators characterized the mission as an "'epic struggle' in which the astronauts were 'pitted' against the 'hostile environment of space.'" (p. 442). NASA spokespersons also described the astronauts who "dare to brave the perils of space" as possessing "bravery, skill, discipline, courage, ingenuity, resourcefulness, teamwork, and character" (p. 442). At the same time, then-president Richard Nixon claimed that the astronauts' actions reminded Americans of their "proud heritage as a nation" (p. 442). This type of imagery provided substance to NASA's claims that the Apollo 13 mission was "A Successful Failure" (Kauffman, 2001, p. 443).

Account Medium.   Finally, it's important to keep in mind that there are many mediums through which verbal accounts may be communicated. Organizations can seek to communicate directly with audiences through paid advertisements, company newsletters, annual reports, Web sites or e-mails. These mediums allow organizational impression managers to craft their accounts to portray specific images (Hearit, 1994). In perhaps the only study of account effectiveness based on account medium, Shapiro et al. (1994) found that face-to-face oral communication of a rejection decision led to more positive reactions from audiences than written communication. This finding suggests that, to the extent that organizational spokespersons can communicate negative news directly to audiences, the more likely they are to manage those audiences' perceptions of the organization effectively.

In other cases, organizations communicate through the news media, where the form and content of their accounts may be altered by the reporter (e.g., an industry-friendly newspaper may report an account of corporate downsizing in a more positive light than would a labor-friendly publication). In fact, it is not uncommon for the media's treatment of the story to create a peripheral controversy, drawing attention away from the facts of the case. For example, *The New York Times* was embroiled in a perception management controversy after they refused to print two sports columns that sided against an organization (the National Council of Women's Organizations, NWCO) that was attempting to get women admitted as members of the Augusta National Golf Club (Johnson, 2002; see Chapter 6 for an in-depth report of this case). This spiking of the news stories led critics to claim that *The New York Times* was making NWCO's crusade their own. In this manner, the newspaper itself became a player in organizational perception management related to the controversy.

Organizational Categorizations and Labels

A second verbal strategy for managing perceptions of organizations is to offer organizational categorizations and labels. In particular, organizations wanting to affirm desired identities use categorizations and labels to define who they are and who they are not.

Inclusion in Social Categories. Social psychologists have shown that, on dimensions that are self-relevant (e.g., one's stand on ideological issues such as gun control), individuals prefer to see themselves as relatively unique compared to others because "similarity [to many others] on self-defining dimensions may imply that one is undistinguished or mediocre" (Wood, 1989, p. 241). As a result, individuals may affirm their distinctive identities by categorizing themselves in ways that display these unique attributes (Brewer, 1991) or by labeling themselves in ways that denote the possession of distinctive attributes (Ashforth & Humphrey, 1995). Researchers have also shown that individuals often prefer social categorizations that emphasize comparisons to inferior social groups as a means of enhancing their self-concepts (Crocker & Gallo, 1985; Wood, 1989). This form of self-categorization tends to be used in response to threats to self-concept or identity (i.e., mistaken inclusion into an undesirable social group such as "right-wing gun enthusiasts"; Hogg & Abrams, 1988).

Recently, organizational researchers have found that members and spokespersons for an organization may perceive these same types of identity threats when the organization to which they belong is categorized in a ways that run counter to their perceptions of its identity. In this manner, Terry, Carey, and Callan (2001) showed that members of a higher status organization that merged with a lower status organization perceived the merger as an organizational identity threat because it diluted the relative status of their organization. Similarly, in their study of business school members' reactions to the *Business Week* rankings, Elsbach and Kramer (1996) found that members experienced cognitive distress or identity dissonance when, as a result of their ranking in the survey, they thought the identity of their school was threatened by what they perceived as inaccurate categorization or misleading (and, by implication, unfair) comparisons to other organizations.

Elsbach and Kramer (1996) showed that, in response to this cognitive distress, members attempted to restore and affirm positive self-perceptions as well as positive perceptions of the identity of the organization by describing their organization in terms of alternate social categories (not included in the *Business Week* rankings) that confirmed its established identity (e.g., being an entrepreneurial school, being a top public institution). These organizational categorizations and labels were most commonly given for attributes that were known to many members of the organization based on their personal experiences. That is, unlike individual categorization and comparison tactics that must be verified only by the claimant, organizational categorizations must be verified by many.

In other cases, researchers have suggested that organizational leaders may wish to clarify their categorization along a number of different identity dimensions, as the identity of the organization becomes more complex (Pratt & Foreman, 2000). Pratt and Foreman suggest that organizations may choose to manage multiple organizational identities by *compartmentalization* (e.g., keeping the identities separate by maintaining multiple identity categorizations), *integration* (e.g., fusing the identities through a single new categorization), *deletion* (e.g., removing some identity categorizations), or *aggregation* (e.g., creating a hierarchy of identity categorizations). Organizations may perceive the need to manage multiple identities as new identities are taken on (e.g., through a change in business practices or a merger or divestiture) or as the value of existing identities change (e.g., a once important line of the business becomes obsolete).

Finally, researchers have suggested that organizations can use distinctive or status-relevant labels or names to indicate and affirm the categorizations to which they belong (Chaung & Baum, 2003; Ingram, 1996). For example, in their study of nursing homes in Canada, Chaung and Baum suggested that nursing homes that included a national chain in their names did so to signal consistency and competency in care, whereas those that hid such connections (by choosing names that did not refer to the national chain) did so to signal that they were a small caring organization, free from the bureaucratic feel of a larger chain. This last naming strategy suggests not only inclusion in a desired category but also, as I discuss next, exclusion from an undesired category.

Exclusion From Social Categories.   In many cases, identity managers may wish to identify categorizations to which the organization does not belong. That is, organizational identity management may underscore disidentification from specific, negatively viewed categories (Elsbach, 1999; Elsbach & Bhattacharya, 2001). For example, organizations that are proactively changing their identities due to mergers, acquisitions, or management directives may want members to give up old identifications so that they can more readily embrace new ones (Pfeffer & Sutton, 1999). However, if new organizational identities are too disparate from existing ones, members may have difficulty understanding and embracing them (Reger, Gustafson, DeMarie, & Mullane, 1994). Understanding the dynamics of disidentification may allow organizations to help their members make this identity transition.

Symbolic Business Behaviors

Symbolic business behaviors involve business activities by an organization or its members that are designed, at least in part, to affect audiences' perceptions of the organization. Symbolic business behaviors are most commonly used as perception management when they are perceived to be visible and salient (e.g., the use of patriotic behaviors such as supporting Veteran's groups has been perceived as much more salient since the events of 9/11) and when they affect a salient aspect of the image or identity of the organization (e.g., introducing a new product or service related to the central mission, such as online education by a renown university). Such behaviors are effective perception management tactics because they literally show the organization "living" its image, identity, or reputation (Arnold, Handelman, & Tigert, 1996). As a case in point, Rao (1994) described how early auto manufacturers (i.e., at the turn of the 20th century) used speed or endurance contests to display specific features of their cars, such as performance in hill climbing or reliability on a rugged, cross-country course to legitimate automobiles as viable alternative to horses, and, as noted earlier, to build their reputations for performance in these areas.

However, for maximum impact, symbolic behaviors are often coupled with verbal accounts or communications that explain them. Thus, Rao (1994) found that auto manufacturers used newspaper advertisements to publicize their contest wins and increase public awareness about the capabilities of their automobiles. In another case, Arndt and Bigelow (2000) found that hospitals that adopted a diversified corporate structure during the 1990s (in place of their previous traditional not-for-profit structure) used verbal accounts in their annual reports that justified the change as a response to the institutional environment (e.g., pressures on hospitals from HMOs to carry out such restructuring) and as an effort to maintain high status in their relevant comparison groups (e.g., other hospitals of our caliber are making these changes, so we must also change to keep up).

Organizational research points to four primary forms of symbolic business behaviors used to manage perceptions of organizations: behaviors related to primary business activities, treatment of employees or prospective employees, visible affiliation with groups or organizations, and escalation behaviors. Each behavior may be coupled with verbal accounts that explain and underscore its meaning to organizational audiences.

Behaviors Related to Primary Business Activities.   The most common forms of symbolic business behavior used as organizational perception management involve visible actions (e.g., attacking competitors, recalling products, or complying with government regulations) related to primary business activities (e.g., serving customers or manufacturing products; Weigelt & Camerer, 1988). For example, research from the domain of management strategy suggests that organizations may attempt to signal a reputation of toughness by enduring performance losses (e.g., by pricing below cost or by proliferating their product lines to fill every market niche, even unprofitable ones) to deter other firms from entering their markets (Kreps & Wilson, 1982; Milgrom & Roberts, 1986; Schmalensee, 1978). In other cases, firms may attempt to signal a reputation for high quality by lavish expenditures on advertising (Nelson, 1974), social causes, or costly office furniture (Milgrom & Roberts, 1986). Finally, organizations may attempt to build reputations for distinctive competencies (e.g., the research orientation of a business school) by offering specific products and services (e.g., large number of faculty on editorial boards, the presence of an academic press associated with the school; D'Aveni & O'Neill, 1992).

As an example, Bansal and Clelland (2004) found that organizations with low *environmental legitimacy* (i.e., "perceptions that the firm's corporate environmental performance was not desirable, proper, or appropriate," p. 94) could protect themselves from unsystematic risk in stock prices by displaying a commitment to the natural environment. Actions such as purchasing environmentally friendly equipment or joining environmentally progressive associations signaled that the firm was committed to protecting the environment and was dedicated to improving its environmental legitimacy in response to audience concerns. As Bansal and Clelland (2004) noted: "By expressing commitment to the environment, the firm can deflect the negative criticism by signaling that it does actually care about the environment ... by not expressing commitment to the environment, the firm may be signaling to investors that it is unresponsive to them" (p. 96).

Treatment of Employees. Symbolic behavior related to the treatment of employees (or prospective employees) can also be used to enhance or affirm the identity or reputation of an organization (Turban & Greening, 1997). Murrell (2001) found, for example, that firms that engaged in employment practices that promoted family life (e.g., good advancement opportunities for women, available on-site childcare, leave for childbirth, job sharing, flextime, and work-at-home options) signaled an identity categorization of "family friendly" and were recognized by *Working Mother Magazine*. Similarly, researchers of organizational justice have suggested that fair and equitable treatment of employees in decisions regarding hiring, firing, promotion, performance evaluation, and compensation are important to maintaining distinctive identity categorizations of fairness and trustworthiness (Folger & Cropanzano, 1998). For example, research on hiring decisions has shown that applicants view cognitive ability tests, personality tests,

drug screens, and biographical inventories as unfair means of employment selection (Folger & Cropanzano, 1998). Further, applicants subjected to these types of procedures are more likely than those who are
not tested to view the organization negatively (e.g., perceive the organization as having an image of unfairness; Smither, Reilly, Millsap,
Pearlman, & Stoffey, 1993; Stoffey, Millsap, Smither, & Reilly, 1991).

In addition, recent empirical studies have described how managers or organizational leaders can enhance organizational reputations for trustworthiness among employees through daily interactions. A recent review of
this work (Whitener, Brodt, Karsgaard, & Werner, 1998) suggests five behavioral characteristics that are important to achieving organizational reputations for trustworthiness among employees. First, they suggest that
behavioral consistency (i.e., reliability or predictability) by leaders increases employees' confidence in the competence of the organization and
its willingness to take risks on their behalf (Butler, 1991; Robinson &
Rousseau, 1994). Second, behavioral integrity (i.e., telling the truth and
keeping promises) by leaders reduces the risk employees associate with
working in an organization (Mayer et al., 1995). Third, a leader's willingness to share control enhances employees' abilities to protect their own interests and affirms their self-worth as valued parts of their organization,
thereby increasing their perception of the organization's benevolence (Tyler & Lind, 1992). Fourth, accurate, open, and thorough communication by
leaders about decisions and organizational issues helps employees to feel
that they are sharing and exchanging ideas, and increases their perceptions
of the organization's integrity (Butler, 1991; Hart, Capps, Cangemi, &
Caillouet, 1986). Finally, demonstrating concern for employees' well-being (e.g., showing consideration and sensitivity for employees' needs and
interests, acting in a way that protects employees' interests, and refraining
from exploiting employees) by leaders helps employees to perceive the organization as loyal and benevolent. In support of these recommendations, a
14-month field study of management performance appraisal systems by
Mayer and Davis (1999) showed that enhancing perceived benevolence, integrity, and competence by implementing a new performance appraisal system increased employees' willingness to let top management have control
over employee and organizational well-being.

Affiliation With Other Groups or Organizations. A third symbolic business behavior that has been used as an organizational perception
management tool involves formal or informal affiliation with other

groups or organizations. In some cases, affiliation behaviors and their advertisement can be used to manage the identity of an organization. For example, visible affiliation with a high-status or distinctive organization (e.g., advertising one's recent inclusion in *Fortune Magazine*'s "most admired" list) can enhance identity by creating the impression that the organization is in the same league as other, perennially admired companies (Elsbach & Kramer, 1996). At the same time, visible disidentification from a low-status or distinctive organization (e.g., touting one's title as the corporation "most hated" by the National Rifle Association) underscores that a company is not in their league (Elsbach, 1999).

Affiliation with well-respected groups can also be used to manage organizational images of legitimacy. For example, research on the uses of philanthropy by organizations (Himmelstein, 1997) shows that many

"All I'm saying is, giving a little something to the arts might help our image."

organizations that are facing legitimacy threats donate money to prestigious causes and organizations as a means demonstrating that their underlying values and ideals are aligned with those of the recipients (e.g., the oft-attacked tobacco giant, Phillip Morris, has sponsored the arts for over 40 years, including donating money to Lincoln Center, The Whitney Museum, The Dance Theater of Harlem, and the Alvin Ailey Dance Theater; Sisario, 2002).

Escalation Behaviors. Finally, a fourth symbolic business behavior that has been used to manage organizational images of correctness and consistency is escalation of commitment to a previously chosen course of action (Brockner, 1992). Such escalation behaviors commonly occur in the following situations:

> ... decision makers allocate some resources ... in the hope of attaining some goal or goals. After having made an investment, however, ... they receive negative feedback suggesting that, at the very least, they have not yet attained their goals; moreover, they are not certain that additional investments will be sufficient to bring about goal attainment. (p. 40)

Organizational theorists suggest that, in these situations, the decision makers continue to invest resources toward their originally stated goals as a symbolic means of self-justification (i.e., to justify that their past actions were correct). Further, such actions demonstrate consistency in behavior over time, which has been shown to be a valued trait (at least in Western societies; Staw & Ross, 1987).

Research has suggested that these symbolic goals motivate organizations and their leaders to continue devoting resources to a failing course of action (Ross & Staw, 1986, 1993). As noted earlier, Ross and Staw (1993) described this phenomena in their discussion of escalation behaviors during the construction of the Shoreham Nuclear Power Plant in Long Island, New York:

> ... external justification effects are particularly strong among those who are politically vulnerable or whose initial policy choice has met with resistance. In constructing Shoreham, [Long Island Lighting Company (i.e., LILCO)] management continually faced the need to assure external constituencies, such as shareholders and the public utilities commission, that its investment was a wise one.... It seemed that as the management of LILCO's commitment was challenged, each challenge was met with renewed justification [and investment], only serving to further increase commitment to Shoreham. (p. 717)

Physical Markers

Physical markers include temporary or permanent physical artifacts that are displayed, at least in part, to signal the images, identities, and reputations of an organization. In connection with organizational perception management, such physical markers commonly include size, style, and location of office buildings (e.g., investment banks located on or off Wall Street), type of furnishings (e.g., traditional vs. contemporary office furnishings), and decor (e.g., the presence or absence of artwork and live plants), as well as company logos, signs, and letterheads (Elsbach, 2004a).

Research from the area of environmental psychology (Sundstrom & Altman, 1989; Sundstrom & Sundstrom, 1986), suggests that physical

markers are most often used to manage perceptions of long-term and enduring identities and reputations (Olins, 1995). Proponents of the visual school of corporate identity, for example, suggest that the visible and tangible decor, design, and structures of an organization may be viewed as manifestations of its identity (Balmer, 1995). Perhaps because physical markers such as buildings and furnishings are relatively permanent they are viewed as a natural means of symbolizing and managing perceptions of the enduring and central character of an organization (Elsbach, 2003b). Along these lines, Ornstein (1986, 1992) found that the design of public reception areas in corporate office buildings conveyed organizational identity categorizations of either authoritarianism—signaled by displays of flags, pictures of organizational leaders, and chairs facing each other—or nonauthoritarianism—signaled by displays of artwork, live plants, and couches and chairs at 45 degree angles. Similarly, Arnold et al. (1996) found that patriotic displays in retail stores (e.g., Wal Mart) were used effectively to communicate and build a long-standing reputation for community involvement and concern for customers. Finally, Ridoutt, Ball, & Killerby (2002) found that organizations that displayed wood in their interior design were most preferred by observers and were most likely to be described by identity categorizations such as innovative, energetic, and comfortable (vs. rigid, unpleasant, and impersonal, which were assigned to organizations without wood in their interiors).

3. Organizational Spokespersons

Organizational spokespersons convey symbolic actions (e.g., verbal accounts, symbolic business behaviors, display of physical markers) to organizational audiences. Spokespersons include anyone who is perceived by audience members as representing the organization. Spokespersons do not have to be members of the organization or hold formal or official titles or roles that designate them to speak on its behalf.

Speaking on behalf of a large and diverse organization presents unique challenges for organizational impression managers. Most notably, these spokespersons must often manage multiple organizational impressions with multiple audiences. This situation is difficult not just because there are many distinct impressions to track but also because these impressions are, at times, incongruent. Elsbach and Kramer (1996) found, for example, that a business school may find it challenging to maintain its reputation for top quality teaching while also trying to maintain an identity as a preeminent research institute. The role of the spokesperson in such situations becomes crucial to success.

Empirical organizational research reveals that the most common types of organizational spokespersons are: (a) organizational leaders or public relations professionals, and (b) rank-and-file employees.

Leaders and Official Spokespersons

Visible organizational leaders or official public relations professionals are most commonly recognized as organizational spokespersons for several reasons. First, they are typically the authors of formal, published accounts following both positive and negative organizational events (Pearson & Clair, 1998). For example, in annual reports, the letter to shareholders explaining company performance is always signed and thus presumably written by the company leader (Staw et al., 1983). Researchers have found that audiences react most positively if, in these letters, leaders take responsibility for both organizational successes and failures (Salancik & Meindl, 1984). Audiences expect leaders to take both credit and blame for the performance of their organizations because to do so signals that the leader is in control and, at least, making important decisions if not wise ones (Meindl & Erlich, 1987; Sutton & Galunic, 1996).

Second, organizational leaders are best suited to actually carry out symbolic behaviors on behalf of the organization, such as presenting promises of restitution to harmed parties following industrial accidents (Marcus & Goodman, 1991). Conlon and Murray (1996) found that responses to letters of complaint about poor product quality typically came from an official organizational spokesperson in charge of customer satisfaction and product quality. When the harm done is most serious (e.g., physical harm or death caused by an organization), studies suggest that the company president or CEO is likely to respond. For example, Ford Motor Company CEO Jacques Nasser announced Ford's program to replace faulty Firestone tires on its Ford Explorers following publicity about numerous deaths that resulted from Explorer accidents (Damage Control, October 8, 2000). In all these cases, the promise of restitution is more likely to be credible if it comes from an organizational leader who is, presumably, able to direct funds toward harmed parties.

Finally, because they are often involved in the choice or design of company buildings and work spaces, organizational leaders are capable of signaling distinctive organizational identities through prominent physical markers. The sprawling, campus-like environment of the Microsoft Headquarters in Redmond, Washington, is often used as an affirmation of the youthful, "all-nighter" identity of the company and is attributed to founder Bill Gates (Meyer, 1994). Similarly, John Chambers, CEO of Cisco Systems, is given responsibility for signaling the collaborative spirit and identity of his company through his design of corporate offices that have him working in a cubicle alongside subordinates (Donlon, 2000).

Employees

For perception management on a smaller and less controversial scale, rank-and-file organizational employees may be used. The management of day-to-day impressions is often carried out by these front-line employees—who routinely interact with the public—because they are in position to provide credible information about the organization. For example, Elsbach et al. (1998) showed how customer service staff in hospital billing departments engaged in symbolic behaviors in their interactions with customers (e.g., threatening to send a patient's bill to an outside collection agency if it wasn't paid on time) to portray the hospital as an intimidating and threatening organization that should not be challenged in its billing procedures.

In some situations, the employees as a group are symbolically defined as the spokesperson in organizational perception management. This can occur when the organization is dominated by an employee union that speaks on behalf of the rank and file or when the employees come together in support of a common cause or goal. In this manner, Cowden and Sellnow (2002) described how the employees of Northwest Airlines were represented as the "organization" in a contentious battle with the National Airline Pilots Association and its decision to strike. In a series of full-page newspaper advertisements, rank-and-file Northwest Airlines employees portrayed themselves as a group committed to meeting the needs of customers but also a group that was handcuffed by a small band of rogue pilots. In this way, the identity of the organization became linked to the values of the majority of employees who were not members of the striking pilots' union.

4. Organizational Audiences

Organizational audiences include all the parties who are targets of organizational perception management. These audiences may be made up of persons external to the organization, such as members of other organizations (e.g., regulatory agencies, competing organizations, suppliers), public interest groups (e.g., consumers, environmental activists, voters), and the general public. Alternatively, audiences may be made up of persons internal to the organization, such as employees, volunteers, dues-paying members, and students.

External Audiences

The general public is the most common external audience studied by researchers of organizational perception management. It is often the largest group affected by organizational events that threaten short-term organizational images and includes consumers or potential consumers who hear about faulty products or services, citizens of communities harmed by organizational actions such as polluting, and citizens in communities affected by corporate decisions such as large-scale layoffs (Marcus & Goodman, 1991). Because these groups include so many people, their complaints receive substantial attention from the popular media (Lamertz & Baum, 1998). In addition, because of the diversity of members within these groups, multiple and complex perception management messages are often required to address adequately all of the members' concerns following a negative organizational event (Sutton & Callahan, 1987). Thus, potential stockholders of an organization that has made large-scale layoffs in some of its manufacturing facilities may be most interested in the long-term justifications for the actions (i.e., how will this affect the value of the stock), whereas citizens of the local community may be most interested in short-term excuses and remedial actions (e.g., how laying off some employees allowed the company to remain solvent and how some laid-off employees may be transferred to other plants).

When there is no immediate crisis or public event to respond to or prepare for, the external audiences that are most likely to scrutinize organizations are members of special interest groups, including customers, competitors, and activists. These audiences pay special attention to routine symbolic behaviors of the organization and its permanent display of physical markers because these actions are most indicative of the enduring identities or reputations of an organization (Fombrun & Shanley, 1990). For example, in ranking corporations in the *Fortune Magazine* survey of most admired companies, Fombrun and Shanely (1990) found that corporate executives, outside directors, and securities analysts (i.e., the participants who filled out the *Fortune* survey) were strongly influenced by routine behaviors, including advertising intensity, contributions to charity, and choice of risky strategies, rather than onetime actions such as a single response to an organizational failure or performance downturn.

A final external audience important in organizational perception management is the media. Both popular and specialized media outlets, including print, television, and radio communications act as interpreters and reporters of organizational actions. Recent research suggests that such media outlets may influence broad public perceptions of an organization by increasing pure exposure of the firm and by framing organizational actions in positive or negative terms (Pollock & Rindova, 2003; Rindova, Pollock, & Hayward, 2005). For example, in their study of over 250 initial public offerings (IPOs) of corporate stock during the year 1992, Pollock and Rindova (2003) found that greater exposure in popular print media led to less underpricing and higher turnover in stock price on the first day of trading. Further, they found that positively framed media coverage, over a threshold level, also led to greater turnover and less underpricing. Pollock and Rindova suggested that these outcomes resulted from the increased organizational legitimacy that was gained through media exposure and framing. As Pollock and Rindova reported,

> Since media coverage contains a high degree of information generated by opinion leaders such as journalists, industry experts, and financial analysts, the positive and negative information it provides is likely to be used as social proof of the legitimacy of IPO firms. Further, to the degree that the media makes such expressed evaluations widely available in public discourse, it creates availability cascades that increase the tendency to perceive expressed evaluations as more plausible (Kuran & Sunstein, 1999). (p. 634)

Internal Audiences

Organizational perception management aimed at internal audiences has received much less attention than that aimed at external audiences. Recent research has begun, however, to examine how managing the perceptions of internal audiences may require additional or distinct tactics (Elsbach, 1999). Specifically, because organizational identities are important to internal audiences, identity management tactics becomes important. This is especially true when internal audiences perceive that the status or distinctiveness of the organization is threatened or that its identity is internally conflicted. For example, Elsbach (2001a) found that long-time staffers working for the California State Legislature connected with the policymaking identity of that organization, whereas newer and short-term staffers often identified with the political-campaigning identity of that organization. Maintaining these two identities was a difficult act for many members, who used tactics such as split or schizo-identification to affiliate themselves with one of these identities but not the other.

SUMMARY: COMPONENTS OF ORGANIZATIONAL PERCEPTION MANAGEMENT

In this chapter I have used empirical studies to explicate the specific types of organizational perceptions, symbolic actions, organizational spokespersons, and organizational audiences that are involved in organizational perception management processes. This discussion outlines how perception management unfolds in organizational settings. It also suggests how organizational perception management may be distinct from its individual-level counterpart relative to the four key components defined here.

First, the research presented here describes a variety of perceptions of organizations that may be managed through perception management (i.e., images, reputations, and identities). Although individuals may manage the same kinds of perceptions of themselves, it is clear that particular perceptions are more relevant to organizations. For example, organizations' preoccupation with images of legitimacy may result from society's more stringent regulation and requirement for standardization of organizational practices than of individual practices. Because organizations are increasingly confronted with both formal and informal certification requirements (from meeting accounting standards to fulfilling social norms about donations to charity), it seems natural that managing perceptions of legitimacy should be a priority for organizational (vs. individual) impression managers. Similarly, organizations' emphasis on status (vs. distinctiveness) components of identity may result, at least in part, because organizations are increasingly ranked in public surveys. By contrast, individuals are not commonly subjected to such public rankings, and thus may focus more on the distinctiveness dimensions of their identities.

Second, the empirical findings reviewed in this chapter suggest that symbolic actions for an organization include many of the same categories of tactics used by individual impression managers, including verbal accounts, verbal categorizations and labels, symbolic behaviors, and the display of physical markers. Yet these findings also reveal how such tactics are uniquely deployed within the domain of organizational perception management. Organizational accounts, for example, commonly include industry norms or trends as content that backs up excuses or justifications. Elsbach (1994), for example, found that cattle industry spokespersons used denials of food safety violations that they backed up with references to their use of industry norms and guidelines. Similarly, in accounts of corporate performance included in annual reports, Bettman and Weitz (1983) found that excuses for poor performance were bolstered by references to industry trends, such as higher prices for materials or a slowdown in the industry. By contrast, individual-level accounts of failures at work are more likely to refer to broad social norms rather than industry norms (i.e., I was late for work because I had to care for a sick child; Riordan, James, & Runzi, 1989). Because the actions of organizations (vs. individuals) are more likely to be evaluated in the context of industry norms (vs. social norms), it may be more appropriate for organizational accounts to refer to such norms.

In addition to differences associated with verbal accounts, organizational actions and physical markers appear to be operationalized differently by organizations compared to individuals. Organizations can devise, publicize, and enact corporate strategies that incorporate a number of activities designed to signal a desired image or reputation. For instance, a corporate strategy of environmental awareness can be enacted through a recycling program that involves actions by marketing, manufacturing, and research and development groups as well as the display of physical markers such as the construction of energy-efficient buildings and plants (Gotsi & Wilson, 2001). In this manner, organizations can enact a desired image or reputation through multiple, simultaneous activities and displays of physical markers that reach diverse audiences. It would be difficult for an individual to manage images or reputation on so many fronts through so many simultaneous actions. Instead, individuals are likely to focus on one type of perception management at a time, perhaps vary their focus over time. Regarding this distinction, Chen and Meindl (1991) described how the image of People's Express Airline founder, Donald Burr, evolved slowly over time through press coverage that was, at least partially, constructed by Burr's own perception management efforts.

Third, the research reviewed in this chapter documents how organizational perception management may be carried out by a variety of organizational spokespersons, many of whom have no link to the specific organizational event or controversy that prompted the perception management. That is, unlike the individual impression manager who is primarily responsible for his or her own images, identities, and reputations, organizational impression managers are responsible for the images, identities, and reputations of a collective. Further, more than one spokesperson may manage the perceptions of this collective. Speaking or acting on behalf of an organization (vs. on behalf of an individual) presents additional dilemmas, such as dealing with the often inevitable inconsistencies between various images, identities, and reputations that define an organization as well as inconsistencies in the expectations held by various internal and external organizational audiences.

Finally, this chapter identifies both internal and external audiences of organizational perception management. In the same way that organizational spokespersons are a diverse group, audiences of organizational impression vary in their size and characteristics. Demands for identity management from employees, an internal audience, may focus on maintaining a distinct culture (e.g., smallness and intimacy). At the same time, external audiences, such as consumers, may desire other organizational reputations (e.g., growth and competitiveness). In other cases, external audiences that routinely interact with the organization (e.g., consumers) may pay most attention to routine symbolic behaviors and communications from leaders, whereas external audiences that only casually observe the organization may pay most attention to crisis communications or communications in anticipation of controversial events. For size reasons alone, the diversity and potential number of these internal and external audiences is likely to be greater for organizations than for individuals. Further, because organizations are scrutinized by a number of media outlets, they may have their actions more routinely observed and interpreted by these influential sources of information.

Taken together, these findings suggest that organizational (vs. individual) perception management involves a consideration of unique strategic issues. This may explain why some researchers refer to organizational perception management as strategic projection (Rindova & Fombrun, 1999). In particular, the findings reported here suggest that organizational perception management involves strategically matching spokesperson actions to audiences' interpretations of salient perception forms (i.e., images, reputations, or identities) as well as to organizational norms and strategies. The key to successful organizational perception management starts with recognizing how different types of triggering events (e.g., crises, controversy, identity change) focus audiences' attention on specific forms of organizational perceptions and specific strategic issues (i.e., coping with audience conflicts, coordinating multiple spokespersons). Interestingly, this perspective suggests that the major mistakes that spokespersons can make in carrying out organizational perception management are not, for example, the use of the wrong types of accounts or symbolic behaviors to manage a threatened organizational image. Rather, the major mistakes such spokespersons can make are to identify incorrectly the form of organizational perception that needs to be managed (e.g.,, using identity management responses when reputation management is called for) and the strategic issues that need consideration (e.g., disregarding how perception management tactics fit with the overall performance strategy).

Still, there are many cases that illustrate how such organizational perception management may be effectively carried out. As one case in point, let us return to the trials of the National Rifle Association, originally discussed at the beginning of this chapter.

The NRA: Follow-up

In the months and years following Handgun Control Inc.'s prediction of the demise of the NRA, the NRA leadership undertook a series of campaigns to manage audiences' perceptions of the organization. First, it attempted to improve its current images of legitimacy and morality with external and internal audiences by electing a new leader. In the Spring of 1997 the NRA elected screen icon Charleton Heston to be vice president. Members elected him as president of the organization one year later. Heston was seen as a legitimate, mainstream gun owner and a morally and ethically sound spokesperson for the organization (most American's remember him in his roles as Moses and Ben Hur; Getlin, 1998).

Second, the NRA reaffirmed its central, distinctive, and enduring identity as a mainstream organization by producing a series of magazine and newspaper advertisements that described its role in mainstream life. These advertisements featured famous and widely respected members of the NRA (e.g., Heston, former NFL quarterback and congressman Steve Largent, and television star Tom Selleck) who claimed, "I am the NRA," in full-page advertisements (Janofsky, 1998). Their statements equated the NRA with their personalities (e.g., mainstream, upstanding, legitimate role models).

Finally, the NRA attempted to influence its widely perceived reputation by publicizing its links to other well-established and well-respected organizations and by engaging in symbolic actions that highlighted its status. For instance, it publicized its affiliation with the Boy Scouts of America in promoting shooting safety, and the NRA cartoon mascot Eddie the Eagle was used in gun safety programs designed by the group and used by the Boy Scouts and other community organizations (Moscoso, 2000). The NRA also designed and taught a college curriculum on gun safety that was offered for credit at Colorado's Trinidad State Junior College (Curtin, 1999).

Together, these tactics were credited with major improvements in audience perceptions of the NRA. By the summer of 2001, LaPierre (now the CEO) reported that membership of the "New NRA" was at an all-time high of 4.3 million members, that approval ratings for the organization based on national polls were running at a 20-year high of 60 to 65%, and that state-supported right-to-carry firearms laws were now in place in 32 states (up from only 6 states a decade earlier; "NRA chief," 2001). Although it is likely that other events also helped to produce this turnaround (e.g., the replacement of a Democratic president with a Republican), it seems probable that LaPierre was correct in crediting the makeover of the images, identities, and reputations of the organization for its improved pubic support. That is, the NRA appears to have implemented organizational perception management successfully.

II

Organizational Perception Management in Context

3

A Typology of Organizational Perception Management Events

Perception management is a ubiquitous activity in organizations today. It is used in daily interactions with customers and employees as well as prior to major organizational product introductions and following severe organizational crises. The variation in the design and strategic use of perception management tactics parallels the variation in the contexts of its use.

In this chapter, I develop a typology of common contexts for organizational perception management that serves as an outline for the next four chapters of the book. This typology describes six different categories of perception management events that vary along two primary dimensions that define those events. In the following sections, I describe these dimensions and categories of perception management events.

DIMENSIONS OF ORGANIZATIONAL PERCEPTION MANAGEMENT EVENTS

Organizational perception management events are situations in which organizational members determine that organizational perception management is needed and take action to respond to that need. Organizational perception management events occur in response to triggering events such as crises (e.g., a strike by employees), identity changes (e.g., a merger with another organization), or organizational performance reviews (e.g., the publishing of industry rankings) that signal the need to engage in organizational perception management. However, it is important to note that the triggering events and the perception management events (which may range from a single press release to a year-long advertising campaign) are separate entities. Only when organizational spokespersons begin to carry out perception management tactics has an organizational perception management event occurred.

A review of the organizational perception management literature reveals two primary dimensions that appear to define most organizational perception management events: (a) why organizational perception management is needed and (b) when organizational perception management occurs. These two dimensions define the primary contexts in which organizational perception management occurs.

Why Perception Management Is Needed

There are two primary reasons why organizations engage in perception management: to deal with perception-enhancing triggering events and to deal with perception-threatening triggering events (Schlenker, 1980; Tedeschi, 1981). Perhaps because organizations are unwilling to take on the risks of protesting their legitimacy too much (i.e., based on the notion that those who are legitimate need not proclaim it; Ashforth & Gibbs, 1990), there is much more evidence about how organizations deal with perception-threatening events than about how they deal with perception-enhancing events.

Dealing With Perception-threatening Events

Events that threaten the images, reputations, or identities of an organization typically occur when organizational members perceive that key audiences' perceptions of the organization are negatively inconsistent with those that members would like to convey (Ginzel, Kramer, & Sutton, 1993). That is, members' construed images, reputations, or identities are more negative than their desired images, reputations, or identities.

When organizational members perceive that audiences have wrongly identified the existence of a negative event or have wrongly attributed a negative event to the organization (Elsbach & Sutton, 1992), organizational members may determine that they need to correct and update audiences' views of the organization. For example, an image of legitimacy may be threatened if customers believe the organization has been acting in a morally illegitimate fashion (e.g., a cigarette company is perceived to be using cartoon characters in its advertising to entice children to smoke) or has been engaging in practically illegitmate actions (e.g., a chemical company releases legal but high levels of toxic emissions, leading investors to sell their shares of company stock; Bansal & Clelland, 2004). Similarly, an identity as a top-tier institution may be threatened if employees perceive that the organization has lost its former status (e.g., members of a business school perceive that the status of their school is lowered after its industry ranking falls; Elsbach & Kramer, 1996).

Dealing With Perception-Enhancing Events

Events that enhance the images, reputations, or identities of an organization typically occur when organizational members perceive that key audiences' perceptions of the organization could be more positively consistent (i.e., consistent but in a more positive direction) with the current images, identities, and reputations of that organization (Ginzel et al., 1993). That is, members' construed images, reputations, or identities are positively inconsistent with the current images, reputations or identities of the organization.

The small but growing set of organizational studies on perception-enhancing events suggests that such events occur for the mirror opposite reasons that identity-threatening events occur. That is, organizational members believe either that the positiveness of an organizational action is not fully known or that an organization's responsibility for a positive event is not fully recognized (i.e., "it was better than you think" and "we were more responsible than you think"; Ginzel et al.,1993; Elsbach & Sutton, 1992). For example, Ginzel et al. (1993) described how the defense contractor Raytheon experienced a perception-enhancing event when their Patriot missiles proved to be so effective against the Iranian SCUD missiles during the Persian Gulf War. In another case, Sutton and Kramer (1990) described how, in the aftermath of the Iceland arms talks between President Reagan and Chairman Gorbachev, the Reagan administration spokespersons focused on the fact that the arms talks led both sides to agree to begin dismantling nuclear weapons, despite the fact that the goals set at the outset—complete nuclear disarmament by the Soviets—were not achieved.

When Perception Management Occurs

There are three occasions when organizational perception management typically occurs: after organizational events, during organizational events, and before organizational events. These three occasions for perception management interact with the two reasons why perception management is needed (described previously) to produce six categories of organizational perception management events. These six categories are displayed in Table 3.1.

TABLE 3.1
Typology of Organizational Perception Management Events

	After Organizational Events	*During Organizational Events*	*Before Organizational Events*
Dealing with perception -threatening events	-Scandals -Accidents -Product Failures	-Contentious negotiations -Controversial identity changes	-Upcoming performance reviews -Introduction of controversial products/services/facilities -Introduction of new identity or vision
	Chapter 4	Chapter 5	Chapter 6
Dealing with perception -enhancing events	-Poor ranking or rating by industry groups	-Overcoming hardship	-Achievment of desired goals -Positive ranking or rating by industry groups
	Chapter 7	Chapter 7	Chapter 7

After Organizational Events

Most organizational perception management research focuses on the use of remedial tactics to repair, maintain, or enhance organizational images, identities, or reputations following either positive or negative events. This category includes organizational perception management after perception-threatening events—covered in Chapter 4 of this volume—such as scandals, accidents, and product failures that threaten images of legitimacy, reputations for integrity, and identities related to status and distinctiveness. This category also includes organizational perception management following perception-enhancing events—covered in Chapter 7 of this volume—such as anticipated performance reviews by industry analysts or rankings by industry publications (e.g., the Fortune 500) that may enhance the reputation of an organization for quality and distinctiveness.

In these contexts, audiences have determined that a noteworthy event has occurred and appear to search for clues suggesting that the organization has considered their concerns and needs in responding to the event. Thus, after organizational events, organizations are required to provide informational cues that support their accounts or acclaims of the triggering event (Bies, Shapiro, & Cummings, 1988; Dutton & Dukerich, 1991; Elsbach, 1994).

During Organizational Events

Theorists have also proposed that organizational perception management may evolve over time, through cycles of communication between organizations and their audiences (Ginzel et al., 1993; Sutton & Kramer, 1990). This category includes organizational perception management during evolving, perception-threatening events—covered in Chapter 5 of this volume—such as contentious negotiations and controversial identity changes that threaten images of legitimacy and identities of status and distinctiveness. This category also includes organizational perception management during evolving, perception-enhancing events—covered in Chapter 7 of this volume—such as the resolution of an organizational problem or the recovery from an organizational setback (e.g., response and recovery from a product failure, such as tainted food product) that may enhance the images of legitimacy and trustworthiness of the organization.

Ginzel et al. (1993) described evolving perception management as a "reciprocal influence process" (p. 235) between the audience and the organization. That is, over time, the organization refines and updates its perception management tactics based on the influential feedback of audiences. If audiences are not sympathetic to the initial accounts of a controversy, for example, the organization may have to rework its perception management strategy to be more accommodative of audience concerns.

Before Organizational Events

Finally, tactics that are used to influence organizational images, identities, and reputations associated with upcoming events are defined as anticipatory organizational perception management (Elsbach et al., 1998). This category includes organizational perception management before anticipated, perception-threatening events—covered in Chapter 6 of this volume—such as anticipated negative performance reviews, introduction of controversial products, services, or facilities, and introduction of new visions or identities that threaten images of trustworthiness and legitimacy and reputations for superior performance. This category also includes organizational perception management before anticipated, perception-enhancing events—covered in Chapter 7 of this volume—such as the anticipated achievement of a long-sought organizational or industry goal (e.g., the development of an effective cancer drug) that may enhance the distinctiveness and status identities of an organization.

Pfeffer's (1981) work on symbolic administrative action suggests that, in addition to mollifying audiences during or following controversies, sym-

bolic acts such as the development of organizational language or the selective release of information may be used to influence the perceptions of
organizational audiences prior to an anticipated organizational event (i.e.,
get employees to buy into and implement an upcoming change in work
strategies). Organizational research suggests that organizations or their
members use preemptive explanations, disclaimers, or self-handicapping
excuses to attenuate the responsibility of the organization for potential failures or to minimize the perceived negativity of a future event (Shapiro &
Bies, 1994; Sitkin & Bies, 1993; Snyder et al., 1983; Sutton & Kramer,
1990). Related research on organizational justice (Greenberg, Bies, &
Eskew, 1991) and organizational trust (Brockner & Siegel, 1996) also suggests that communications about the rationality and consistency of decision procedures may serve as a form of preemptive perception management
to promote images of fairness and trustworthiness prior to an unpleasant
decision outcome (e.g., announcements about layoffs).

4

Organizational Perception Management Following Crisis Events

What should an oil company do following an oil spill by one of its tankers? How should a university respond to a lawsuit claiming that it discriminates against women? What kinds of messages will be most effective in regaining consumer trust following food poisoning at a restaurant belonging to a national chain? In this chapter, I discuss how organizations and their spokespersons may use perception management effectively following such crisis events. Public relations researchers have studied crisis events for decades, and these types of events comprise the bulk of the cases studied by organizational perception management researchers over the past 20 years (see Pearson & Clair, 1998, for a review).

However, despite the common occurrence of crisis events, there is little consensus among business leaders about how organizations should manage audiences' perceptions in response to them (Burnett, 1998; Pearson & Clair, 1998). Further, there are inconsistent findings about the types of responses that are most effective in repairing organizational images, reputations, or identities as distinct types of organizational perceptions that may be threatened by organizational crises (see Elsbach, 2001b). In this chapter, I take a closer look at the research on organizational crisis management and public relations in an effort to develop guidelines for tailoring organizational perception management effectively to follow specific types of crisis events.

In the following sections, I first define the most common types of organizational crisis events and their effects on organizational audiences. I then discuss the most common perception management tactics that organizations use following crisis events as well as what appears to make these tactics effective (or ineffective). I next discuss some common pitfalls that organizations may encounter when carrying out perception management following crisis events. Finally, I provide a detailed illustration of organizational perception management following a crisis event with a case study of Sears' Auto Centers and their 1992 indictment for fraud.

DEFINING ORGANIZATIONAL CRISIS EVENTS

Organizational crisis events are recognizable by their relative discreteness (i.e., they are definable as individual events) and their clear threat to organizational perceptions (i.e., at least some audiences perceive them as negative). They are distinct from the evolving perception-threatening events that are discussed in Chapter 6 (e.g., such as a long-term negotiation or merger) because they become known to audiences rather suddenly and, although their cause is often unknown, they are clearly perceived as threats to positive organizational perceptions that must be dealt with swiftly. In this manner, Pearson and Clair (1998) defined an organizational crisis as "a low-probability, high-impact event that threatens the viability of the organization and is characterized by ambiguity of cause, effect, and means of resolution, as well as by a belief that decisions must be made swiftly" (p. 60).

Common Forms of Crisis Events

Pearson and Clair (1998) suggest that common forms of organizational crisis events include the following:

* extortion
* hostile takeovers
* product tampering
* plant fatalities
* copyright infringement
* environmental spills
* computer tampering
* security breaches
* product boycotts

* work-related homicides
* malicious rumors
* natural disasters
* bribery
* sabotage
* terrorist attacks
* sexual harassment
* counterfeiting
* customer assault
* product recalls
* escape of hazardous materials

While these events represent a variety of motivations and causes, but the perception management implications of these events rest primarily on two of their attributes: the identifiability of crisis event victims (i.e., whether or not there are clear links between organizational actions and victim injuries) and the degree to which audiences perceive the crisis to have been preventable (i.e., is the crisis the result of organizational incompetence or lack of concern for human well-being—which could have been prevented, or is it the result of human error or poor judgment—which are difficult to prevent?; Marcus & Goodman, 1991). Based on these dimensions, Marcus and Goodman defined three general forms of crisis events: accidents, which involve concrete victims but high preventability; scandals, which involve more diffuse and obscure victims but low preventability; and product failures, which involve moderate levels of preventability and victim identifiability.

Accidents

An oil spill caused by human error in navigating an oil tanker between icebergs and by a reef. A horrible chemical leak linked to faulty safety equipment. A plane crash caused by unstable chemicals in the cargo bay. These are all examples of accidents that may cause perception management crises for organizations. These types of events are often severe in their damage (i.e., they typically damage plants and equipment and may cause human injury or death). As a result, accidents are widely reported by the media and quite visible to the public (Small, 1991). Consequently, accidents are likely to injure short-term images of quality, safety, and legitimacy because they provide salient evidence that the organization is fallible.

At the same time, accidents are typically perceived to result from human error, rather than from utter incompetence or lack of concern for human well-being. Further, the public is often sympathetic to the fact that all organizations are at risk of human error. By contrast, they aren't so forgiving of an organization that does not respond to an accident in ways that show consideration of public concerns (Small, 1991). As a result, the effects of accidents on long-term reputations are often strongly mediated by the perception management that follows the accident (Fombrun & Shanley, 1990). Thus, as discussed later in the chapter, although accidents almost always harm the short-term images of a firm, they may not be as damaging to the long-term reputation of that firm if swift and appropriate perception management is carried out.

Scandals

The disclosure that auto corporation executives had driven more than 60,000 cars with unhooked odometers before selling them as new. The revelation that corporate accountants had kept millions of dollars of losses off the books to improve performance indicators. The reporting of widespread overcharging of auto repair customers linked to an organizational quota system for selling brakes and other common parts. These are all examples of organizational scandals that, all too commonly, may threaten audiences' perceptions of an organization.

Scandals may vary greatly in their damage to organizational audiences, but in most cases this damage is financial and emotional. Many scandals, such as the unhooked odometer scandal described previously (which occurred at the Chrysler Corporation; Hearit, 1994), may have had very small effects on the value of products bought or used by customers. By contrast, scandals such as the ENRON accounting scandal (Bryce, 2002) may cost organizational consumers, employees, and stockholders millions of dollars in lost income in the short term and cost communities that depend on the financial impact of the corporation's economic stability in the long term.

In many of these cases, it is difficult to ascertain the exact numbers and types of audiences harmed. In the ENRON case, for example, it appears that energy consumers in California were harmed by the scandal because they bought energy brokered through ENRON (a company based in Texas) at highly inflated prices. In turn, these increased energy prices may have played a role in the bankruptcy of many California firms already hurting due to the economic downturn in the high-tech sector. In the terminology of Marcus and Goodman (1991), the victims of this corporate scandal were low in identifiability.

Regardless of the degree and diffuseness of financial and emotional damage done by an organizational scandal, most audiences view such scandals as the result of avarice by top managers of the organization. That is, according Marcus and Goodman (1991), most corporate scandals would be seen as high in preventability. As a result of this high preventability, organizational audiences tend to be severely critical of organizational scandals, even if they are not personally harmed by such events. This critical judgment commonly affects immediate images of legitimacy and trustworthiness because it signals immorality among organizational decision makers. Further, if the scandal is perceived to be the fault of those at the very top of the organization, audiences may question the organization's long-term reputation for integrity (i.e., they may feel that all past reputation-enhancing events are also tainted and that the organization does not deserve its enduring categorization as a high-status company). Finally, scandals that arise at the top of an organization may cause employees to perceive that the organization is not what they thought it to be. As a result, they may question the organization's identity, especially if that identity was linked to the distinctive categories of integrity and honesty.

Product Failures

Media reports of automobile gasoline tanks that easily ruptured in rear-end collisions. A medical report that revealed that it was common for breast implants from one company to leak after implantation. A widespread product recall resulting from glass shards found in a popular brand of baby food. These are all examples of product failures that immediately threatened audiences' perceptions of organizations.

These types of product failures often create crisis situations for organizations not only because they harm audiences but because they are perceived to be the result of either lack of concern for those audiences or corporate incompetence (Hearit, 1994). In this manner, product failures are viewed as at least moderately preventable. In addition, although product failures may not harm audiences in large group events (i.e., they typically injure one consumer at a time over the course of many days, weeks, or months), they often cause severe harm (i.e., human injury or death), and they may affect large numbers of victims over time. Thus, they are viewed as at least moderate in victim identifiability.

As a result of their moderate preventability and victim identifiability, product failures often call into question the viability and legitimacy of the organization as a whole because they demonstrate a lack of ability in carrying out the most basic organizational objective—delivering the product

(Kauffman, 2001). In particular, product failures may threaten distinctiveness categorizations, such as high quality or reliable, which help define organizational images and identities. Over time, repeated product failures along these lines may call status categorizations into question, threatening the reputation of the organization (e.g., most admired company).

Interestingly, however, product failures may be less damaging to organizational perceptions of legitimacy in the long run if they can be framed as the result of honest incompetence (Hendry, 2002), which can be overcome through learning. In this way, although accidents may be more severe in their human costs than are scandals, they may be less threatening to organizational perceptions because the sin of incompetence is less damning, over the long term, than the sin of immorality (Elsbach, 2005). I discuss this issue in more detail in my discussion of the Catholic Church sex abuse scandal in Chapter 8 of this volume.

ORGANIZATIONAL PERCEPTION MANAGEMENT FOLLOWING CRISIS EVENTS

Although there are many aspects to what is popularly known as crisis management (e.g., determining the cause of the crisis, containing and repairing physical damage, resuming operations, altering safety procedures; Mitroff et al., 1996), this chapter focuses solely on actions taken to repair organizational images, identities, and reputations. It should be noted that actions that have substantive effects in crisis management (e.g., providing restitution to repair harm done to the general public) may also have symbolic perception management effects, especially if these actions are widely reported. In the following sections, I describe three of the most commonly studied contexts in which organizational perception management is used following a crisis event. I also discuss the effective use of perception management in each of these contexts. These contexts include: managing organizational images of legitimacy following accidents or scandals, managing organizational reputations for integrity following scandals, and managing organizational identities related to status or distinctiveness following product failures.

Managing Organizational Images of Legitimacy Following Accidents and Scandals

Accidents and scandals reveal either incompetence or avarice by organizational decision makers. As a result, they tend call into question the legitimacy of an organization and its leadership (i.e., would a legitimate organization make such mistakes? Would a legitimate organization be motivated by such base instincts?). In this way, they lead audiences to wonder if an organization and its leadership are behaving in desirable, proper, or appropriate manners (Suchman, 1995) and if they should continue to support this organization in substantive and symbolic ways (Pfeffer, 1981).

In responding to threats to images of legitimacy caused by accidents and scandals, organizations have been found to use two common strategies effectively: accounts that include denials of wrongdoing, coupled with symbolic behaviors that provide evidence of organizational rationality following accidents; and accounts including justifications for organizational actions, coupled with symbolic behaviors that provide evidence of organizational consideration of audience views following scandals (Elsbach, 2001a).

Denials of Wrongdoing and Rational Symbolic Behavior Following Accidents

A common organizational perception management strategy used in the wake of accidents is to deny wrongdoing, and to back up that claim with symbolic behaviors or references to symbolic acts that had been previously carried out that demonstrate that the organization was behaving rationally when the accident occurred. For example, in a study of the radical environmentalist organization Earth First!, Elsbach and Sutton (1992) found that, in cases where the organization was blamed for human injury resulting from tree spiking (i.e., loggers were hurt when their chainsaws hit metal spikes that had been driven into trees to prevent them from being cut down), organizational spokespersons swiftly denied responsibility and showed the media an Earth First! tree-spiking manual that specifically required that all spiked trees be marked with spray paint so that loggers would know they were spiked and not try to cut them down. The organization made the argument that any real Earth First!er would follow these strict guidelines to prevent injury and thus any injury caused by tree spiking must not be due to its members. The symbolic behavior of compiling and distributing the tree-spiking manual portrayed the organization as rational in its pursuit of saving trees and backed up its denial of responsibility for the loggers' injuries. In turn, this perception management strategy was shown to increase the legitimacy of the organization with at least some constituencies (e.g., members of other pro-environment organizations; Elsbach & Sutton, 1992).

In a similar way, Marcus and Goodman's (1991) study of organizational crisis management by large corporations showed that managers commonly offered denials following company accidents (e.g., oil spills, plane crashes, nuclear power plant failure), coupled with references to their previously existing safety procedures that were designed to prevent any foreseeable problems. In these cases, denials included claims that the accidents were due to technical failure, sabotage, or isolated human error, all of which were unforeseeable and for which they should not be held accountable. Again, these tactics were designed to show that the organization was rational in its actions and that the accident was "An 'act of God' ... that the company could not have foreseen or prevented ... and does not reflect underlying inadequacies in either the company, its management, or its way of doing business" (p. 286). In turn, Marcus and Goodman found that the use of such denials following accidents was associated with improvements in stock price for the organization in question.

Research in the area of procedural justice and equity (Folger & Cropanzano, 1998) provides some insight into the underlying reasons for the effectiveness of denials coupled with rational symbolic acts following accidents. This research suggests that individuals act as intuitive accountants in evaluating organizational explanations for decisions (Walster et al., 1978). From this perspective, people are viewed as legitimacy bookkeepers, who make rational assessments of the legitimacy of an organization based on a mental balance sheet of fair and unfair acts. Factors shown to enhance perceptions of rationality and justice include consistency in the application of decision procedures (Kim & Marborgne, 1993), advance notice of decision processes (Brockner et al., 1994), correctability of decisions (Magner & Johnson, 1995), and application of measurement standards in decision making based on documented evidence (Taylor et al., 1995).

Such signals of rationality and technical proficiency may indicate that an organization is adhering to normative guidelines and lead audiences mindlessly to accept that the organization is more credible than its detractors and thus not deserving of a decline in legitimacy (Meyer & Rowan, 1977). In essence, following accidents, references to rational thinking and decision processes may be thought of as the most that any organization could have done, given the information at hand (Elsbach, 2001a).

Justifications and Consideration of Audience Concerns Following Scandals

Perception management tactics that combine justifications with symbolic behaviors (or references to past symbolic behaviors) demonstrating sensitivity to audience concerns are often used following scandals. These tactics suggest that an organization had good reasons for taking the actions in question and that those reasons were based, at least in part, on their attempts to satisfy audience needs. For example, following a scandal at Chrysler, in which cars were sold as new although they had been driven by Chrysler executives with the odometers disconnected, Chairman Lee Iacocca justified the practice by claiming that it was a legitimate and normative industry practice that was done to check the quality of new cars. As he noted, "For years, spot checking and road testing new cars and trucks that come off the assembly line with the odometers disengaged was standard industry practice.... In our case, the average test mileage was 40 miles" (Hearit, 1994, p. 119).

As additional evidence of consideration for audience needs, such justifications for negatively perceived actions are often backed up by relabeling the event in terms that suggest that the actions were normative and in line with audience concerns (Ashforth & Humphrey, 1995). Thus, Iacocca labeled their practice as "road tests" for a "valid quality assurance program," which differentiated them from the fraudulent "executive perks" that media reports had identified (Hearit, 1994, p. 119).

Research in the areas of procedural justice and organizational perception management suggests that combining justifications with considerate symbolic behaviors may be most effective following foreseeable organizational controversies, such as scandals (Tyler, Boeckmann, Smith, & Yuen, 1997). In these cases, researchers have suggested that justifications combined with considerate symbolic behaviors indicate that the organization had good intentions and had listened to audience concerns before taking the actions that led to the scandal (Elsbach, 2001a). Proponents of this "value-expressive perspective" argue that audiences react positively to "having the chance to state their case, irrespective of whether their statement [actually] influences the decisions of the authorities" (Tyler, 1987, p. 333) or whether or not the outcome is favorable.

In this manner, Shapiro and Brett (1991) found that providing disgruntled employees with the opportunity to voice their grievances during an arbitration or mediation enhanced their perceptions of procedural justice if they felt the arbitrator or mediator had considered what they said. By contrast, voicing grievances did not improve perceptions of fairness if employees believed their remarks were ignored. In the same manner, Lind, Kanfer, and Early (1990) found that experimental participants who were told their opinions about the fairness of a task-related goal would be "taken into account" perceived more fairness in the procedure than did participants who believed their opinions would not be taken into account.

One of the best illustrations of the importance of combining justifications with behaviors that show consideration of audience concerns following foreseeable crises comes from the case of the initial response to the Exxon Valdez oil spill (Small, 1991). Although the spill itself was viewed as an unforeseeable accident, the poor initial response to the spill was viewed as a foreseeable crisis (i.e., Exxon could have foreseen that an oil spill from one of its tankers would happen and should have had a better response plan in place). Instead, Exxon spokespersons wasted precious time denying the extensive nature of the spill and arguing with local authorities about who was responsible for cleaning up.

Exxon's failure to show consideration of audience concerns has been called "a textbook example of what not to do when an unexpected crisis thrusts a company into the limelight" (Holusha, 1989, p. D1). In particular, the response to the Valdez spill was criticized as arrogant and insensitive to the concerns of the public (Small, 1991). This view of insensitivity by Exxon leaders was primarily blamed on the absence of Exxon's CEO, Lawrence Rawl, from the media spotlight in the early days following the crisis and by his later remarks when interviewed. As *Fortune Magazine* (Anonymous, 1989) noted,

> Rawl's *inability to consider his situation from the public's point of view led to much folly*. At first he seemed to be hiding from the press ... for six days, as reporters around the world spread the news of wheezing waterfowl and oil slicks the size of states, the most visible Exxon spokesman was Frank Iarossi, the head of the company's obscure shipping division. Then, when Rawl entered the public view, speaking to PBS's *MacNeil-Lehrer NewsHour, Fortune*, and others, he sometimes made matters worse with heedless remarks. On CBS's *This Morning* he said his job was not to know details of a highly technical cleanup plan [emphasis added]. (Quoted in Small, 1991, p. 20).

Managing Organizational Reputations for Integrity Following Scandals

Scandals involving severely unethical or morally illegitimate actions (e.g., corporate fraud, human rights abuse, tyranny) can damage even longstanding organizational reputations for quality and integrity. The case illustration at the end of this chapter describes one such scandal. In a matter of weeks, the revered retail giant Sears Roebuck & Co., whose overall positive reputation for integrity and quality was synonymous with its logo, "Sears, you can count on us," had all but lost that reputation following a multistate investigation of its auto repair centers (Gellene, 1992b). This investigation revealed corporate-wide fraud, which cost consumers millions of dollars in unnecessary auto repairs and replacement of parts (Gellene, 1992b). The magnitude of this scandal caused consumers to question their long-held trust in the company and their perceptions of its reputation for integrity. As a result, in the months following the scandal, Sears had its first quarterly loss since the Great Depression (Associated Press, 1992). As the case illustrates, Sears' response to this scandal served only to make matters worse. By contrast, other organizations in similar situations have demonstrated that reputations can be saved, even in these most dire of situations. These examples suggest that, following scandals, apologies and reparative actions may be the most effective means of managing organizational reputations.

Apologies and Reparative Action Following Scandals

Because scandals are typically shown to be the result of deliberate organizational actions, accounts that deny responsibility for them (e.g., excuses or denials) are not likely to be viewed as credible. Instead, apologies or justifications (which admit responsibility for the scandalous actions but argue that these actions were justifed) are more likely to be accepted by audiences. Of these two types of accounts, apologies are often preferred following scandals that call into question the integrity of an organization because such scandals often involve actions, such as criminal activities, that are hard to justify at any level (Hearit, 1994).

Effective apologies combine both an admission of blameworthiness (e.g., "we were wrong") with a promise that the problem that led to the scandal has been isolated and resolved (e.g., "we won't let this happen again"; Hearit, 1994). In this way, apologies are designed to convince audiences that the undesirable event should not be considered a "fair representation" of what the organization is really like (Schlenker, 1980, p. 154). As Schlenker noted, in terms of individual apologies, "Blame must be attached to a 'self' that no longer exists or has changed sufficiently that audiences do not need to be concerned about a repeat of the offense. Thus, a current 'good' self is split off from the past 'bad' self that was responsible for the undesirable offense" (p. 154).

One of the most effective means of proving that an organization is currently distinct from the organization that caused a scandal is to take reparative actions that alter its core structures or procedures (e.g., instituting new compensation schemes, changing leadership, reorganizing subunits). Such reparative actions demonstrate a concern for the welfare of harmed audiences, and provide proof of a commitment to righting the wrong in situations where mere explanations and accounts would be met with suspicion

(Marcus & Goodman, 1991). In addition, reparative actions that involve changes to fundamental organizational structures and practices help audiences focus on the future of the organization, rather than on its past. Such a focus allows organizational leaders to concentrate on re-establishing a history of credible behavior and re-earning a reputation for integrity.

An example of successful reputation management through the use of apologies and reparative actions involves the investment bank, Solomon Brothers, and the scandal over its illegal attempts to corner the Treasury securities market in 1991 (Fombrun, 1996).[1] At the time of the scandal, Solomon Brothers was viewed as the most powerful and respected broker on Wall Street. Then, in August of 1991, Solomon Brothers announced that it had committed, "irregularities and rule violations in connection with its submission of bids in certain auctions of Treasury securities" (quoted in Fombrun, 1996, p. 365). By the end of the year, the company faced 46 lawsuits over charges of fraud, price manipulation, and misrepresentation in its securities dealings. Shares in the company lost almost $500 million in market value in the first week following the scandal, and credit regulators downgraded its debt and stock ratings (Fombrun, 1996). Shortly after the scandal broke, an editorial in *The New York Times* characterized Solomon Brothers as a company governed by "a culture of greed, contempt for government regulations, and a sneering attitude toward ethics or any other impediments to earning a buck" (editorial, August 22, 1991). Clearly, the scandal had damaged Solomon Brothers' reputation for integrity.

In response to the scandal, Solomon Brothers carried out a textbook case of effective reputation management. In addition to accepting responsibility for their actions, the Solomon board undertook swift and sweeping reparative actions designed to correct the problems that led to the fraudulent bidding behavior and to prevent it from happening again.

First, the board appointed Warren Buffet as the interim chairman of the bank. Known as "Mr. Clean," Buffet maintained a personal reputation for integrity that sent a strong signal to outsiders about the values of the bank. In turn, Buffet appointed another veteran officer of Solomon, Deryck Maughan, known as "Mr. Integrity," to act as chief operating officer. Second, Buffet cooperated fully and openly with the regulators who had been assigned to investigate the bank and hired an outside firm, Coopers and Lybrand, to conduct an internal audit of the entire trading operations for the company. Third, Buffet undertook a major restructuring of the corporation,

---

[1] An earlier version of this case appears in Elsbach (2005).

including firing more than 140 analysts, bankers, and traders, reducing the power of the investment banking subsidiary of the company, and revising the pay systems that been largely blamed as a motivator for fraudulent trading behavior (Fombrun, 1996).

Together, these actions demonstrated that the company was committed, over the long run, to operating in a trustworthy and ethical manner, not just to overcoming the short-term obstacles that had resulted from the scandal. Such acts also helped focus the audience's attention on the future of Solomon Brothers, rather than on the past actions that led to the scandal. By 1996 Solomon Brothers had re-emerged as the largest and most influential bank on Wall Street (Fombrun, 1996).

Managing Organizational Identities Following Product Failures

A final crisis situation that organizations may commonly encounter is a threat to organizational identity following product or service failures. Such crises may result in threats to either status categorizations that define organizational identity (e.g., a ranking by industry analysts that suggests that a firm that thought its products or services were top tier is, in fact, second tier) or distinctiveness–categorizations that define identity (e.g., an organization that defined itself through its wholesome all-natural products finds out that some of those products are making consumers sick).

In these situations, organizations have been shown to use two techniques to affirm and enhance their pre-existing identities. First, organizational members and leaders may attempt to highlight distinctiveness along dimensions others than those under attack (Elsbach & Kramer, 1996). Second, organizational members and leaders may attempt to highlight their affiliation with other organizations that have suffered from similar product failures but remain, nevertheless, high status (Thomsen & Rawson, 1998).

Distinctive Categorizations Following Product Failures

When a product or service failure leads members to question the positive value of distinctiveness categorizations (i.e., when that failure is visible and is clearly the fault of the organization) that define the identity of their organization, those members often look to other distinctive dimensions of the organization as means of affirming positive distinctiveness (Aronson, Blanton, & Cooper, 1995). Such categorizations present the organization's identity as multifaceted and suggest that the organization isn't all bad because it has many positive dimensions to its identity. For example, Elsbach and Kramer (1996) found that members of some U.S. business schools, who felt that the distinctive identities of their schools as high-status teaching institutes were threatened by poor *Business Week* rankings, attempted to reaffirm positive organizational identities by highlighting distinctiveness on other dimensions, such as research quality, collegial culture, and nontraditional students. Social identity research suggests that such behavior is adaptive for organizational members because specific identity dimensions may be more or less valued depending on context or audience (Brickson, 2000). For example, a doctor may find that her organization is viewed as more positively distinct when she is attending a medical conference than when she is attending her child's school play (Steele, Spencer, & Lynch, 1993).

An illustration of successful organizational identity management using just such distinctiveness categorizations following a product failure is the case of the Odwalla's e. coli poisonings in 1997 (Thomsen & Rawson, 1998). Odwalla, a manufacturer of fresh juices, was launched in 1980 in Danville, California. From the beginning, the organization maintained a distinctive identity based on its product, processing, and mission. This identity was largely based on the distinctive categorizations of "all natural" and "fresh" (Thomsen & Rawson, 1998). Odwalla's vision statement defined the company as "a breath of fresh intoxicating rhythm" and noted its commitment to "nourishing the body whole" (quoted in Thomsen & Rawson, 1998, p. 36). A primary part of this fresh and nourishing identity was the shunning of heat treatment or pasteurization in its juice processing. Instead, Odwalla kept the juices cold during the entire production and distribution process to maintain the naturalness of the product (Thomsen & Rawson, 1998).

Unfortunately, the very process that was central to Odwalla's identity became a huge liability when it was revealed that the deadly e. coli bacteria could survive in unpasteurized apple juice. This information came to light in the fall of 1996, after several people became ill and one child died following e. coli poisoning that was traced to unpasteurized Odwalla apple juice. This product failure created a severe threat to Odwalla's identity. As Thomsen and Rawson noted, "Odwalla now realized that it faced the ultimate challenge. It would have to change the production process that had given the company its identity without further alienating what remained of its loyal audience.... It would have to ... differentiate itself from the old Odwalla, and build a 'new' Odwalla that would still preserve and maintain the old values" (p. 42).

At this point, Odwalla's leaders decided to focus on a slightly different but still distinctive aspect of its identity. Thomsen and Rawson (1998) saw this new identity as focusing more on nourishment than all naturalness, bringing to the fore the concept of learning. As they reported:

> The "new" Odwalla would remain a "nourishment" company, but would now also become a "learning" company. "Learning," which had been mentioned as a value in previous company literature, now would be more of a major focus, or root metaphor, in its new rhetoric: Odwalla had learned from the past and the new company would continue to learn.... After all, "learning" implies that the company is being responsive to its audiences and business environments. That, in itself, is a highly regarded value, one that audiences would expect from such a caring and concerned company. (p. 42).

This new, distinctive identity categorization not only helped the organization to focus attention away from the now negatively perceived categorizations of all natural or fresh beverage, it also helped focus attention toward the future of the company and the distinctive categorizations with which it hoped to become identified. Combined with a number of corrective actions (e.g., using a flash pasteurization process, helping to form and fund an industry group committed to consumer health and safety), Odwalla's new identity helped save the company and allowed it to recover from the product failure crisis within two years (Thomsen & Rawson, 1998).

Affiliation With High-status Groups Following Product Failures

Product failures may also threaten the identity of an organization by calling into question its relative status or rank in comparison with other organizations. In these cases, product failures suggest that the organization should occupy a relatively lower status position compared to other organizations in terms of overall quality and performance (e.g., an airline that is consistently ranked last in on-time performance may be seen as lower status than its competitors).

In response to such identity threats, organizations may attempt to display or affirm their close affiliation with other, more highly ranked organizations as a means of reestablishing their status. Elsbach and Kramer (1996) found that members whose business schools were ranked lower than expected by the *Business Week* rankings commonly perceived the rankings as an identity threat and responded by suggesting that their organization was affiliated with other organizations that had suffered a similar fate, despite the fact that they were widely regarded as high status (e.g., "we're like many other high quality public universities that were ranked low because of our focus on research rather than teaching"). This type of recategorization serves two purposes. First, it suggests that, despite its poor performance on the ranked dimension, the organization in question may have qualities, similar to those of the other high-status organizations, that are positively valued. That is, these organizations have high status because of their performance on many dimensions, not just the one that is associated with the product failure. Second, it suggests that the status rankings may be, in fact, flawed because it rated other highly respected organizations lower than expected.

In the Odwalla case, the organization used affiliation with other high status organizations to shift focus away from their production process and toward problems faced by the fresh juice industry as a whole. First, they claimed that the organization lacked the new information that now suggested that e. coli bacteria could survive at the acidic levels contained in fresh apple juice—suggesting that this was a problem of which the entire juice industry was unaware (Thomsen & Rawson, 1998). Second, they promised to team up with several well-known universities and consulting companies, as well as other fresh juice makers, to form and lead the American Fresh Juice Council, which would pioneer new ways to promote food safety in the juice industry, just as Johnson and Johnson had pioneered tamper-proof packaging following the Tylenol poisonings (Thomsen & Rawson, 1998). These two actions suggested that Odwalla was in the same league as other respected juice makers as well as respected research institutes and other organizations that had successfully responded to product failures (e.g., Tylenol). As noted, Odwalla's response to their product failure was widely viewed as a success and a model for responding to such organizational crisis events.

PITFALLS OF ORGANIZATIONAL PERCEPTION MANAGEMENT FOLLOWING CRISIS EVENTS

Most of the examples described in this chapter detail successful deployment of perception management tactics following crisis events. However, as illustrated by the Exxon Valdez oil spill case, perception management does not always proceed smoothly or effectively. Instead, perception managers may fall prey to a number of cognitive errors and biases that lead them to engage in ineffective or even damaging perception management. In particular, researchers have identified three common pitfalls that may threaten the effectiveness of organizational perception management: threat rigidity responses, dysfunctional sensemaking, and protesting too much.

Threat Rigidity

Threat rigidity refers to an organization's or individual's narrowing of focus, conservation of resources, and reliance on well-worn procedures when confronting a control-reducing threat (e.g., a regulatory agency introduces policies that limit organizational discretion in production processes, budget cuts restrict organizational choice in daily operating procedures; Chattopadhyay et al., 2001 Staw, Sandelands, & Dutton, 1981). Theorists reason that threat rigidity responses are attempts by organizations and their leaders to exert control in situations where they perceive their control is diminishing (Chattopadhyay et al., 2001).

Crisis events that engender threat-rigidity responses may also jeopardize the image or reputation of the organization. As D'Aunno and Sutton (1992) noted, for example, "Funding decreases [as a control-reducing threat] may be interpreted by key exchange partners as a sign of managerial incompetence and organizational ineffectiveness. As a result, leaders are likely to be blamed and replaced when financial performance is poor (Meindl, Ehrlich, & Dukerich, 1985; Pfeffer & Salancik, 1978)" (p. 118). In these cases, the perception management that follows may also be narrow in focus, conservative, and uncreative. For example, organizations that have faced only minor performance setbacks in the past due to economic downturns and responded with rational excuses for these events may rigidly use the same form of perception management following a major product failure, such as filing for bankruptcy after making a poor acquisition choice. However, as noted, the types of responses that audiences look for following crisis events are quite different depending on the degree of preventability attributed to the crisis. A bankruptcy following a poor acquisition may be seen as more preventable (and thus harder to excuse) than cyclical downturns due to the economy. Using a one-size-fits-all response for both types of events ignores this critical distinction.

In other cases, organizations who are unaccustomed to dealing with crisis events (either because they have never had a crisis or because they have a reputation for quality that allows them to explain most negative events easily) may exhibit threat rigidity in responding to a rare product failure, accident, or scandal and treat the event like just another routine business problem rather than a full-blown crisis. This type of case is illustrated by the response of Daimler–Benz to a major failure in its 1997 Mercedes A-Class sedan (Puchan, 2001). The crisis happened when the A-class sedan—a car that Daimler–Benz hoped would earn car of the year honors—toppled over during a test run by Swedish motoring journalists. The car overturned at relatively low speed (40 mph) on an obstacle course (chosen to simulate the common occurrence of deer and elk running onto the roads in Sweden) and injured the four journalists who were taking the test drive. The crash occurred during the same time as the International Motor Show in Tokyo, where the new A-class was being introduced. Such a major product failure was unheard of for the prestigious Mercedes line of autos and was unexpected by Daimler–Benz.

In response to the rollover, however, Daimler–Benz reacted much like a deer in the headlights. For the next few days there was no official word from Daimler–Benz about the crash. Worse, at the Tokyo motor show, interested journalists were told that the event was not worthy of a corporate response: "The board [of Daimler–Benz] does not think it is necessary to provide an official statement, simply because somewhere a car has toppled over" (quoted in Puchan, 2001, p. 43). Finally, one Daimler–Benz board member called the test results "hare-brained" and threatened to sue one of the Swedish journalists for submitting such a damaging report (Puchan, 2001, p. 44). These responses suggest that Daimler–Benz leaders were caught off-guard by the crisis and felt threatened by the accusations that one of their prized products was unsafe. To cope with this threat, these leaders responded by treating the crisis as a familiar production problem and made the hasty decision to threaten legal action against the Swedish reporters (long before they had any evidence about the validity of the reports).

Unsatisfied with explanations for the reported crash from Daimler–Benz, auto journalists from around the world attempted to replicate the crash with their own testers. These test proved to be an image nightmare for Daimler–Benz, as all of the test cars left the road on two wheels and one toppled over, this time on film (Puchan, 2001). Further, this new information led many to speculate about the future financial wellness of the company (Puchan, 2001). Although Daimler–Benz ultimately admitted to problems in the design of the A-class, the initial damage done by their threat-rigidity response to the crisis led them to lose over $300 million in profits and tarnished the once-spotless reputation of the organization.

Dysfunctional Perception Management: Self-Deception, Trivialization, and Scapegoating

In some crisis situations, organizations are faced with the fact that their actions (which caused the crisis) were not in concert with their stated beliefs and values (e.g., the juice maker Odwalla, discussed previously, found that its products and processing methods were harmful to consumers rather than wholesome and nourishing). Such belief–act discrepancies often threaten the self-perceptions of organizations and their members and may lead them to make changes in structures and procedures to prevent future discrepancies of the same manner (Brown & Jones, 2000). As Odwalla CEO Greg Steltenpohl noted, "I've made my life's work focused on health nutrition. Now to find our company linked to a problem that has affected public health has been very difficult" (quoted in Thomsen & Rawson, 1998, p. 41). In turn, Odwalla significantly changed the juice processing (e.g., added heat treatment of apple juice) to prevent future belief–act discrepancies (Thomsen & Rawson, 1998).

In some cases, however, these discrepancies are resolved by dysfunctional perception management tactics that allow organizations and their members to deny personal responsibility for undesirable actions and maintain positive self-perceptions (Brown & Jones, 2000). Specifically, researchers have suggested that through the use of self-deception (i.e., claims that the organization was unaware it was committing an undesirable act), trivialization (i.e., claims that the undesirable act was not important), or scapegoating (i.e., blaming others for the undesirable act) organizations and their members may preserve collective and individual self-esteem despite involvement in negative events such as scandals, accidents, or product failures (Brown & Jones, 2000). The obvious downside of such tactics is that the organization does not perceive the need to change its structures or procedures (which may have caused the negative event) and leaves itself open to future crises of the same type.

One of the most deadly illustrations of such dysfunctional perception management following crisis events comes from Firestone's perception management following early reports of tread separation on its ATX and Wilderness AT tires, leading to rollover crashes for the cars (mostly Ford Explorer SUVs) on which they were installed (Blaney, Beloit, & Brazeal, 2002). First, it appears that Firestone was self-deceiving regarding early reports of tread separation on its tires. Although it had received reports of tread separation beginning in 1998, a Firestone memo "said it wasn't aware of a problem until July 2000. And then, it only knew, ... because an impatient Ford analyzed the tire company's reports of incidents involving injury or damage" (Healy, 2000, p. 3B).

Second, Firestone trivialized the role of the tires in the rollover crashes. Even after they began recalling tires in the fall of 2000, their president,

Yoichiro Kaizaki, claimed that the "fatal accidents blamed on [Firestone] tires weren't caused by defects" and noted, "we didn't recall the tires because we found a defect that caused the accidents" (Stoddard, 2000). These comments implied that some minor problem merited the recall but that this problem was not the cause of the deadly crashes.

Finally, Firestone scapegoated Ford for advising consumers to keep the tires underinflated and thus causing the rollover accidents (Blaney et al., 2002). As Kaizaki noted, "under inflation of tires or poor maintenance are known to be causes of the tread belt separations and punctures that caused the accidents" (quoted in Blaney et al., 2002, p. 383). This scapegoating of Ford eventually led Firestone to sever their 100-year-old relationship with the automaker. According to Firestone's newly appointed CEO and President John Lampe, this act was fueled by "Ford's refusal to admit that the Explorer's design played a role in the tires' tread separations, which have been linked to 174 deaths and 700 injuries" (quoted in Blaney et al., 2002, p. 384).

All three of these perception management tactics (i.e., self-deception, trivialization, and scapegoating) have been blamed for Firestone's slow response to the crisis and potentially for the high number of fatalities that resulted from consumer unawareness of the problem. As Blaney et al. (2002) noted: "Had corrective action been implemented immediately, it seems likely that many deaths and injuries could have been avoided" (p. 388).

Protesting Too Much

A third pitfall of organizational perception management following crisis events is the tendency for organizations to protest their legitimacy (or trustworthiness or competence) too much (Ashforth & Gibbs, 1990). As Ashforth and Gibbs noted, "[o]rganizations that are perceived by constituents as legitimate simply do not need to protest legitimacy as strongly" (p. 185). That is, organizations that have preexisting and strong reputations as legitimate and high-status organizations do not need to promote their organizational legitimacy because their everyday deeds and performance speak for themselves (Greenberg, 1990). Because most audiences understand this phenomenon, organizations that protest their legitimacy too loudly may be viewed as less legitimate than those who are subtler in their perception management. Jones and Pittman (1982) called this outcome the "self-promoters paradox: Since protests of competence are more likely when actual competence is problematic or unknown, individuals tend to discount such protests" (as cited in Ashforth & Gibbs, 1990, p. 186).

Ashforth and Gibbs (1990) defined three types of organizational actors whose perception management may come across as protesting too much. First, they defined the clumsy actor as an organization that is unethical, heavy-handed, and insensitive in its perception management. Clumsy actors often attack those who question the legitimacy of the organization (O'Day, 1974) and may use threats or bribes in attempts to silence their detractors (e.g., Daimler–Benz's threats to sue the journalists who claimed their A-class sedan had toppled over in a test drive). Second, they defined the nervous actor as an organization whose perception management appears dogmatic, intolerant, and evasive. Nervous actors may respond to crisis by paying meticulous attention to legal regulations and by carefully defining how their actions adhered to the letter of the law (e.g., Firestone's claim that underinflation of its tires caused rollover crashes, not defects in the tires themselves). Their defense of their actions often comes across as righteous indignation (Ashforth & Gibbs, 1990). Finally, Ashforth and Gibbs defined the overacting actor as an organization whose audiences perceive its perception management as self-aggrandizing, inflammatory, and overreacting. Overacting actors tend to make claims of legitimacy that are far beyond what even a highly legitimate organization could claim (e.g., Exxon's claims that the beaches of Prince William Sound were completely restored to their prior conditions after only a few months of cleanup) and may use inflammatory rhetoric to discredit a competitor or detractor (e.g., referring to a hostile takeover as a "rape"). In all three cases, the perception management that was intended to repair or restore legitimacy following a crisis may have the opposite effect and further reduce the legitimacy of the organizations who use them.

CASE ILLUSTRATION: REPUTATION MANAGEMENT AND SEARS AUTO CENTERS

In this chapter, I have discussed how organizations may manage audiences' perceptions of their images, reputations, and identities following crisis events. The research and theory reviewed in this chapter suggests that effective perception management is possible in these contexts, especially if spokespersons understand how to tailor their perception management to the specifics of the crisis. Nevertheless, I have described several situations in which perception management may be flawed and have defined the most common pitfalls faced by organizations attempting perception management. In the remainder of the chapter, I describe, in detail, an illustrative case of flawed perception management. This case shows how providing the wrong types of verbal accounts following a scandal can be viewed not only as unresponsive to the crisis but as an indication that a longstanding reputation for quality has been unearned. This is the case of Sears Auto Centers.[2]

By the early 1990s, the retail giant Sears, Roebuck & Co. operated over 1,500 auto repair centers in the United States, performing routine maintenance and repairs for private customers (*Times* staff, 1995). National sales from auto repairs were over $3 billion in 1992. Against this backdrop, on June 11, 1992, the California Attorney General's Office announced that it had conducted an 18-month undercover investigation of 33 of the 70 Sears Auto Centers in the state. State consumer affairs director Jim Conran reported that the investigation uncovered "a consistent pattern of abuse" linked to corporate reward and quota systems that encouraged mechanics to recommend unnecessary repairs (Gellene, 1992c).

According to the report, undercover agents working for the California Department of Consumer Affairs took cars in top condition to Sears for mechanical inspection and were overcharged an average of $223 for repairs (Gellene, 1992c). The scandal did not stop there. As the *Los Angeles Times* reported, "Besides making unnecessary repairs, Sears mechanics also charged some undercover agents for work that was never performed.... In a few cases, Sears mechanics damaged cars: one undercover auto that went in for a brake inspection left Sears without brakes ..." (p. A1).

As Consumer Affairs Director Conran put it: "these are not honest mistakes.... This is the systematic looting of the public" (Gellene, 1992c, p. A1). Further, Conran directly threatened Sears' legitimacy by claiming, "People go to Sears because they feel they will get good service. They believe it is a company you can depend on. Unfortunately, that is not the case" (p. A1). As a result, Conran's agency said it would seek to revoke Sears' license to repair autos in California. The same day, the California Attorney General's Office reported that it too was investigating Sears Auto Centers in response to consumer complaints and threatened to seek monetary damages from the retailer (Gellene, 1992a).

Given the overwhelming evidence in support of the charges against Sears as well as the apparent intentional nature of the controversy, the Sears Auto Centers crisis appears to qualify as a scandal (Marcus & Goodman, 1991) that was based on the deliberate design of Sears' incentive and compensation system for auto mechanics. In such cases, the previous discussion suggests that justifications that show consideration for audience concerns would provide the best response. However, this was far from Sears' initial response.

---

[2]An earlier version of this case is published in Elsbach (2001a).

Primary Accounts

Counter to the suggestions in this chapter, Sears' initial responses involved denials based on rational arguments that contained extensive technical jargon. Thus, the day after the indictment a Sears' spokesperson denied the government charges by claiming, "There may have been some honest mistakes, but there was no fraud" (Gellene, 1992a, p. D1).

This spokesperson also reported that

> The department's undercover investigation was faulty because the agency used older cars with signs of wear that tricked Sears' employees into thinking certain repairs were needed ... [for example] at least two cars received new master cylinders because the department had aged the parts with acid to look old. In addition, there were signs that brake fluid had leaked from faulty master cylinders replaced by the department before taking the cars to Sears. (p. D1)

In addition to these remarks, Sears placed full-page advertisements in major California newspapers (e.g., *Los Angeles Times,* June 14, 1992) two days later. These ads claimed,

> With over 2 million automotive customers serviced last year in California alone, mistakes may have occurred. However, Sears wants you to know that we would never intentionally violate the trust customers have shown in our company for 105 years.... You rely on us to recommend preventative maintenance measures to help insure your safety, and to avoid more costly future repairs. This includes recommending replacement of worn parts, when appropriate, before they fail. This accepted industry practice is being challenged by the Bureau.

These statements were primarily denials (e.g., "fraud didn't happen") based on rational arguments (e.g., "we weren't making unnecessary repairs; we were performing preventative maintenance"), communicated through technical jargon (e.g., "dirty or acid stained master cylinders look the same as worn ones") and in reference to industry versus social norms (e.g., "accepted industry practice" vs. consumer concerns). As the earlier discussion in this chapter suggests, these accounts were not effective in repairing Sears' legitimacy. Sales in Sears Auto Centers slowed, Sears stock dropped, and a flurry of class-action suits were filed against Sears in the days following the initial reports (White & Maier, 1992).

Secondary Accounts

Two days after Sears' full-page denial, the Attorney General's Office in New Jersey said it too had found evidence of fraud at Sears Auto Centers

(Gellene, 1992b). The New Jersey Consumer Affairs director said that its undercover agents had taken 12 cars with disconnected alternator wires (a $10 repair) to Sears Auto Centers, and had been recommended unneeded repairs ranging from $30 to $406.

In response to this new evidence, a Sears spokesperson denied a connection between the California and New Jersey investigations, supporting the company's claim that there was no system-wide fraud based on incentive systems. Instead, Sears continued to deny any wrong-doing and claimed that they were only following technical procedures and company norms. As one Sears spokesperson was said to have reported,

> While Sears' preliminary diagnostic equipment may have indicated a defective battery or alternator, a mechanic might have discovered the loose alternator wire once work began.... One thing we're checking is how visible the loose wire was ... in a smaller shop, a mechanic might spot the loose wire right away. At Sears, a car is first inspected by a service advisor, or salesman, who evaluates the problem, provides an estimate and refers it to a mechanic. (Gellene, 1992b, p. D2).

As before, these denials did not improve Sears' legitimacy. In fact, several industry experts suggested that Sears' defensive stance was only making things worse. As Gerald Meyers, former chairman of American Motors Corp. and professor of management at Carnegie Mellon University, noted three days after the New Jersey report,

> Sears' first mistake was getting defensive.... Their message? It isn't true, and even if it were, it's not serious, and even if it's serious, don't worry about it, we guarantee our work. That's not good enough. Thousands of Californians trusted Sears to service their cars and install good parts—and only when necessary. If anything disturbs customers more than being bilked, it's having their safety threatened. That's exactly what these fraud charges sound like to consumers.... Sears may very well win in court, but management should concentrate first on protecting and getting customers. (Meyers, 1992, June 19, p. B7)

To make matters worse, three days later, Florida's Attorney General's Office reported that they had recently undertaken an investigation of Sears Auto Centers in response to the large number of complaints they had received following the California and New Jersey reports (Gellene & White, 1992).

Final Accounts

In the face of the enormous evidence supporting claims of fraud, Sears chairman Edward Brennan admitted, on June 23, 1992 (11 days after the initial investigation announcement), that their incentive system for auto mechanics led to overbilling in car repairs (Trager, 1992). Two days later, Brennan gave the details of Sears' pay policy in a full-page advertisement in national newspapers (*Los Angeles Times,* June 25, 1992) and a nationally televised commercial. This testimonial account included an acknowledgment of the problem and of consumer concerns (i.e., their concerns about trusting their auto mechanics), a justification for the recommendation of unneeded parts (i.e., we stressed preventive maintenance because consumers said they wanted it, and it's safer), and an extensive list of responsive actions that showed consideration of consumer views and desires (i.e., discontinue incentive pay, use outside auditors to check on us). Furthermore, this account replaced technical references and language with more common terms (e.g., terms like *folks* and *shopping audits* instead of specific repair terms). Excerpts from the advertisement included the following:

> We are confident that our Auto Center customer satisfaction rate is among the highest in the industry. But after an extensive review, we have concluded that our incentive compensation and goal-setting program inadvertently created an environment in which mistakes have occurred. We are moving quickly and aggressively to eliminate that environment....

> We have eliminated incentive compensation and goal-setting systems for automotive service advisors—the folks who diagnose problems and recommend repairs to you.... Rewards will now be based on customer satisfaction....

> We're augmenting our own quality control efforts by retaining an independent organization to conduct ongoing, unannounced "shopping audits" of our automotive services....

> We have written to all state attorneys general, inviting them to compare our auto repair standards and practices with those of their states in order to determine whether differences exist....

> And we are helping to organize and fund a joint industry–consumer–government effort to review current auto repair practices and recommend uniform industry standards....

> Our policy of preventive maintenance...recommending replacement of worn parts *before* they fail...has been criticized by the California Bureau of Automotive Repair as constituting unneeded repairs. We don't see it that way. We recommend preventive maintenance because that's what our consumers want, and because it makes for safer cars on the road. In fact, 75 percent of the consumers we talked to in a nationwide survey last weekend told us that auto repair centers should recommend replacement of parts for preventive maintenance. As always, no work will *ever* be performed without your approval.

These accounts appeared to end the crisis for Sears, as evidenced by the sharp decline in press coverage and no further reports of undercover investigations in other states, yet in the long run, these accounts may have been too little, too late. In 1993, Sears Auto Centers were doing so poorly the company dropped most of its repair services, including oil changes and tune-ups, leaving tire and battery sales and installation as its major auto repair business (Gellene, 1995).

5

Organizational Perception Management During Evolving Controversies

Whereas most research on perception management following crisis events has focused on relatively circumscribed controversies (i.e., related to a single event at a single moment in time), some controversies are much more loosely defined. For example, controversies that linger for more than a few months often evolve as new information or interested audiences arise. In other cases, controversies may evolve quickly but substantially as powerful and influential parties become involved in the dispute. The involvement of the Clinton Administrations involvement in the Monica Lewinsky scandal, the controversy over the 2002 merger between the computer giants Hewlett-Packard and Compac, the Pacific Lumber Company's year-long controversy over tree-sitter Julia Butterfly Hill—these are all examples of controversies that evolved in terms of the perceptions, audiences, tactics, and spokespersons that were involved in them. One of the attributes that distinguishes such controversies from the crisis events discussed in Chapter 4, then, is the need to adapt and evolve perception management to match the changing nature of the controversy. As Ginzel et al. (1993) put it, "[Organizational] impression management is [often] a process of reciprocal influence in which the presence of the organizational audience affects both the initial attempts to explain an organization's actions or performance, as well as ongoing attempts to resolve interpretive conflicts" (p. 229).

DEFINING EVOLVING ORGANIZATIONAL CONTROVERSIES

A look at controversies that evolve over time reveals two primary categories of events that are most likely to fit this definition: contentious negotiations and controversial identity changes.

Contentious Negotiations

When an organization and another party (e.g., another organization, the public, a group of customers) disagree about the details of an important decision (e.g., how to insure the safety of organizational products), the two sides may decide to negotiate the terms of the decision. Entering in negotiation means that neither side has the power or the desire to use the power to get its own way (Fisher & Ury, 1991). Sometimes this negotiation is carried out in a formal fashion, such as labor contract negotiations between an organization and a workers' union. Other times it is carried out informally, such as the negotiation in the press and the court of public opinion about how to handle an accounting scandal. In either case, such negotiations have the potential to become long-term, evolving controversies.

Contentious negotiations typically occur because there is some initial disagreement or ambiguity about the legitimacy of an organizational decision or action and initial organizational accounts do not satisfy some audiences in terms of justifying or excusing the action. As Ginzel et al. (1993) noted:

> We contend that top managers will try to develop initial accounts that provoke as much sympathy and as little antagonism as possible, that top managers often make errors in judgment about which accounts will provoke the most widespread sympathetic response, and that when initial accounts provoke more antagonism than anticipated, antagonistic audience members may pressure top managers to change their accounts over time. (p. 235)

For example, if there is ambiguity over the moral legitimacy or social "rightness" of an organizational decision (Suchman, 1995), organizational leaders may want to pull back from their initial stance and take stock of public reaction before offering an alternate decision. Such a process may occur, for instance, after an organization announces an impending change to its products or services (e.g., an airline announces that it will begin charging larger passengers the price of two seats instead of one). In these cases, the negotiation between the organization and its audiences evolves as these audiences become more aware of the controversial issues (e.g., organizational customers hear about larger passengers being charged double) and the organization becomes more aware of audiences' views on these issues (e.g., some passengers complain that higher rates for larger passengers is stigmatizing, whereas others praise the decision as preventing crowding by large seatmates).

In other cases, there may be a conflict between perceptions of the practical versus the moral legitimacy of a decision. An organizational decision that is viewed as having practical legitimacy is one that is seen as serving the practical interests of organizational stakeholders (Suchman, 1995). Thus, a decision to use foreign labor may be viewed as having practical legitimacy by some organizational audiences because it lowers costs to consumers and increases profits for organizational stockholders. At the same time, such a decision may also be viewed as morally illegitimate by other audiences because it takes advantage of weak child labor laws and poor working conditions in foreign countries.

Finally, in some cases, organizations and their audiences may have conflicting interpretations of the practical legitimacy of a decision or action. For example, contract negotiations between the players' union and owners of Major League Baseball teams have often become contentious as both sides view the other's demands as damaging to the viability of the industry. In the case of the 2002 baseball negotiations, many Major League owners claimed that they needed to institute a luxury tax on high-payroll teams to level the playing field between powerful and rich teams, like the New York Yankees, and most of the rest of the teams in the major leagues (Torry, 2002). Such a leveling, they claimed, would allow more teams to be profitable. The players, however, did not see the need to penalize teams for paying top dollar to great players and worried that a luxury tax would reduce the salaries of all players. Players' union representatives suggested that taxing high-payroll teams would amount to penalizing the players for poor management (Torry, 2002).

Controversial Identity Changes

Evolving controversies may also arise during organizational identity changes. When an organization announces that it plans to adopt new leadership, merge with another organization, significantly change its products or services, or sever its relationship with longstanding partners, audiences may anticipate major changes in the structures and procedures that define everyday life in the organization. In some cases, audiences may push back against the impending or proposed identity changes. In other cases, audiences may be the driving force in causing the identity change, and organizational leaders may push back against their efforts.

The difficulty with accepting such identity changes arises because organizational members often must give up or disidentify with their organization's previous identity before they can accept its new one (Elsbach, 1999; Reger et al., 1994). In some cases this disidentification may mean cutting ties to long-standing and cherished social groups (e.g., partnerships with failing financial services firms) that nevertheless now threaten an organization's status. In other cases, disidentification means shedding traditional categorizations (e.g., being known as an online stock trading firm), which, while distinctive at one time, now make the organization appear undistinctive. In addition, because the adoption (or attempted adoption) of such changes often unfolds over several months, conflicts between organizations and their audiences may continue to arise and evolve over a period that may begin prior to the change and continue for several months after the change has occurred.

ORGANIZATIONAL PERCEPTION MANAGEMENT DURING EVOLVING CONTROVERSIES

Perhaps because evolving controversies require organizations to respond quickly as new events arise, various forms of verbal accounts and categorizations are the most commonly used tactics for responding to them. These verbal tactics also allow organizational spokespersons to tailor their messages to particular audiences, when more than one issue and one audience is involved in the controversy (Zbaracki, 1998). In addition to accounts and categorizations, organizations use their primary business practices as a form of symbolic behavior to manage their perceptions during evolving controversies. Salient business activities, such as changes in routine safety procedures, manufacturing protocols, and quality control programs, can be a powerful tools for influencing perceptions of organizations in evolving controversies because they demonstrate active responsiveness to increasing audience concerns (Arnold et al., 1996).

The use of verbal tactics and primary business activities to manage perceptions of organizations in evolving controversies can be illustrated in the two common contexts of: contentious negotiations and controversial identity changes. In contentious negotiations, as noted previously, the most commonly threatened perceptions are images of organizational legitimacy. In controversial identity changes, the most commonly threatened perceptions are those of distinctive and status-oriented organizational identities.

Managing Images of Legitimacy During Contentious Negotiations

Over the course of contentious negotiations, audiences may reject the initial accounts given for an organization's position as new information arises, new developments occur, or new inconsistencies or inaccuracies in past statements and evidence are uncovered. In these cases, research suggests that progressive accounts that demonstrate that the organization has adapted its position in response to new information may be most effective (Ginzel et al.,1993). However, it appears that for such progressive accounts to be effective, they must be coupled with the undertaking of new business activities that convincingly show that the organization is not just talking about how its position in the negotiation has changed but is demonstrating that position in its day-to-day activities. Case studies of progressive accounts coupled with changes in business activities suggest that these tactics are most effective when they are used either to illustrate consideration of audience needs or concerns or to illustrate rationality in organizational decision making.

Progressive Accounts and Business Activities That Illustrate Consideration

When conflicts arise between audience and organizational views of the moral and practical legitimacy of a decision or action taken by an organization, organizational spokespersons may respond with progressive accounts and changes to primary business practices that, over time, demonstrate that the organization is taking audiences' views into consideration and rethinking the controversial decision or act. When such accounts and behaviors demonstrate a concern for audience views of moral and practical legitimacy, they are highly effective in repairing threats to legitimacy.

One example of the effective use of progressive accounts and business activities comes from the case of Southwest Airlines' 2002 decision to enforce its longstanding policy of charging large passengers (i.e., those who cannot sit in their seats with the arm rest down) for two seats (St. John & Zamora, 2002). Southwest claimed that this move was made in response to customer complaints. In the summer of 2002, spokesperson Angela Vargo reported that 90% of all complaints the airline received from passengers were from those who had been seated next to large passengers who spilled over into the next seat and caused discomfort to seatmates (St. John & Zamora, 2002).

Immediately after the decision to enforce extra charges for large passengers was announced, on June 19, 2002, a flood of angry responses appeared in national newspapers. Advocates for the obese, including the National Association to Advance Fat Acceptance, claimed that the enforcement of policies requiring large passengers to purchase two seats was unfair and arbitrary because it left the decision about who should have to purchase a second seat up to the individual judgment of ticket agents (St. John & Zamora, 2002). Newspaper travel writers also claimed that the rules were stigmatizing and insensitive to obese people and that they resulted purely from profit motives by the airlines (Molyneaux, 2002). A travel editor for the Houston Chronicle put it this way:

> What angers me the most is that heavy people as an entity are being stereotyped. I've sat on airplanes next to dozens of babies who screamed for the duration of a flight, next to adults who chatted incessantly for hours, next to passengers who were rail-thin but stunk like a sewer. Do we kick them all off the plane?

He added,

> The saddest part about all this is that airlines could easily adjust to suit consumer needs if they weren't so greedy. [They] could establish perhaps just one row on each aircraft that includes four seats instead of six to allow for the rare extremely obese passengers—thus ensuring comfort for people of all sizes and for those seated adjacent to them. (quoted in Molyneaux, 2002, p. K1)

In response to these complaints, Southwest Airlines spokespersons showed consideration of audience concerns by claiming that the policy was designed for the safety and comfort of large passengers, in addition to those seated around them. Southwest spokesperson, Beth Harbin, noted, using sensitive language, that

> This policy is designed for the customer of size, to give them room to be comfortable and safe on the aircraft. Certainly, we understand this will be a bit of a transition, and we will work on that with each individual customer. (quoted in Hensel, 2002, p. B1)

Harbin also noted that

> The preferred method is for the customer to make the decision [about needing an extra seat]. If there is any question or any doubt, the airline will offer to pre-board the passenger. A passenger could then sample a seat out of sight of most other passengers. If a larger passenger is required to purchase an extra seat and empty ones are available, the customer can get a refund. (quoted in Hensel, 2002, p. 1)

Although these responses quieted some of the criticism from large passengers and their advocates, the issue remained in the news as advocates for "normal sized" passengers began to speak up in *favor* of the policy. David

S. Stempler, president of the Air Travelers Association, sided with this group when he noted,

> [T]he reality is that when passengers of size are taking up the space of another passenger, that passenger is inconvenienced. It is also a safety issue. The really telling point is if you cannot get into or out of the seat with the armrests down, you need to use another seat. ("Large passenger policy," 2002, p. E3).

Then, in October of 2002 the controversy evolved as a lawsuit filed by a passenger, who was seated next to an obese seatmate, was settled. The court ruling—which granted compensation to Virgin Atlantic passenger, Barbara Hewson, after she suffered a blood clot, torn leg muscles, and sciatica after an 11-hour flight next to an obese passenger—included the statement that passengers have the right to be moved to alternative seats if they are obstructed by large or overweight seatmates (Miles, 2002). After the announcement, Hewson's husband and attorney claimed that they hoped more airlines would follow the lead of Southwest Airlines and ask people who cannot fit into a single seat to purchase a second (Miles, 2002).

Shortly after this news was reported, Southwest, who had been relatively silent on the controversy for several months, reported that their new policy had, so far, been a win–win for both large and more average-sized passengers. Southwest Airlines President Colleen Barrett claimed that the airline had flown about 6 million passengers in a recent month and had enforced the policy for only 100. Of those 100 passengers, 92 were given refunds (Reuters News Service, 2002). This symbolic action sent the signal to large passengers that the policy would not be enforced in an aggressive and arbitrary manner but also let other passengers know that they would not be inconvenienced or injured by an obese seatmate. Together, these actions and accounts appeared to satisfy large passengers as well as their smaller sized traveling neighbors, as the issue was completely dropped from the headlines.

An example of a less effective response to a contentious negotiation comes from the case of the Exxon Valdez oil spill cleanup. The initial response to the oil spill by the Exxon Valdez was discussed in Chapter 4 as an example of crisis event, but the long-term cleanup of the oil spill represents an example of an evolving and contentious negotiation. Over the course of a year, Exxon officials negotiated the image of the organization with the general public and local residents as the cleanup effort continued. This contentious negotiation began about a week after the initial spill.

At that time, Exxon CEO Lawrence Rawls commented to the press on the cleanup effort for the first time. In response to criticisms about the slowness of the initial cleanup response, Rawls arrogantly blamed the U.S. Coast Guard and officials from the State of Alaska for holding up their progress (Small, 1991). Over the course of the next year, this arrogance and lack of consideration of audience concerns was demonstrated repeatedly. For example, only a few months after the spill occurred, Exxon executives appeared to suggest that the company had the cleanup well in hand and claimed in a memo that Exxon alone would determine when they should demobilize their cleanup crews for the winter and whether or not they would return in the spring (Small, (1991).

Over a year into the cleanup effort, critics who were still unsatisfied with the cleanup progress continued to point to the apparent insensitivity of Exxon to public concerns. When a *Time* interviewer asked CEO Rawls if he was arrogant, Rawls angrily replied,

> ... Let's talk about that word arrogance.... We said we would do all we could after the Alaska spill: we took responsibility, we spent over $2 billion, and we gave Alaska fishermen $200 million on no more than their showing us a fishing license and last years' tax return. And we're arrogant? That bothers the hell out of me. Maybe "big" is just arrogant. Or maybe I get emotional and that's arrogant. Or maybe I say things people don't like to hear. Is that arrogance? You tell me. (quoted in Small, 1991, p. 18)

Together, these denials of wrongdoing and excuses for the slow cleanup, coupled with an apparent lack of sensitivity to audience concerns severely damaged the organizations legitimacy with consumers and industry critics and ultimately caused Exxon to drop from 10th to 110th on *Fortune Magazine*'s list of the most admired companies.

Progressive Accounts and Business Activities That Illustrate Rationality

Organizations may also respond to extended and contentious negotiations by using progressive accounts and business activities that, over time, demonstrate that the organization has and is using rational procedures in its decision making. These accounts are most likely to be effective with industry experts or organizational insiders, who understand the logic and science behind such rational procedures. However, as illustrated by Dow Corning Wright and the 1991 controversy over the safety of their silicone gel breast implants, accounts and behaviors that signal rationality may be limited in their appeal to the general public. This case was originally reported by Ginzel et al. (1993).

In late December, 1991, Federal Department of Agriculture (FDA) Commissioner David Kessler issued a press release warning women about the risks of leakage from silicone gel breast implants (commonly used in reconstructive breast surgery in cancer patients; Ginzel et al., 1993). Leakage from the silicone implants was reported to cause severe pain, infection, and in some cases death in women patients. A few weeks later, the FDA took the more extreme stance of stopping all sale of silicone gel implants, noting, "'Physicians should cease using [implants] and manufacturers should stop distributing them,' adding that the FDA 'cannot assure women of their safety at this time'" (quoted in Ginzel et al., 1993, p. 232).

This FDA action represented a clear threat to the legitimacy of Dow Corning Wright, the organization that had manufactured a majority of the silicone gel implants. It suggested that the company was manufacturing and selling a product that was unsafe.

In response to this threat, Dow Corning Wright first used denials coupled with references to the rational and scientific basis of their views that the implants were, in fact, safe. Dan Hayes, President and CEO of Dow Corning Wright, suggested that the action of the FDA was based on flawed decision making and noted, "If this review is [re]done with experts in immunology, we're confident the process will support the safety of breast implants" (quoted in Ginzel et al., 1993, p. 239). Dow also made selective internal memos and scientific documents available to the press, and their head of health care business claimed at a press conference that, "[the] cumulative body of credible scientific evidence shows that the implants are safe and effective" (quoted in Ginzel et al., 1993, p. 246).

These accounts showcasing the rational and scientific basis for support of silicone implants were accepted by some members of the medical community (e.g., The American Society for Plastic and Reconstructive Surgeons), satisfied patients, and other makers of silicone breast implants—all audiences who had benefited from Dow's product. However, many other members of the medical community, activist groups for breast cancer patients, and a large number of dissatisfied patients found these claims inadequate. These audiences claimed that Dow appeared both unconcerned with the women who had suffered from leaking implants and uncooperative with the highly respected FDA (Ginzel et al., 1993). In addition, these audiences pointed to newly leaked, internal documents that revealed that scientists at Dow were concerned about the unsystematic testing of the implants (Ginzel et al., 1993).

Dow responded again with appeals to rationality. In response to the leaked memos, they replied, "Internal memos are not science ... they are a printed record of one side of a two-way conversation." (quoted in Ginzel, 1993, p.

24B). However, only two days later, Standard and Poors announced that it was lowering the debt rating for Dow because it expected a number of lawsuits to be brought against the company. On the same day, a competing manufacturer of breast implants announced that it was switching to another design that used saline solution instead of silicone gel (Ginzel et al., 1993). These events showed that even previously sympathetic audiences had now begun to doubt Dow's accounts.

Finally, on February 11, 1992, Dow made several changes in its primary business activities that signaled consideration of audiences' concerns. First, it replaced its CEO. It also changed its precautions to doctors about the use of the implants, warning them that patients should not massage the implants to reduce scar tissue, as such actions may cause the implants to leak. Finally, it instituted a registry for tracking implant users and offered to provide financial assistance to implant users who wanted to have them removed but could not afford it. These actions were met with widespread, positive press and appeared to satisfy most of the organization's critical audiences (Ginzel et al.,1993).

Managing Identities of Distinctiveness and Status During Identity Change

In managing perceptions of the identity of an organization during a controversial identity change, spokespersons typically rely on organizational categorizations and comparisons that help to clarify the organization's status and distinctiveness in relation to its new identity. In this way, the management of controversial identity change is similar to the management of other organizational identity threats. What is distinct, however, is that in managing evolving controversies related to identity changes, managers may find it necessary to invoke more specific forms of categorization and comparison as audiences put pressure on the organization to become more specific and clear about the new identity. In particular, organizational spokespersons may employ the use of disidentification tactics (e.g., categorizing the organization as completely separate and distinct from other groups or audiences), or schizo-identification (i.e., splitting the organization's identity into distinct parts and showing identification with some parts and disidentification with other parts; Elsbach, 1999; Elsbach & Bhattacharya, 2001). In addition, organizations may employ any number of tactics for maintaining multiple identities (e.g., aggregating or integrating multiple identities through categorization tactics; Golden-Biddle & Rao, 1997; Pratt & Foreman, 2000).

Organizational Categorizations and Comparisons That Signal Status

To the extent that status (vs. distinctiveness) categorizations are central to the identity of an organization, they will be more aggressively reaffirmed and defended following events that question that identity. Such status affirmations typically include communications and actions that make clear exclusivity or entry barriers (e.g., only the top 1% of test scorers are admitted to a university). For example, status affirmations may be made through disidentification with a proximal but lower status category with which an organization feels it may be mistakenly associated (Elsbach, 1999; Elsbach & Bhattacharya, 2001). Currently, one of the most popular forms of this type of disidentification is to claim "we are not Wal-Mart" as a means of separating any "high quality" organization from the monolithic discount chain. In this way, exclusivity and disidentification (as contrasted with inclusivity and identification) may be used as identity management tactics in cases where status is critical to organizational identity (Jost & Elsbach, 2001).

As an illustration of this tactic, in the case example discussed later in this chapter, I describe how the Augusta National Golf Club managed a perceived a threat to its identity status when a large women's rights organization called for it to admit a female member. In this case, the exclusivity of the club and its right to admit whomever it chose were important components of the identity of the organization. In response to this threat, the club president carried out a number of symbolic actions that clearly categorized the private club as separate from public organizations that were expected to respond to the demands of activist groups. These actions were extreme and included removing all outside sponsorship from the upcoming Masters Golf Tournament (one of the most prestigious tournaments in professional golf) and conducting its own poll of so-called "average citizens" to verify that most believed a private club, such as Augusta, could admit (or not admit) anyone it wanted. Clearly, in this case, the importance of maintaining exclusive status was important enough to the organization that it was willing to forfeit millions of dollars of sponsorship to maintain that status.

Organizational Categorizations That Signal Distinctiveness

Managing Changing Identities. In some cases organizations desire to manage a deliberate change to a distinctive organizational identity.

In these cases, an organization may want to signal that it has given up a previous distinction, with which it wants members to disidentify, and taken on a new one, with which it wants members to identity. This process of disidentifying with an old identity before identifying with a new one is an example of perception management during an evolving controversy and is illustrated by the automaker, Saturn (Pfeffer & Sutton, 1999).

In the early 1990s, when Saturn began making cars under a separate identity from its parent company, General Motors, executives used disidentification claims as an initial identity management tactic. For instance, to prepare audiences for its new, innovative identity, Saturn used the slogan, "A different kind of car company. A different kind of car," to distinguish and distance itself from General Motors. In its commercials and print advertising, the company also spent considerable effort separating itself from the stereotype of General Motors as big, impersonal, and adversarial. In one advertisement, an African-American man talked about how his father was treated unfairly by a big-company car salesman in the 1950s and how his approach, as a salesperson at Saturn, was designed to provide a contrast to that experience. This tactic appeared designed to help audiences disidentify with the outdated and undesirable identity of the traditional car company and thus to make it easier for them to identify with the "different kind of car company" Saturn professed to be.

Subsequently, in later commercials, Saturn turned attention to identification with its desired identity as personal and customer friendly. In one of these commercials, for example, Saturn showed a grade-school teacher who had written a letter to Saturn about how much she appreciated the customized options included in her car and how she felt like her Saturn was designed especially for her, rather than for some nameless market segment. These commercials were effective in portraying Saturn as a friendly and personal company, at least in part, because Saturn had previously distanced itself from the impersonal and unfriendly identity of a large, traditional automaker.

Managing Multiple Identities.   In other cases, an organization that is growing and taking on multiple identities may want to take actions to maintain and affirm its distinctive identity over the course of this growth process. In these cases, evolving controversies may arise if organizational members perceive a loss of organizational distinctiveness because the organization is not known for doing one thing (Pratt & Foreman, 2000) or because integrating these multiple identities, which are based on conflicting ideals, is difficult (Golden-Biddle & Rao, 1997). Such difficulties with multiple identities often come to light, for example, when an organization acquires a new identity through merger, new business lines, or leadership changes. In other cases, diverse outside audiences may expect the organization to act in line with all its identities, even when those identities are in clear conflict. For example, in their study of the New York City Port Authority and its multiple identities of caring community citizen (concerned with dealing sensitively with homeless people who frequented their bus terminals) and effective transportation manager (concerned with the safety and cleanliness of its facilities), Dutton and Dukerich (1991) found that, in response to growing public concern about the homeless in public transportation facilities, the Port Authority could not affirm one identity without jeopardizing the other. In these cases, researchers have found that finding ways either to maintain plural identities or to merge those identities synergistically may allow organizations to maintain their distinctiveness (Pratt & Foreman, 2000).

In some cases, for example, organizations may find that it is important to keep all the distinct identities that define the organization because critical stakeholders value those identities. For example, a university that has both great teaching traditions and research traditions may find it necessary to aggregate those two identities into some overarching theme of learning or discovery when pressed by writers of college guidebooks to define its distinctive niche. In this way, the organization can maintain a unified and distinctive identity while recognizing the diverse dimensions of that identity (Reger et al., 1994).

Of course, in some cases, it may be difficult or impossible to link diverse identities under one overarching identity. Humphreys and Brown's (2002) account of the campaign by Westville Institute to achieve the status of university provides an example of one such case. Members of the Westville Institute, a UK-based institution of higher education, grappled with several different identity conflicts in its quest to move from a local provider of higher education focused on teaching to a national university focused on research. These conflicts included self-categorizations as a teaching or research institute and as a local or national player in higher education. It became clear, as the campaign wore on, that many of the Institute's members had perceptions of the organization as a local, teaching institute, which would be hard to aggregate with other members' perceptions of the Institute's future as a national university. As one faculty member noted in a discussion about changing to a research institute, "Your ultimate identity lies with what you teach" (Humphreys & Brown, 2002, p. 434). Other faculty members feared that the push toward national university status would allow outsiders to view all faculty as one and the same, essentially removing the distinctive identities of different groups. For example, a psychology lecturer asked to teach within another subject group as part of the new university curriculum said that he didn't want to be associated with what he saw as an "academically inferior discipline" (Humphreys & Brown, 2002, p. 434). In the end, the quest for national university status failed, partly as a result of poor morale and low support from many faculty who did not buy into the new identity.

In other cases, an organization may find it is desirable to integrate its diverse identities and arrive at a new, single identity that benefits from the synergies of the distinct dimensions of the organization (Pratt & Foreman, 2000). For example, Cheney (1991) described how the Catholic Church managed its two identities of religious leadership and policy leadership through the use of rhetoric. Cheney described, for example, how at the 1983 National Conference of Catholic Bishops, the American Bishops integrated their policy on pacifism as a stance on war with the Catholic doctrine on just wars by claiming that both identities were aligned under the common presumption against the use of unprovoked force. In another example, Elsbach and Kramer (1996) described how some business school members who felt threatened by the *Business Week* rankings of U.S. business schools (e.g., because the rankings showed their school to be of lower status than members had presumed) used the tactic of changing the focus of their identity categorizations to highlight alternative and more integrative categories that defined their organizations. For instance, members of the business school at the University of California, Berkeley, talked about how their school, which was known as a research institute and a public institution, was the highest ranked public school in the *Business Week* survey. Thus, they combined their ranking with their public/research identity to form a new integrative identity of high-status public institution.

PITFALLS OF ORGANIZATIONAL PERCEPTION MANAGEMENT DURING EVOLVING CONTROVERSIES

The dangers of managing perceptions during the course of an evolving organizational controversy are great. Because organizational spokespersons must manage multiple issues and multiple audiences over time, the complexity of the perception management problem may become overwhelming. As Ginzel et al. (1993) noted:, "[I]t becomes less obvious to top management what crucial issues need to be addressed in their accounts and who the primary targets of the account should be" (p. 255).

Two of the primary pitfalls that perception managers may encounter in such complex and evolving controversies are an escalation of commitment to a failing course of action (Brockner, 1992; Staw, 1976) and an inconsistency over time and across audiences in the organizational perceptions affirmed.

Escalation of Commitment to a Failing Course of Action

Escalation of commitment to a failing course of action involves the continued support (through time and resources) of a chosen strategy, even though evidence suggests that the strategy is failing to provide positive and desired outcomes (Staw, 1976). For example, Ross and Staw (1986) described how the provincial government of British Columbia, Canada, continued to support and prepare for the 1986 World's Fair (i.e., Expo '86), despite increasing evidence that the fair would run a deficit instead of a profit.

Researchers have found that such escalations may have three types of determinants: psychological, social, and structural (Ross & Staw, 1986). First, early commitments to an organizational stance may cause organizational decision makers to engage in biased information searches that focus only on information that confirms their initial strategies or choices (Brockner, 1992). Second, organizational decision makers may feel pressure to act consistently with past claims and decisions, even if those decisions are now shown to be faulty, because consistency is a highly valued social trait and because acting inconsistently with past decisions would be tantamount to admitting that past decisions were wrong (Cialdini, 1984). Finally, structural forces, such as involvement by other organizations and groups, contribute to the escalation of commitment to the failing course of action. For example, in the case of Expo '86, Ross and Staw (1986) found escalation behaviors were supported by nonrefundable commitments placed by participating vendors, hotels, and transportation companies, along with reputational commitments made by the local government.

Of these three determinants, the second may be especially relevant when organizational perception management is a concern of organizational decision makers. That is, if decision makers believe that their own personal images, as well as images of their organizations, are threatened by admitting that a chosen course of action has been a mistake, they will be more likely to escalate their commitments to that course of action. In such cases, spokespersons may believe that protecting images of correctness and consistency are more important than stopping the flow of resources into a failing project (Ross & Staw, 1993).

In light of these perception management pressures, Ross and Staw's (1993) examination of the escalation of commitment to building the Shoreham nuclear facility in New York suggests that exiting a failing project may require making the project less important to the identities or images of the organization. For example, they found that removing the project from center stage by labeling it as a pilot project and emphasizing its peripheral nature with respect to the core business of the firm reduced pressures to continue supporting the nuclear plant and made it easier to drop support altogether (Ross & Staw, 1993).

In sum, perception managers must be aware of the pressures to maintain images of consistency with regard to supporting a given project or pressures to maintain identities that are tied to single projects. If those image- or identity-relevant projects begin to fail, it may be difficult to extricate the organization from them without image or identity threat. In such cases, perception managers need to take steps to make the images and identities of the organization less dependent on the project.

Inconsistency over Time and Across Audiences

Inconsistency in perception management messages may occur because the number of issues and audiences relevant to the controversy become too great for spokespersons to manage. Dutton and Dukerich's (1991) study of the New York City Port Authority and its handling of homelessness issues in its bus and train terminals provides an example of the difficulties of dealing with multiple audiences over time. As Dutton and Dukerich explained, spokespersons for the Port Authority initially interpreted complaints from customers about homeless persons inhabiting their bus and train terminals as a security issue to be dealt with by the police. In response, Port Authority spokespersons sought to communicate to customers that the Port Authority was a safe and clean business. Later, however, it became clear that many audience members were advocates for the homeless and demanded that the Port Authority treat the problem as a social issue, requiring a humane response. Thus, Port Authority officials took actions, such as forming a homeless project team and funding a study of the problem. These actions were designed to communicate to homeless advocates that the organization was a caring community citizen. Eventually, however, it became clear that the homeless issue was a no–win situation in which one audience (i.e., either customers or advocates for the homeless) would be dissatisfied with the responses of the Port Authority. In the end, organizational spokespersons decided to become quiet advocates for the homeless and push the issue out of the limelight, rather than to attempt to meet the expectations of all audiences (Dutton & Dukerich, 1991).

CASE ILLUSTRATION: IMAGE, IDENTITY, AND REPUTATION MANAGEMENT BY THE AUGUSTA NATIONAL GOLF CLUB

In this case, I examine organizational perception management that encompasses identity, image, and reputation management by a focal organization as well as by organizations that were associated with that firm. As such, it provides an interesting illustration of not only the tactics involved in managing organizational perceptions over time but of the ways that the perception management of the organization may be intertwined with that of others. Further, it provides evidence that extreme identity management tactics, which include disidentification with all organizations that threaten an organization's identity, can be a catalyst for escalating commitment to a failing cause (Staw et al., 1983).

The case involves two primary parties, The National Council of Women's Organizations (NWCO) and the Augusta National Golf Club (home of the Masters Golf Tournament). Over time, a number of peripheral organizations also became involved in the controversy. These organizations included corporate sponsors of the Masters Golf Tournament (e.g., Coca-Cola, IBM, Citigroup), organizations run by prominent members of the Augusta National Golf Club (e.g., General Electric, previously run by member Jack Welch; the U.S. Olympic Committee, headed by member Lloyd Ward), CBS television, the Professional Golfers' Association (PGA), sponsors of high-profile professional golfers (e.g., Nike, associated with member and Masters Champion Tiger Woods), national and local newspapers (e.g., *The New York Times*), and finally, civil rights organizations (e.g., the NAACP).

The controversy centered on the NWCO's campaign to get Augusta National to admit women as members of its club and Augusta National's refusal to do so at any cost. The controversy evolved over the course of a year and was punctuated by four specific events: (1) an initial letter sent by NWCO to Augusta National urging them to admit women as members, (2) hints from NWCO that it may write to the corporate sponsors of the Masters Golf Tournament urging them to discontinue their associations with the

Tournament if Augusta National does not admit women, (3) pressure from NWCO on CBS, the broadcaster of the Masters Golf Tournament, urging it to pressure Augusta National to admit women, and (4) letters sent to prominent members of the Augusta National Golf Club, many of whom were CEOs of large, public companies or held elected offices, urging them to pressure Augusta National to admit women. I discuss of these four events and the organizational perception management that followed each of them in the following sections.

1. The Controversy Arises: The Letter From NWCO to Augusta National

On June 12, 2002 the NCWO—a six million member council representing over 160 groups (e.g., the National Organization for Women, the YWCA, and the League of Women's Voters)—sent a letter to the Augusta National Golf Club urging the all-male club to allow women to become members before the April, 2003, Masters Tournament. Augusta National had only recently welcomed African American men to its ranks, including Lloyd Ward, the CEO of the U.S. Olympic Committee. During the 2002 Masters Tournament, Ward commented that he would lobby to broaden membership at Augusta National to include women (News Services, 2002a). In a reference to Ward's comments, NCWO chairwoman Martha Burk noted in the letter to Augusta National, "We know that Augusta National and the sponsors of the Masters do not want to be viewed as entities that tolerate discrimination against any group, including women" (News Services, 2002a, p. D2).

In later comments to the press, Burk also noted that the NWCO had focused attention on Augusta National (vs. the numerous other all-male golf clubs in the United States) because "they host one of the most prestigious tournaments in the world ... they should be at the forefront of having non-discriminatory membership practices" (Brown, 2002b, p. D4).

Initial responses: Identity threat and management by Augusta National

Almost one month later, on July 10, 2002, Burk got a response from Augusta National president, William "Hootie" Johnson. In a three-sentence statement, Johnson called the letter from NWCO "offensive and coercive" and said that "there would be no more discussion with NCWO because Augusta membership matters are private" (News Services, 2002a, p. D2).

The same day, in what appeared to be an attack on the attackers (Ohbuchi & Kambara, 1985) as well as an organizational identity affirmation, Johnson made the following statement to the press:

> We want the American public to be aware of this action right from the beginning. Dr. Burk's letter incorporates a deadline tied to the Masters and refers to sponsors of the tournament's telecast. These references make it abundantly clear that Augusta National Golf Club is being threatened with a public campaign designed to use economic pressure to achieve a NCWO goal. We expect such a campaign would attempt to depict the members of our club as insensitive bigots and coerce the sponsors of the Masters to disassociate themselves under threat, real or implied, of boycotts and other economic pressures. We will not be bullied, threatened or intimidated. Obviously, Dr. Burk and her colleagues view themselves as agents of change, and feel any organization that has stood the test of time and has strong roots of tradition and does not fit their profile, needs to be changed. We do not intend to become a trophy in their display case. There may well come a day when women will be invited to join our membership, but that timetable will be ours, and not at the point of a bayonet. We do not intend to be further distracted by this matter. We shall continue our traditions and prepare to host the Masters as we have since 1934. (Brown, 2002b)

These remarks suggest that Johnson perceived the request by NWCO as an identity threat to his organization and, by extension, to himself. His comments about the organization having "stood the test of time" and having "strong roots of tradition" indicate a perceived threat to the enduring categorizations of the organization—a primary component of organizational identity (Albert & Whetten, 1985). In addition, Johnson noted that Burk intended to "change" the organization because it did not "fit their [the NWCO's] profile." These statements also suggest a perceived threat to the distinctive and enduring categorizations that define the organization, which are essential to its identity.

As a possible response to these identity threats, Johnson also offered the following organizational identity affirmation in his prepared statement to the press: "Augusta National and the Masters—while happily entwined—are quite different. One is a private golf club. The other is a world-class sports event. It is insidious to attempt to use one to alter the other. The essence of a private club is privacy" (Potter, 2002). This statement includes a clear distinctiveness categorization of the organization, that is, "a private golf club," which underscores and affirms the exclusive and nonpublic nature of the organization. It is also used to differentiate (but not completely dissociate) Augusta National from the Masters Tournament. This identity management claim was repeated extensively in the initial news coverage following Johnson's press conference.

On hearing these remarks, Burk commented that she was "surprised that Hootie Johnson reacted so strongly" and that "I thought the club was already leaning in the direction of adding women, and I thought that his could be a quiet discussion." (Brown, 2002b, p. D4). In fact, many journalists commented on the unexpectedly "arrogant" and strong reaction by Johnson to Burk's letter (Hiskey, 2002). This kind of strong reaction further suggests that Burk's letter was not viewed as merely a temporary image threat but a threat to the central, distinctive, and enduring identity of the organization and its members.

2. The Controversy Escalates:
Pressure on Corporate Sponsors

In response to Johnson's statements, Burk suggested that the next step for her organization would be to go after sponsors of the Masters Golf Tournament, including Coca-Cola, IBM, and Citigroup (News Services, 2002a). Burk was willing to make this an organizational image controversy for these corporate sponsors. Further, if these sponsors pulled out of the Masters Tournament, the departures could be viewed as a reputation threat to Augusta National (i.e., the club would lose some perceived status by outsiders). In the days following these comments, there was a flurry of media coverage of the issue, as interested stakeholders—including prominent members of Augusta National Golf Club, sportswriters, fans, broadcasters and sponsors of the Masters Tournament, officials from the Professional Golfers Association (PGA), and average golfers—weighed in. The opinions of these stakeholders were split, with vocal support shown for both Augusta National and the NWCO.

Support for Augusta National

Support for Hootie Johnson and Augusta National came from sportswriters, fans, and some professional golfers. Some groups justified Augusta National's all-male membership as a traditional form of male bonding. As Denver Post sportswriter Mark Kiszla (2002) wrote,

Good for Hootie.... The National Council of Women's Organizations is trying to nag, nag, nag Augusta National into admitting females into its 300-member club for men.... Will women never get it? Guys like to sneak away to the golf course for exactly the same reason that red-blooded, American males brave flesh-eating mosquitoes to go fishing and enjoy hunkering down in the haze of a blue smoke to deal poker until two o'clock in the morning. Why do men enjoy these games? There are no women around to discuss feelings, make a honey-do list or generally bug 'em.

But most of those supporting Augusta National echoed Johnson's claim that a private club can and should make its own decisions regarding membership. As Coca-Cola spokesman Ben Deutsch said, "Our sponsorship is of the Masters golf tournament, a one-week, public event that is viewed and enjoyed annually by millions of sports fans in every corner of the globe. It would be inappropriate for Coke to comment on the club's policies" (Sheeley, 2002, p. D1). Similarly, Atlanta Mayor Bob Young noted: "[Augusta National] is entitled to set their own membership policies, and I respect that. This country is built on individual rights and freedom of assembly" (Sheeley, 2002, p. D1).

In addition, the Masters Tournament organizers, television broadcasters, prominent members of the Golf Club (e.g., IBM CEO Lou Gerstner, Former GE Chairman Jack Welch), and several of its sponsors were all unwilling to argue against Johnson's stance, offering tacit support for his claim that this was a private matter. As golfing hall-of-famer Jack Nicklaus said, " I think that's not my issue. That's Hootie's issue.... The club has its policies and I'm not involved in the policies of the club. I'm just a member" (Sheeley, 2002, p. D1).

In a few cases, corporate sponsors appeared to disidentify with Augusta National in an attempt to distance themselves from the fray. However, in most cases, these claims appeared to support Augusta National's claim that they were a private club, separate from the Masters Golf Tournament. In this manner, Deb Gotheimer, spokesperson for IBM, noted, "The Masters and Augusta are separate and we're a sponsor of the Masters which is open and public. We're not a sponsor of Augusta" (Sandomir, 2002b, p. D2). Similarly, Jeff Kuhlman, a spokesperson for Cadillac, claimed, "We're the official car of the Masters, not for Augusta" (Sandomir, July 18, 2002b, p. D2).

Support for the NWCO

Taking the side of the NWCO were a number of sportswriters and other journalists. In a column written on July 11, 2002, Washington Post writer Leonard Shapiro suggested that the time for admitting women to Augusta National Golf Club "ought to be now" (Shapiro, 2002a, p. D7). Shapiro went on to note that the PGA and LPGA had decreed in 1990 that "they no longer place any of their tournaments at clubs that discriminated against minorities" (p. D7). This decree apparently arose after there was protest over the 1990 PGA Championship being played at the all-White Shoal Creek Golf Club in Birmingham, Alabama. Although the Masters is not technically a PGA tour-sponsored event, Shapiro noted that it is an official event recognized by the PGA and players' statistics and earnings at the Masters are considered official PGA tour statistics and earnings. These comments appeared to refute the suggestion that Augusta National was just a private club with an identity distinct from the Masters Tournament.

Columnists from the *Atlanta Journal Constitution,* the major newspaper in Augusta National's home state of Georgia, also supported the position of NWCO (Hiskey, 2002). Further, they refuted Johnson's claim that the Masters Tournament should not be linked to the policies of Augusta National. As reporter Michelle Hiskey wrote, "Augusta National is no more just a private club than the Masters is simply a tournament. For one glorious week in April, it's a private business with a product that draws its value not only from tradition, but vast public support" (p. 3D).

Finally, *The New York Times* (Greene, 2002, p. H11) ran a story by a prominent law professor that attacked the position that Augusta National was merely a private club, with no responsibility to end its discriminatory practices. As Professor Linda Greene of the University of Wisconsin Law School reported,

> [Augusta National] is the 21st century host of a multimillion-dollar, corporate sponsored, nationally-televised tournament, as well as a club that includes chief executives from Fortune 100 corporations. Now the private club claim sounds like a jaded resurrection of an ancient rationale for the maintenance of Jim and Jane Crow.... Some argue that the end of the male-only policy would have limited significance. It is true that neither the abandonment of the policy nor the admission of a single woman will work a power transformation. But symbols are important and symbolic actions are often important first steps. Just as the elimination of "white-only" signs signaled the possibility of equal justice to all irrespective of race, the elimination of male-only policies at PGA tournament clubs would have similar significance for women.

Again, these statements appeared to refute Augusta National's identity claims that it was a private club and to categorize the club as a backward, discriminatory organization that owed its livelihood to public support. In addition, this last statement concerning the "symbolic" meaning of a change in policy illustrates how such a seemingly small action may be viewed as such an important threat to organizational identity. That is, a change in policy would be symbolic of the abandonment of the "private" identity of the club.

Responses: More Identity Management by Augusta National

In a reported attempt to shield corporate sponsors from pressure by the NWCO, Augusta National Golf Club chairman Hootie Johnson announced on August 31, 2002, that the 2003 Masters Golf Tournament would be put on without the support of sponsors (including major sponsors IBM, Coca-Cola, and Citigroup) and would be televised commercial-free. (Sandoval, 2002, p. D1). Johnson made the following statement concerning this unprecedented action:

> We have told our media sponsors that we will not request their participation for the 2003 Masters. The telecast will be conducted by the Masters Tournament.... We are sorry, but not surprised, to see these corporations drawn into this matter but continue to insist that our private club should not be "managed" by an outside group. As I previously said, there may come a day when women will be invited to join our club, but that decision must be ours. We also believe that the Masters and the club are different, and that one should not affect the other. Augusta National is NCWO's true target. It is therefore unfair to put the Masters media sponsors in the position of having to deal with this pressure. (Harig, 2002. p. 1A)

The action of dismissing the sponsors from the Masters Golf Tournament may be viewed as a symbolic act of identity management. Specifically, it appears to be an attempt by Augusta National to disidentify with these publicly-traded corporate sponsors and, by extension, to disidentify with the notion that the club has a relationship with the public. In his statement, Johnson also reaffirmed the club identity as private and distinguished it from the Masters Golf Tournament, whose revenue from ticket sales and merchandising would cover the expense of putting on the tournament and televising it.

Sports industry consultants offered initial shock at the news that the Masters had fired their sponsors. Further, these experts found the action "over the top" as a means of affirming the club's right to privacy. As Jim Andrews, editorial director of IEG Sponsorship Reports, industry newsletter, remarked, "[Johnson] is being a little disingenuous, using the sponsors in a way to make a statement that 'nobody comes in and tells me what to do'" (Sandomir & Elliott, 2002, p. A1).

Despite this extreme event, the NWCO was not deterred. Martha Burk, chairwoman of the NWCO, responded with the claim, "I think they're doing what they can to avoid having a woman member. They're willing to pay a lot of money to continue to discriminate. That's what it comes down to" (News Services, 2002b, p. D2).

3. Continuing Pressure: Pressure on CBS and Prominent Members

Pressure on CBS

Following Augusta National's announcement that they would put on the Masters Golf Tournament without the benefit of corporate sponsors, the NWCO vowed to continue its fight to get women admitted as members at Augusta National by putting pressure on CBS, the television network that had covered the Masters for 46 years. In a statement to the press, Burk noted, "We expect to have a conversation with CBS. It will be about whether they want to broadcast an event held in a venue that discriminates against half the population, and what kind of statement that makes about CBS as a network" (News Services, 2002b, p. D2). These statements were clearly designed to threaten the image of CBS as a legitimate organization (i.e., one that does not condone discrimination).

In response to these statements, CBS spokesperson Leslie Ann Wade made the brief comment that "CBS will broadcast the Masters in April" (McCarthy, 2002, p. 12C). Spokespersons for other networks were not surprised, given the prestige that the tournament adds to the sports calendar for a network. As Chet Simmons, former president of NBC Sports and founder of ESPN, noted, "It would take every woman in the country saying that she wouldn't watch CBS anymore to make them give up the Masters. And that's not likely to happen" (Borden, 2002, p. 106).

Undaunted, Burk sent a letter to CBS on September 20, 2002 ,urging them not to broadcast the Masters Golf Tournament in 2003 if the Augusta National Golf Club "continues to discriminate against women by excluding them from membership" (Shapiro, 2002b, p. D1). CBS Sports President Sean McManus immediately wrote back with the following justification for the decision to telecast the upcoming Masters:

> I very much appreciate you sharing your position on CBS Sports' broadcast of the Masters. However, as a sports television programmer serving millions of men and women who eagerly anticipate and avidly watch the Masters broadcast each year, CBS will cover the Masters as it has done for the last 46 years. To not do so would be a disservice to fans of this major championship. Please do not hesitate to stay in touch with our organization on issues you feel of importance. (Shapiro, 2002b, p. D1).

Throughout this exchange, Hootie Johnson and Augusta National were silent, offering no response to these continued actions designed to threaten the images of organizations associated with the club.

Pressure on Members

A week after receiving affirmation that CBS would telecast the Masters, the NWCO started a letter-writing campaign to prominent members of the golf club, many of whom were leaders of large, public organizations. These members included U.S. Congressman Amo Houghton (R-N.Y.), CEO of the U.S. Olympic Committee Lloyd Ward, former U.S. senator turned Coca-Cola board member Sam Nunn, Citigroup CEO Sam Weill, Motorola CEO Christopher Galvin, and J. P. Morgan Chase CEO William Harrison (McCarthy & Brady, 2002). In the letters, Burk described Augusta National as "publicly flaunting its practice of sex discrimination" and asked members to reconcile their public or corporate positions on diversity with the male-only policy of the club (Sandomir, 2002a, p. D3). Again, these letters were designed to threaten the images and reputations of the organizations that these men headed. By suggesting that the leaders were hypocritical in their stance toward diversity issues, the letters threatened the organizational images of legitimacy and their reputations as respected institutions. In one pointed letter to USOC chairman Lloyd Ward, Burk wrote that Ward's membership at Augusta "… sends a message to the public that the USOC's statements and policies on nondiscrimination are not taken seriously by the leadership, and indeed, give the impression that the organization approves of Augusta's exclusion of women" (Sandomir, 2002a, p. D3).

Responses: Image and Identity Management by Augusta National and Its Members

Although Hootie Johnson offered no official response to these events, a number of other club members began to speak out about their distress over the chairman's strong stance against the NWCO. Breaking the rule of silence, a dozen members, whose names were kept confidential, spoke to *The New York Times* about their concerns. These members reportedly claimed to be attempting to soften Johnson's stance from within the organization. According to reporters Bill Pennington and Dave Anderson, several members also "said they intended to seek a face-saving middle ground, one that might mean welcoming one or two women as members before or shortly after the Masters next April" (Pennington & Anderson, 2002, p. H1). As one member stated, "Even those among us who agree with the position in principle are puzzled and amazed by the course followed. There has to be another path" (p. A1). Another noted, "It could have been handled quietly. Now, we need to do something. I need to do something just to get my daughter off my back" (p. A1). Finally, some prominent members, including Citigroup CEO Sanford Weil and USOC CEO Lloyd Ward, publicly announced their intentions to work within the organization to change the club's policy toward women (Shapiro, 2002c, p. D7). These comments and actions suggested that some members of the organization perceived that not only was the identity of the organization threatened by the controversy but that Augusta National's response to the controversy was threatening its image as a legitimate organization as well as threatening the reputations of its members and their corporations. Further, they included some image management by implying that remedial action would be taken to correct the situation.

Finally, on November 12, 2002, Hootie Johnson offered interviews to several newspapers regarding the controversy. It was the first official statement from the organization since they announced the dismissal of their sponsors on August 31st and included the most extensive perception management yet enacted by the organization. In his interviews, Johnson steadfastly maintained that Augusta National would not be pressured by the NWCO to admit a woman to the club before next year's Masters and noted that it may be several years or longer before a woman was invited (Brown, 2002a). In a number of identity claims, Johnson affirmed the independence and privacy of the club and also affirmed its traditional and spiritual nature. Johnson conceded that the organization would have trouble altering its identity but also affirmed that this identity was legitimate:

> There has been so much speculation about when we are going to add a woman member. First of all, I'd like to say we have no timetable. Second, our membership has enjoyed camaraderie and a kindred spirit that we think is the heart and soul of our club. It's difficult for us to change something that has worked so well.... We are where we are. And we're right. And right usually prevails. (Brown, 2002a, p. A1)

In addition to these identity management claims, Johnson offered, for the first time, a number of image management actions. First, through defensive verbal accounts, Johnson justified the men-only status as a legitimate, American tradition. As he put it:

> What's really gotten me is that this woman calls us discriminatory. She calls us bigots. And the media jump all over this. If we discriminate, do the Girl Scouts discriminate? Do the Boy Scouts discriminate? Does Spelman College discriminate? Does Smith College discriminate? Do social fraternities and sororities discriminate? Single-gender organizations are good, and part of the fabric of America. Nobody has stopped to think about that. Nothing has been written about it. But it's a fact.... We are a private club. And that's just a fact. I don't feel uncomfortable being associated with the Girl Scouts and the Boy Scouts and the Junior League. And no one else should. (Brown, 2002a, p. A1)

Further, Johnson used references to institutional norms and procedures to back up defensive claims that single-gender organizations were not discriminatory:

> They're totally different; racial issues and gender issues. You've never hear a constitutional lawyer say they were the same thing. You've never heard a civil rights activist say they were the same thing. And if they were the same thing, maybe they would've been put into the Civil Rights Act. So they're totally different.

These justifications suggested that the organization was following normative and valued procedures in choosing not to admit women and, as a result, should be viewed as legitimate.

In addition to these verbal accounts, Johnson and Augusta National carried out the symbolic behavior of conducting a poll, through an independent research firm, to see how Americans felt about the controversy. Conducting this poll demonstrated that Augusta National was willing to listen to the opinions of general public and thus was sensitive to their concerns. Johnson claimed that the results of the poll indicated that the majority of those polled, including women, were supportive of Augusta National's stance. As noted in Chapter 2, indicating such sensitivity to audience concerns is an important indicator of organizational legitimacy (Elsbach, 2001a).

4. Last Resorts: Threats of Picketing, Boycotts

In the days following Johnson's November 12th press interviews, the NWCO began calls to picket the upcoming 2003 Masters Golf Tournament. As Martha Burk commented, "People have been making plans at my request to go down there. It sounds like if nothing changes there probably will be pickets and demonstrators" (Union-Tribune News Services, 2002, p. D4). Further, Burk claimed that the NWCO would be putting up a Web site that contained the names of prominent players who headed large, public companies. As Burk described the Web site:

> We will tell them that we're putting a Web site up that will highlight your company's products, your corporate diversity statements and contact information in case consumers would like to correspond with you about your membership in a club that discriminates against women while your company professes to be diverse and non-discriminatory in its policies. Basically, we're going to highlight the corporate hypocrisy represented in their membership in Augusta National. (Shapiro, 2002d, p. D1).

In addition, several new allies for the NWCO called for a boycott of the 2003 Masters Tournament. First, *The New York Times* published an editorial calling on prominent club members, CBS television, and star players like Tiger Woods to boycott the Masters. As the editorial noted:

> The constitutional right to choose is real, but it is not limited to Mr. Johnson and his all-male choir. If the club that runs the Masters can brazenly discriminate against women, that means others can choose not to support Mr. Johnson's golfing fraternity. That includes more enlightened members of the club, CBS sports, which televises the Masters, and the players, especially Tiger Woods. ("America's all-malek," 2002, p. A18)

Second, the NAACP wrote a letter to *The New York Times* calling on all players and members of Augusta National to boycott the Masters ("Women at Augusta," 2002, p. A18). Finally, the commissioner of the Ladies Professional Golf Association (LPGA), Ty Votaw, publicly supported the NWCO position and criticized PGA commissioner Tom Finchem for tacitly supporting Augusta National (Shapiro, 2002d).

Response: More Defensive Accounts and Some Disidentification

In response to these events, Augusta National issued its first written statement by a club spokesperson other than chairman Hootie Johnson. Perhaps in an attempt to distance the club from the controversy over Johnson's inflammatory remarks of past weeks, spokesperson Glen Greenspan offered the following legitimating justification, which contained references to social norms, for their decision not to allow a woman member:

> The American public already has voiced overwhelming support for the club and our right to make our own membership choices [based on evidence from their own poll conducted by an outside research agency]. Ms. Burk is obviously trying to generate yet more publicity for herself. The public has rejected her arguments and is clearly tired of hearing this story. (Shapiro, 2002d, p. D1).

This comment also contained an attack on the attackers (Ohbuchi & Kambara, 1985) by claiming that the continuing controversy was merely a means for the NWCO to gain publicity for itself and its leader.

However, in another week, there was evidence of a rift among the members of Augusta National, causing some to speak out as unofficial spokespersons for the organization. Speaking for about 50 to 75 members, Thomas H. Wyman, former CEO of CBS television, claimed that this faction of the membership believed that a woman should become a member. To affirm his identification with this group and disidentify with Hootie Johnson and other members who opposed their view, Wyman resigned his membership over the issue on December 3, 2002, calling Johnson's position unacceptable and "pigheaded." In a statement to the press, Wyman noted, "I am not anxious to make this personal. But Hootie keeps writing that there has not been a single case of protest in the membership. And he absolutely believes this will all go away. I know there is a large number of members, at least 50 to 75, who believe it is inevitable that there will be and should be a woman" (Hopkins, 2002, p. 40).

The official club spokesman, Glen Greenspan, responded to Wyman's comments by noting, "We are disappointed that Mr. Wyman has chosen to publicize a private matter. While we respect the fact that there are differences of opinion on this issue, we intend to stand firm behind our right to make what are both appropriate and private membership choices" (Hopkins, 2002, p. 40).

Scorecard: Report at the Ninth Hole

Six months and more than 500 newspaper stories after the initial letter was sent from NWCO to Augusta National, it appeared that Augusta National's identity was more fractured than ever and that its image as a highly regarded American institution was in severe jeopardy. The timeline of events for this controversy, as reported by Buckley (2002) and Justice (2002) is given in Table 5.1.

At this point in time, it appeared that the use of categorization and disidentification as extreme identity-management tactics had led Augusta National to escalate its commitment to a failing course of action (Brockner, 1992) and had severely damaged its image and reputation. By December 5, 2002, USA Today sportswriter Christine Brennan summed up the status of the controversy as follows:

> I thought I'd give you the score so far in the battle between Martha Burk and Hootie Johnson. ... So far, it's no contest. Martha is stomping all over him. You disagree? All right, let's go back to April. Let's pretend we're at the Masters, let's say I lean over to you and whisper the following prediction: Within eight months, this tournament will have no sponsors. Coke, IBM, Citigroup: They'll all be gone. One of the members of Augusta National will resign because of the club's refusal to admit a female member, calling Johnson's position "pigheaded" and saying that as many as one-fourth of the members of the club support having a woman join. Other influential members will publicly call on the club to open its doors to a woman. The membership policies of Augusta National will leap from the sports pages, to talk radio, cable shows and the network news. *The New York Times* will even write an editorial suggesting Tiger Woods boycott next year's Masters.... To which you would have said, "Yeah, right." (Brennan, 2002, p. 3C).

TABLE 5.1

Timeline of Events for Case on Augusta National Golf Club

Date	Event
4/10/02	U.S. Olympic Committee CEO Lloyd Ward, one of Augusta's few African-American members, says he will lobby to admit women to Augusta National.
6/12/02	Letter from Martha Burk, head of the National Council of Women's Organizations, asks Augusta National to open club membership to women by 2003 Masters.
7/8/02	Augusta National president Hootie Johnson calls Burk's letter "offensive and coercive."
7/9/02	Johnson says the club will not be "bullied, threatened, or intimidated." It may admit women one day, but "that timetable will be ours and not at the point of a bayonet."
8/20/02	PGA Tour Commission Tim Finchem says the tour will still recognize the Masters as one of the four major championships in golf.
8/30/02	Masters drops its corporate sponsors—IBM, Citigroup, and Coca-Cola—to keep them out of the controversy.
9/19/02	Burk appeals to CBS to drop coverage of the Masters, CBS refuses.
10/4/02	Citigroup Chairman Sanford Weill becomes the first club member to publicly support the NWCO.
10/7/02	USOC CEO Lloyd Ward says he will work aggressively to get women admitted.
10/8/02	Kenneth Chenault, CEO of American Express, says he supports women as members of Augusta.
10/16/02	Tiger Woods won't take sides. Says he'd like to see a woman member, but clubs have right to set their own policies.
11/15/02	The Rev. Jesse Jackson says he will protest at the club if it doesn't admit a female member before the next Masters.
11/18/02	A New York Times editorial says Tiger Woods should skip the 2003 Masters.
11/27/02	Thomas Wyman, former CBS executive, resigns from the club to protest the club's refusal to admit women. He calls the club's policy "pigheaded."
11/30/02	An Associated Press poll finds Americans evenly divided over whether the club should have female members; three-fourths believe Woods should skip the Masters.
12/5/02	The Daily News of New York reports that columns by two sportswriters for The New York Times were killed because they disagreed with the paper's editorial position.
12/10/02	John Snow, President Bush's choice for Secretary of the Treasury, says he has resigned his membership at Augusta National.

6

Organizational Perception Management Prior to Anticipated Controversies

Many organizational perception management events are unexpected and become known suddenly (e.g., industrial accidents, product failures, and employee criminal behavior). By contrast, there are a number of types of perception management events that organizations can reasonably anticipate and plan for. In this chapter, I focus on the more common forms of anticipated negative events (I discuss anticipated positive events in Chapter 7). These expected controversies include events such as the opening of an organizational facility that may affect the health and safety of nearby residents (e.g., the opening of a nuclear reactor facility), the introduction of a new product or service that may be viewed by some as incongruent with the identity of the organization (e.g., a large family discount chain that decides to begin selling firearms), or the unveiling of a new marketing campaign that is viewed by some as morally illegitimate (e.g., a cigarette commercial that uses a cartoon character appealing to children).

In all these cases, the controversial event is likely to be consistent with some aspects of the images, identities, or reputations of the organization (e.g., a plant closing may increase shareholder wealth and profitability, which may be important to the legitimacy images of an organization). At the same time, it is clear that these types of events are likely to be viewed as inconsistent with other desired images, identities, and reputations (e.g., a plant closing may be seen as morally illegitimate by local employees or community members who benefit from the income generated by the plant). Because organizational leaders can easily anticipate many of these controversies, they can also implement perception management strategies and tactics designed to minimize the potential protests by audiences who find them illegitimate.

DEFINING ANTICIPATED
CONTROVERSIAL EVENTS

The most common anticipated organizational controversies are associated with events that the organization can control in terms of when and how they are made public. Further, because many of these events are the result of deliberate choices by organizational leaders, they are more likely than other types of controversies to be managed strategically to affect long-term reputations and identities rather than short-term images. These types of events include anticipated performance reviews or rankings that may threaten the reputation of an organization for status or quality and planned identity changes that result from the introduction of new products, services, and facilities or the announcement of new identity statements.

Upcoming Performance Reviews or Rankings

Organizational performance is reviewed and ranked by internal and external auditors on a regular basis. When the stock of an organization is publicly traded, the results of the performance review are typically conducted by internal auditors and made available to stockholders and the general public through annual reports (Staw et al., 1983). In cases where performance is reviewed by external auditors, the results are typically revealed through industry rankings or ratings (Fombrun, 1996). Because both types of performance reviews are announced at predetermined times and through formal communication channels (e.g., the publication of *Fortune Magazine*'s annual issue on the most admired companies or an annual report for a company), organizational members can anticipate their effects on audience perceptions of the organization. For example, the announcement of industry survey results is viewed as a highly legitimate measurement of organizational reputations because surveys are generally conducted by independent third parties. As such, the announcement of performance rankings provides an opportunity for managing organizational reputations. As Fombrun (1996) noted,

[Awards or rankings] confirm achievements that might not otherwise get widespread notice in the marketplace.... Since the publicity that surrounds an award is created by the awarding organization—and so comes from a third party—it often appears more credible than a company's self-serving promotions. That's why most companies welcome awards given by credible judges. (p. 167)

However, as Fombrun (1996) also noted, when the news is bad, organizations face an anticipated controversy associated with the rankings publication: "[A] pristine reputation is like a magnet—for employees, customers, investors, and local observers—whereas a bad one sends them running to rivals" (p. 179).

Identity Changes

Planned events that affect a longstanding organizational identity are likely to be controversial for at least some audiences. There are two types of planned events that commonly affect organizational identities: the introduction of new products, services, or modes of operation that may contrast with the core features of established organizational identities; and the deliberate introduction of new vision or identity statements that are meant to reflect a strategic organizational change.

Introduction of New Products, Services, or Modes of Operation

When new products, services, or modes of operation contrast in some salient manner with existing products, services, or operations they are likely to affect perceptions of the distinctive identity of the organization, especially if that identity is centered on these distinctive products, services, or operations. For example, in the case discussed at the end of this chapter, the sportscar icon Porsche found many of its loyal customers to experience identity threats when it announced that it would be producing its first sports-utility vehicle (SUV), the Cayenne. For Porsche, which had a proud history of Monte Carlo racing, the introduction of a family-style SUV represented a strong contrast with its distinctive sportscar identity (Taylor, 2001). Unhappy about this threat to the Porsche identity, sportscar loyalists from around the world vowed to shun the Cayenne from Porsche rallies and claimed that they would not recognize the car as a "true" Porsche (Frankel, 2002).

In other cases, if these new products, services, or modes of operation take the organization into a new area of interorganizational competition, they may threaten the status identity of the organization. An organization known for being a top player in one industry may dilute that status by entering into other industries. For example, when the catalog and e-tailer giant of men's and women's clothing, J. Crew, ventured into the retail stores market, many industry insiders predicted that the company would lose its identity as a high-quality, high-service organization (Kaufman & Atlas, 2002). These analysts predicted that the mall stores would not be able to carry the extensive line of J. Crew clothing (which can be tailored to just about any specification) and had already made mistakes in some of their early-opening stores by carrying the wrong merchandise. Together, these anticipated changes led many to foretell threats to the J. Crew identity as the company closed in on its first year in the retail market.

Introduction of New Identity Statements

Another common type of anticipated controversy is the deliberate introduction of new visions or identity statements by organizations. When organizations make major and strategic changes to their core structures (i.e., through merger or acquisition, changing leadership, or divestiture), they often accompany those changes with revised or totally new statements about the identity of the company (Pfeffer & Sutton, 1999). Accompanying these new identity statements are a number of organizational identity management tactics, including press releases about the new identity, changes in physical structures and company logos, and changes in routine operating procedures (Fombrun, 1996).

An example of one such planned identity change involved the agribusiness company ConAgra Inc. In 2002, ConAgra Inc. changed its name to ConAgra Foods, as a reflection of its growing business in consumer food products (e.g., Hunt's Ketchup, Healthy Choice frozen dinners) rather than agribusiness (e.g., grain milling, meat processing; Goldberg & Vargas, 2003). ConAgra was also in the process of divesting many of its agribusiness units (e.g., meat processing). Accordingly, the company was attempting to transform its identity from "an agribusiness giant to America's favorite food company" (Goldberg & Vargas, 2003, p. 10). As Goldberg and Vargas reported, "ConAgra carried the baggage of a commodity company image ... investors were more likely to compare ConAgra with Cargill than with Kraft ... ConAgra was going through an identity crisis.... Despite the prevalence of ConAgra products in kitchen cabinets across the country, few people knew the 'good names behind the good names'" (p. 10).

However, when existing organizational members and audiences have strong identifications with the previous organizational identity, these strategic identity shifts may be met with resistance. In addition, organizational audiences may not know how to think about the new organization in terms of its competitive and market niches. Thus, it took ConAgra several months before business writers appeared to view ConAgra as a food company and talk about it in that way (Goldberg & Vargas, 2003).

ORGANIZATIONAL PERCEPTION MANAGEMENT PRIOR TO ANTICIPATED CONTROVERSIES

In the anticipatory perception management contexts described above, organizations and their spokespersons have been shown to use a variety of perception management tactics to prepare audiences for the potential controversies. These tactics include: anticipatory accounts, avoidance behaviors, and cognitive separation through recategorization.

Pre-empting Threats to Performance Reputations

When organizational leaders anticipate negative or controversial performance reviews, they may use both anticipatory accounts and avoidance behaviors to mitigate threats to their performance reputations that they believe will accompany these reviews.

Anticipatory Accounts

Most pre-existing research on anticipatory perception management examines the use of anticipatory excuses or anticipatory justifications by individuals (Snyder et al., 1983). Hewitt and Stokes (1975) called these anticipatory accounts "disclaimers" (p. 2) and noted that they create "interpretations of potentially problematic events intended to make them unproblematic when they occur." Some common forms of anticipatory excuses used by individuals include claims that a person was impaired by factors outside his or her control, claims that most typical people would have performed similarly in the same situation, and claims that this was a special case that is not indicative of a person's normal performance (Snyder et al., 1983). Common forms of anticipatory justifications include claims that ends justified the means, claims that performance evaluations were unfair, and claims that evaluations were wrong or inaccurate (Snyder et al., 1983).

More recently, researchers have shown that the same forms of anticipatory excuses and justifications may be used by organizations, through the design of special press releases or media reports prior to an anticipated controversy (Higgins & Snyder, 1989). For example, in their study of CEO compensation, Porac, Wade, and Pollock (1999) found that corporate boards used anticipatory ends–means justifications in their annual announcements of CEO compensation. These researchers suggested that growing public criticism of highly paid CEOs (despite poor corporate performance) made the announcements and justifications of CEO pay an anticipated controversy. As they noted,

> The 1992 SEC reporting rules ensure that shareholders have clear and detailed salary information. This makes it much easier for shareholders to assess any pay-for-performance linkage, thereby increasing the salience of company performance graphs and their peer comparisons. Within this newly opened disclosure process, high CEO salary is a potentially explosive issue. (p. 120)

In response, Porac et al. (1999) found that when CEO pay was especially high, board members would construct and announce a comparison group that included more peers from lower performing industries. This comparison group made the CEO's performance look better than it would have without the addition of low-performing peers and thus, protected his or her reputation as a high-quality and high-status performer, deserving of high pay.

In other cases, organizations have been shown to rely on anticipatory excuses to minimize responsibility for poor performance outcomes. In this manner, a series of organizational studies on corporate annual reports suggests that, when performance is poor, organizations design their annual reports to serve as anticipatory excuses prior to the announcement of quarterly earnings (Bettman & Weitz, 1983; Salancik & Meindl, 1984; Staw et al., 1983). For example, in Staw et al.'s study of explanations of corporate performance through annual reports, the researchers found that, when relaying upcoming negative news (e.g., impending announcements of poor quarterly performance), organizations placed blame on the industry or environment rather than on the organization (e.g., they provided an environmental excuse for poor performance, such as the introduction of new regulations that hampered their performance). Similarly, Bettman and Weitz's (1983) study of corporate annual reports revealed that organizations were more likely to attribute anticipated unfavorable outcomes to external, unstable, and uncontrollable causes, whereas they attributed favorable outcomes to internal factors (e.g., management prowess).

Avoidance Behaviors

Organizations may also use anticipatory avoidance behaviors to minimize audience scrutiny of impending negative performance reviews. A common method of scrutiny avoidance is to prevent audiences from evaluating organizational performance. In some cases, this means selectively withdrawing from performance contests (Snyder et al.,1983). For instance, in building a reputations for quality and status, U.S. business schools may showcase their performance in industry rankings that are based on either a research-oriented, scholastic model (e.g., the *U.S. News and World Report* rankings) or a teaching-oriented, practitioner model (e.g., the *Business Week* rankings; Fombrun,1996). Interestingly, many schools that do well on one performance measure (e.g., research) do less well on the other (e.g., teaching). In these cases, organizational spokespersons have been shown to avoid publicity associated with one set of rankings while seeking recognition for the other set (Fombrun, 1996). Anectdotal reports suggest that some schools have discussed removing themselves completely from one or more ranking competitions as a means of avoiding the pressures associated with these performance reviews.

In other cases, avoiding scrutiny in association with an upcoming performance review means making performance difficult to measure. For example, in their study of anticipatory perception management through hospital billing activities, Elsbach et al. (1998) found that hospital spokespersons used obfuscation behaviors to prevent hospital patients from scrutinizing their hospital bills and subsequently from requesting audits of their bills (e.g., they created difficult procedures for auditing bills and confused patients about the nature of bill auditing process). In a similar, study, Erfle, McMillan, and Grofman (1990) found that large oil companies waited to raise their prices until government regulators were busy with more pressing needs or until environmental factors could be viewed as a cause for rising gas prices. In these cases, the oil companies appeared to be taking advantage of naturally occurring events that helped them to avoid scrutiny before engaging in a potentially controversial action that could affect performance evaluations or ratings.

Pre-Empting Threats From Identity Changes

To pre-empt threats to organizational identities when identity changes are anticipated, organizations and their spokespersons may attempt to justify the identity change through anticipatory accounts or to smooth the transition to a new identity through recategorization tactics.

Anticipatory Accounts

When the introduction of a new product, service, or mode of operation suggests a change in organizational identity, organizations may wish to explain this change in ways that help organizational members and audiences accept that change (Elsbach, 1999). In particular, as a means of facilitating acceptance of identity changes, anticipatory accounts may be designed specifically to portray impending identity changes as "middle-range" rather than extreme (Reger et al.,1994). Reger et al. described "middle range" identity changes as "large enough to overcome cognitive inertia and relieve organizational stress [due to a gap between desired identity and current identity], but not so large that members believe the proposed change is unobtainable or undesirable" (p. 565). As a result, Reger et al., argue that identity changes perceived as middle range will be most likely to be accepted by organizational members.

It seems plausible that anticipatory justifications may be useful in achieving the perception that an impending identity change is middle range. For example, in their study of identity management in a volunteer organization, Golden-Biddle and Rao (1997) described an upcoming open forum to discuss the budget as an anticipated controversial event (i.e., it represented a new mode of operation that signaled a threat to the identity as a family of friends who did not openly disagree or debate issues like the budget). In preparation for this open forum, organizational leaders prepared justifications for their budget that showed how the new open-forum discussion could be incorporated into their identity as a family of friends. For example, Golden-Biddle and Rao quote one organizational leader as saying, "There is an attitude that we need to go into the annual meeting with. More than in the entire history of [the organization], we have numbers that are good, numbers that are real in the budgeting process.... We ought to be positive and upbeat.... It's very clear that we have answers for the questions that were asked" (p. 604). This quote suggests that organizational leaders wanted to justify the change in organizational identity (i.e., a change to an identity that allows for debate and open discussion) as good for the organization because it provides better budget numbers, and as consistent with the pre-existing identity (i.e., as a positive and upbeat family of friends). In this way, the identity change was portrayed as moderate. These anticipatory accounts also suggested that the new identity would retain many of the pre-existing identity dimensions.

Recategorization and Renaming

Organizational identity changes often require the integration of multiple identity dimensions into a new whole (e.g., when two organizations merge or an organization takes on a new purpose) or the reorganization of identity dimensions into a smaller whole (e.g., when an organization divests a unit or division; Balmer & Greyser, 2002). In these cases, organizational leaders may use recategorization tactics to show how the new or remaining identity dimensions fit together in the same overarching identity category. Similar to the anticipatory accounts described previously, such recategorization tactics are used to portray the identity change as moderate or middle range by suggesting that the newly acquired identity is really similar to the existing identity in a fundamental manner.

One way that such recategorization is signaled is through changing the name of the organization (Glynn & Abzug, 2002). For example, Balmer and Greyser (2002) described how the British Post Office signaled a change in its identity from a mail delivery organization to one that provided a variety of services, including retail sales of stamps, basic banking services, and the distribution of government benefits packages. To signal this larger, more complex identity, the Post Office changed its name to Consignia but retained the divisional names of Royal Mail, Post Office, and Parcel Force. As Balmer and Greyser noted,

> This enables the company to enter prospective new markets under its corporate name. In essence, the new corporate name intends to reflect a potentially wider range of services in a larger geographic footprint and permits potential global delivery systems under an international identity.... At the same time, the [name] "Post Office" identifies only the retail outlets within the U.K. and provides clarity for customers. (p. 80)

As a result, the British Post Office was able to recategorize itself as an international firm that encompassed its existing national mail delivery systems and its new global delivery services units.

In another example, Balmer and Greyser described how the British firm GEC recategorized itself through a name change when it divested its defense division. As the major British manufacturer of electrical systems and electronics, GEC had established its identity as an electronics firm throughout the 20th century. With the divestiture of its defense division, it intended to recategorize itself as an information technology hardware firm, without giving up the status that the name GEC had come to symbolize. To do this, the organization changed its name to Marconi, which was the name of one of its acquired firms, founded by the legendary Guglielmo Marconi, the inventor of wireless transmission. As Balmer and Greyser noted, "The Marconi name not only reflected the new positioning more strikingly, but also drew on the distinct identity strands of the organization's heritage" (p. 80).

Finally, in some cases organizations have used renaming and recategorization as a means of obfuscation. In many of these cases, organizations wished to minimize all future scrutiny by potentially hostile audiences related to their controversial products or services (e.g., tobacco products, gambling services). For example, in early 2003 the tobacco giant Phillip Morris followed the advice of its image consultants and changed its name to The Altria Group (Smith & Malone, 2003). Internal documents suggested that this name change was made in an attempt to buffer the corporation and its many non-tobacco divisions from the negative scrutiny of anti-tobacco audiences. As Smith and Malone noted,

> "Phillip Morris" will only refer to the tobacco operation companies under the larger "Altria Group" corporate umbrella, thus insulating both the corporation and its other operating companies—notably Kraft General Foods—from the taint of tobacco. Holding the company as a whole responsible for its role in tobacco-related death and disease will thus become more difficult. (p. 553)

Prior to this name change, tobacco control advocates had used the well-known connections between Phillip Morris' tobacco companies and their other food companies (notably Kraft) as a means of organizing product boycotts (Smith & Malone, 2003). In addition, the negative publicity associated with tobacco had been shown to damage the company's marketing success, legislative success, financial ratings, and ability to hire and retain good employees. For example, the investment bank CS First Boston commented that Phillip Morris' stock was undervalued because it was "perceived" to be a tobacco company (p. 554). Under the new name, the company hoped connections between its many non-tobacco companies and the name Phillip Morris would be more difficult.

At the same time, analysts suggested that the company was attempting to make this name change in a subtle manner so that it would not draw "attention to why it shouldn't be accepted by the community of 'good corporate citizens'" (Smith & Malone, 2003, p. 555). Thus, although the real purpose of the name change may have been anticipatory obfuscation of its tobacco business, the new name was presented by corporate spokespersons as a means of clarifying and reflecting the evolution in its products and services.

PITFALLS OF ORGANIZATIONAL PERCEPTION MANAGEMENT PRIOR TO ANTICIPATED CONTROVERSIES

Although the perception management strategies outlined here may be effective for fending off threats to organizational images and identities associated with anticipated controversies, they are not without potential risks.

In particular, the use of anticipatory perception management may lead to at least three pitfalls. First, anticipatory excuses can lead to negative images of control and adaptability. Second, anticipatory justifications can lead organizations to implement defensive routines and procedures that hinder performance. Finally, a focus on anticipated controversies can cause organizations to expend an unwarranted amount of resources preparing for low-probability events.

The Double Edge of Anticipatory Excuses

Anticipatory excuses are popular perception management tactics because they can lead to positive impressions whether or not an anticipated negative outcome occurs. For example, claiming to be hindered by economic trends can excuse poor quarterly performance or make good quarterly performance look that much more remarkable. However, such anticipatory excuses have two potential downsides. First, although anticipatory excuses cause the focal image or identity to be protected from threat, some other image or identity is compromised (e.g., an organization that uses economic environment as an anticipatory excuse may be seen as unable to adapt to market changes). At the individual level, researchers have found that people who use anticipatory excuses are seen as generally less competent than those who don't use such excuses (Arkin & Baumgardner, 1985). For organizations, the same downside may exist. That is, organizations that routinely lower expectations about their performance may be seen ultimately as incapable of high performance.

This is the saga of many U.S. government organizations, such as the U.S. Postal Service and the Federal Aviation Administration. These large, bureaucratic organizations have histories of providing standing excuses for poor performance. For example, in the mid-1990s the U.S. Postal Service was hit with a barrage of bad press when post offices in Chicago and Washington, DC, were shown to have horrendous service records, including housing piles of undelivered mail (McAllister, 1994). The U.S. Postal Service attempted to fend off anticipated complaints from other cities by claiming that individual post offices were often hit by bad weather or had local problems (such as poor morale) that could not be solved by organization-wide changes. Over time, these excuses appeared to lead consumers to perceive the U.S. Postal Service as unreliable and incapable of providing good service (Hein, 1996).

A second pitfall of providing anticipatory excuses for poor performance is that organizational members may come to internalize the excuses. For example, in the case of the U.S. Postal Service, mail carriers reacted negatively to many of the changes implemented in response to poor service reviews. One change was the implementation of delivery point sequenced (DPS) mail systems, which automated much of the mail sorting, previously been done by hand (Neff, 1996). When early trials of these systems led to slowdowns in delivery, mail carriers across the nation picketed in protest. These carriers blamed the national postmaster general for implementing an unworkable system and for keeping employees out of the implementation process (Neff, 1996). In this case, it appeared that the postal employees themselves had lost confidence in the ability of the national organization to manage day-to-day operations—they had come to believe that the Postal Service was incapable of good decision making.

Defensive Overcompensation and Poor Strategic Choices

In response to some anticipated controversies, organizational leaders may implement defensive routines or procedures to fend off expected criticism. Typically, these cases involve organizations that are highly scrutinized, in terms of their legitimacy, by the public or other oversight agencies (Dirsmith, Jablonsky, & Luzi, 1980). In such cases, it is possible for organizations to overcompensate for their contested legitimacy by relying heavily on rational procedures in cases where more strategic and intuitive procedures may be called for. That is, organizations come to trust the numbers over expert opinions to fend off expected attacks on the legitimacy of their decisions. Such actions may lead to poor strategic decisions for the organization.

For example, Dirsmith et al. (1980) described how the U.S. Federal Government used a variety of rational planning techniques (e.g., planning, programming, and budgeting (PPB), management by objectives (MOB), and zero-based budgeting (ZBB)), to legitimate their decision making and planning procedures. As Dirsmith et al. noted,

> As appropriate decision strategies and performance tests shift from computational ... to judgmental ... to compromise ... to inspirational ... the amount of controversy surrounding the decisions being made will become greater. Thus, the introduction of a decision facilitating mechanism which is based upon a computational decision strategy and which uses efficiency performance tests may serve to suppress political controversy. (p. 324)

In particular, these planning techniques helped the Federal Government appear more explicit, transparent, and rational in its decision processes. As Dirsmith et al. reported,

PPB, MBO, and ZBB may be considered as being introduced by the executive branch as a means for providing legislators with a more explicit statement of objectives and anticipated outcomes, and concrete data concerning performance for U.S. Federal agencies and programs.

However, an analysis of the effectiveness of these decision-making routines revealed that they were ill-suited for the institutional, strategic decision making that was required in complex, dynamic environments such as the Federal budgeting process (Dirsmith et al., 1980). Instead, these procedures served mainly to support pre-existing inclinations based on past performance. As Dirsmith et al. concluded,

> These techniques have the potential for encouraging simplistic, past-oriented, closed system logic, computational decision strategy in situations calling for a complex, forward-looking, open system logic, inspirational decision strategy. (p. 319)

Overweighting Low Probability Events

A third pitfall of engaging in anticipatory perception management is the tendency for organizations to become preoccupied with a low-probability controversy and thus expend unwarranted resources preparing for it, in part, through anticipatory perception management. This pitfall arises from the general tendency of people to overweight low probability events, especially if those events are vividly frightening (Kahneman & Tversky, 1979). In turn, these tendencies may lead organizational leaders to expend a disproportionate amount of resources to counter potential but unlikely negative perceptions.

In an example of such behavior, Meszaros (1999) asked the corporate safety directors of six large, international chemical corporations to discuss how they would respond to the news that a planned facility of theirs "might pose a risk" of human injury to local communities. Although the probability of risk varied across the six cases they developed, these managers appeared to treat all cases as equally urgent if they met the threshold condition of being "a potentially ruinous event" (i.e., an event that could potentially lead to the demise of the entire organization). This threshold reasoning appeared to center on maintaining the reputation of the corporations against the backdrop of "anticipated judgment by juries and governmental bodies" (p. 994). As one safety manager reported, "Maintaining reputation in order to maintain the ability to do business. This is what [the corporation] is really concerned with" (p. 986). As a result, decisions were made to spend exorbitant amounts to protect against highly unlikely negative events. For example, one manager noted, "In one instance our company invested $1 billion essentially to save one life per year. We could have saved more lives if we had invested that money elsewhere" (p. 993).

CASE ILLUSTRATION: IDENTITY MANAGEMENT AND THE PORSCHE CAYENNE

As a case illustration of anticipatory perception management, the following text describes how the sportscar icon, Porsche AG (for Porsche Aktiengesellschaft)—hereafter referred to as simply "Porsche"— prepared consumers and car enthusiasts for the introduction of their first non-sports automobile, the sport utility vehicle (SUV), Porsche Cayenne. This case describes how perceptions of the identity and reputation of the venerable sportscar maker were managed in the years and months preceding the introduction of the Cayenne. This case is punctuated by four events: (1) the announcement of Porsche's plans to produce an SUV, (2) the announcement that the SUV would be available in 2002 and would be called the Cayenne, (3) the unveiling of the first prototype images of the Cayenne, and (4) the introduction of the first Cayenne at the 2002 auto shows. The primary parties involved in this case were Porsche, sportscar enthusiasts and members of Porsche's auto clubs, auto industry writers and analysts, and the car-buying public.

The auto designer and manufacturer, Porsche, was established in Stuttgart, Germany, in 1930 by Dr. Ferdinand Porsche. One of Dr. Porsche's first car designs was the 1935 Volkswagen Beetle—the car that eventually became the greatest selling automobile model of all time (Kaplan & Horvath, 1993). After World War II, Porsche concentrated its design and production on building sportscars and racecars. Starting in the 1960s Porsche's success in international automobile rallies, such as the famed Monte Carlo rally and the grueling Paris–Dakar rally, gave the company an international reputation and identity as a premier sportscar specialist (Deutsche Welle Productions, 1999). The company designed, produced, and sold high-end sportscars, centered on the platform of their successful racecar, the Porsche 911. The company stock became publicly traded in 1972 (Kaplan & Horvath, 1993).

By 1998 (the year the company announced it was working on an SUV), Porsche had just two production platforms, the legendary 911 sports/racing car and the new Boxster roadster. These two platforms (and their various models) embodied the essence of the Porsche identity—elegant, flowing lines and powerful rear-mounted engines. Although many other sportscar makers had diluted their identities with myriad models (e.g., the former sportscar specialist, BMW, produced everything from racecars to minivans), Porsche had condensed its line (discontinuing attempts, in the 1980s, at making front-engine sportscars and a four-person passenger car) in a way that amplified its distinctive features and meaning (Deutsche Welle Productions, 1999).

This "pure" sportscar identity was the basis for organizational identification by thousands of sportscar enthusiasts and members of Porsche's hundreds of auto clubs worldwide. For example, auto industry writers often displayed a passion for Porsches that could be described only in poetic terms—as one writer for Autoweek did:

> A Porsche also needs curves to feed its soul.... If we want to know how a Porsche Turbo handles, we go to France, as we did last April for our cover story, which introduced the car and described its many and impressive technical virtues. We drove 450 hard and excited miles there, intoxicated by spring in Provence and victims of love at first feel.... Of course the car has an exhibitionistic personality and character; your eyeballs tell you that as you gape at the composite whale-tail wing and the smooth, fat, sculptured rear fenders housing humongous tires, and when you then have to pull those orbs back into their sockets after a full-throttle burst. (Moses, 1995, p. 18).

It was against this backdrop that Porsche announced it would introduce a new sports utility vehicle to its line of cars.

1. Announcing an SUV: A Porsche SUV is Still a Porsche

In June 1998, Porsche CEO Wendelin Wiedeking said that Porsche would build an SUV in collaboration with Volkswagen ("VW and Porsche," 1998). Wiedeking claimed that the new SUV was good for Porsche's growth and long-term potential: "Our new sports utility vehicle will tap new growth potential. It will also limit our dependency on the traditional market segments of sportscars, convertibles and roadsters" (p. D8). Wiedeking said little about how the SUV would fit in with the identity of Porsche or how it may cause that identity to evolve, remarking only that the SUV would "correspond in full with Porsche's high technical and visual standards" (Proudfoot, 1998, p. D9).

Porsche enthusiasts and industry writers reacted to this news with apprehension. In the days and weeks following the announcement, members of these audiences weighed in with a variety of reasons why the proposed Porsche SUV was a bad idea. Most reasons centered on the potential damage to the central and distinctive features of the organization, or in other words, its identity. As one auto industry writer remarked:

Porsche's decision to jump aboard the sport utility vehicle bandwagon worries those of us who are caught by the belief that Porsche has come closer to realizing its purpose than any other automaker. A Porsche SUV in the year 2002? It'd have to be too high and too heavy to be anything like a Porsche. It'd point Porsche in an entirely different direction. And each time Porsche has tried to expand beyond what it's best known for, rear-engine sportscars, it hasn't worked. Diversifying has succeeded only in blurring Porsche's most precious attribute—its image ... can you picture an SUV with the name Porsche on it? I can't. At which end, I ask you, could the engine be? Not likely in the rear. How sweet might the curves of its fenders and roofline be? Not very sweet, it seems to me, for an SUV needs to be basically box-like ... (Proudfoot, 1998, p. D9).

Even a year later, industry analysts were talking about how the new Porsche SUV would be tough to fit into Porsche's existing identity and brand image. Todd Turner, president of Car Concepts Research Inc. in Thousand Oaks, California, remarked,

It's going to be very difficult for them to bring a sport-utility to market without damaging their brand image.... Porsche used to be the car every kid wanted to drive. Now if you're 18 to 25, a Ferrari is the ultimate fantasy. (Welch, 1999, p. 5)

However, some analysts were more optimistic. As Susan Jacobs, president of the marketing firm Jacobs & Associates in Rutherford, New Jersey, noted,

If Porsche can make it a more versatile extension of its lineup in styling and presentation, it will dilute the lineup less. It is a big brand challenge, but it is possible for them to move Porsche to the next level. (Welch, 1999, p. 5)

While Porsche executives admitted that they had not yet decided how they would market the SUV, spokespersons began their first serious identity management campaign by reiterating that the car would remain true to Porsche's identity. As Richard Ford, CEO of Porsche North America, put it, "We will remain true to what our brand is known for. That's satisfying emotional needs" (Welch, 1999, p. 5). Further, Porsche executives commented that the new SUV would meet the needs of many of its current customers, who already own both sportscars and SUVs (McDonald, 1999). Finally, company spokespersons felt certain that, given its thoroughbred Porsche design, their SUV would "blow everything else out of the water" in terms of the current SUV market (McMahon, 1999).

Together, these statements appeared to be attempts by Porsche to affirm its identity as a premier auto maker that was known for its combination of style and power and whose products were primarily designed to satisfy emotional rather than practical needs of its customers.

2. Introducing the Cayenne: Using Naming as Identity Management

In early June, 2000, Porsche announced that its planned SUV would be called the Cayenne (i.e., after a hot South American pepper; Martin, 2000). Porsche spokespersons claimed that the name "conjures images of spiciness, adventure and a sense of joie de vivre, and fits the driving experience of its off-road rocket" (Martin, 2000, p. 59). As Porsche CEO Wiedeking explained:

> With the terms Carrera, Targa, and Boxster, … our sports cars are not only associated inseparably with the Porsche brand name, but also make a decisive contribution to the strong image and success of these products. So the name of our new SUV must be of substance and must reflect the Porsche philosophy. In this case, not only on the road, but also off-road. We are convinced that the combination of Porsche and Cayenne as a model designation radiates true strength, dynamism, fascination and emotions, and will continue the great tradition of legendary names. ("Cayenne," 2000, p. 1)

This choice of name and its meaning were clearly designed to link the new SUV to the Porsche identity. Organizational researchers have provided significant evidence that company and product names are primary tools for defining and affirming organizational identities (Glynn & Abzug, 2002; Olins, 1995). As Olins (1995) noted,

> Identity is expressed in the names, symbols, logos, colours and rites of passage which the organization uses to distinguish itself. At one level, these serve the same purpose as religious symbolism, chivalric heraldry or national flags and symbols: they encapsulate and make vivid a collective sense of belonging and purpose. At another level, they represent consistent standards of quality and therefore encourage consumer loyalty. (p. 9)

Using the name "Carrera"—the Spanish word for "race"—and the name "Targa"—Latin for "shield"—Porsche had relied on European-sounding names that had an exotic tone and meanings related to strength and speed to signal its identity. The term *Cayenne* continued this theme and added exotic "spice" to strength as the image conjured by the Porsche SUV. This name also contrasted the Porsche SUV with most other SUVs, which carried names such as "Explorer," "Tahoe," or "Navigator" that sounded rugged and outdoorsy but not exotic or spicy. As such, introducing their new SUV as the Cayenne was a form of identity management designed to affirm the identity of the new car as a traditional Porsche.

Still, some car enthusiasts found the name to be too domestic, eliciting images of food and cooking rather than of asphalt and steel, adding to their fears that the SUV would be more suited to soccer moms than racecar drivers. As one writer quipped:

> [a Porsche spokesperson] revealed that "when we announced the name, the very first call we got was from Bon Appetit." Can you imagine a Porschephile, who lives for those moments he or she can slip behind the wheel of a performance machine, rushing to the store, racing to the magazine rack, tossing aside Motor Trend, Car and Driver, and Road & Track for the newest issue of Bon Appetit to get the lowdown on the new motorized gem? (Majeta, 2000, p. C4)

Similarly, the name announcement did little to quell the fears of Porsche auto club members, who remained nervous about the performance of the Cayenne, despite the recognition that the company probably needed the SUV to remain competitive and viable. As Bob Miller, president of the 48,000 member Porsche Club of America, noted, "This was probably a wise management decision. That doesn't mean that members of the club have embraced it 100 percent" (Mertl, 2000, p. C16). Miller went on to add, cautiously, "I would assume it would have great brakes, it would have a great engine, it would have great handling, just because of where it's coming from. But those are issues we're going to have to address a little bit down the road" (p. C16).

3. First Prototype Photos: Using Physical Markers for Identity Management

In February, 2001 some of the first photographs of the Cayenne prototype were revealed in *Fortune* (Taylor, 2001). The photos, reported to have been secretly taken during testing (Taylor, 2001), showed a car that looked more like an off-road station wagon than an SUV. The photo included in *Fortune* was accompanied by the headline, "Can you believe Porsche is putting its badge on *this* car?" The writer then noted that "The idea of Porsche making an SUV is only slightly less jarring than Lafite Rothschild producing a blush wine, or Brioni applying its Italian stitching to a pair of overalls. This is a company that thrives by building cars that go faster than most people can drive them—and cost more than most people can afford" (p. 168).

Countering these comments, Porsche marketing director Hans Reidel noted, "We are doing the sportscar of sport utilities, with on-road performance that is comparable to our other cars" (p. 172). Reidel went on to add, "This will be good for all those fathers who don't want to sacrifice their sportscar to parenthood."

However, Porsche executives were also clearly worried about tarnishing their image as a premier sports and racing car company. Thus, despite the fact that they expected over half their sales of the Cayenne to be in the United States, Porsche decided to build its new manufacturing facilities in Germany (unlike Mercedes and BMW, who had recently built American plants). Porsche apparently believed that a made-in-the-U.S.A. label would detract from the Porsche "mystique" (p. 172). Further, company executives noted that the Cayenne would be a genuine Porsche, recognizable as much by its physical appearance as by its performance. As reported by Taylor (2001), "Although the engine will be in front, the Cayenne will retain such hallowed Porsche eccentricities as an ignition switch placed on the left side of the steering wheel" (p. 172).

Auto writers also noticed the classic Porsche look to the Cayenne. As one Australian writer noted:

> As the photographs show, the Cayenne owes many of its styling cues to its sports-car siblings. The front-end, for example, closely mirrors the style of the current 911 and Boxster ranges by having the indicator and high-beam globes neatly tucked within the lower half of the swoopily styled headlights.... The bullish front bumper on the Turbo model, which features multiple air intakes and twin fog lights, also evokes memories of the brutal 911 GT2 and will leave those ahead on the road in no doubt as to what brand of car is tailing. (Mcgavin, 2002, p. 3)

These physical identity markers (i.e., the manufacturing plant, ignition switch, and front-end appearance) clearly identified the Cayenne as a member of the Porsche family, just as facial characteristics help identify siblings as members of the same family. Such family characteristics have long been used by auto manufacturers to show a common endorsed identity (Olins, 1995) in a variety of automobile lines (e.g., the General Motors lines of Chevrolet, Pontiac, Oldsmobile, Buick, and Cadillac).

Porsche's first official photos of the Cayenne were released a year later, in March 2002. These photos showed a car almost identical to those in the secret prototype photos. In a press release accompanying the photos, Porsche appeared to be downplaying off-road qualities and focusing on power and performance. For example, the press release called the road performance of the Cayenne "outstanding" but the off-road performance only "very good":

"Taking the Porsche experience to a new level, the Cayenne will create the perfect balance of performance and power, delivering outstanding on-pavement performance and very good off-road driving characteristics" (posted in: http://www.us.porsche.com/english/news/pressreleases/020306.htm, March 5, 2002).

Further, Porsche Cars of North America President Frederick J. Schwab linked the Cayenne to its sportscar cousins by focusing on the "sport" dimensions of the car. As Schwab put it, "Porsche has been at the forefront of all-wheel-drive design. From the Lohner-Porsche in 1900 to the Porsche 959 in 1985, Porsche has been engineering four-wheel drive and all-wheel drive vehicles. The Cayenne is a natural for us, and it will put the sport in sport utility vehicles" (http://www.us.porsche.com/english/news/pressreleases/020306.htm, March 5, 2002).

Reinforcing this statement, Schwab also noted that "For a Porsche to be a Porsche, we have to outperform everything on the highway" (Ritzler, 2002b, p. 1S). Together, these statements appeared to further attempt to link the Cayenne with Porsche's distinguished line of sportscars. As such, these statements represented symbolic categorizations of the Cayenne that affirmed its inclusion in the Porsche family while admitting some overlap with the category of SUV.

Despite the hype, many Porsche drivers and enthusiasts were less than thrilled about the look of the Cayenne. Many saw it as too big and as a blown-up (and disfigured) version of the sleek Porsche race car. As car writer Catherine Riley of the London *Times* wrote, "It is monstrous. Quite simply, the Porsche Cayenne is wretched. There has never been a Porsche design I did not like until now, but this, Porsche's belated entry into the SUV market, looks like a backstreet garage's entry into the cut-and-shut car-of-the-year award. Boxster meets Nissan Terrano" (Riley, 2002a).

Other critics remained concerned about the effect of the Cayenne on Porsche's identity. Thus, after seeing the photos of the Cayenne and realizing that Porsche's new car would look substantially different from its classic sportscars, Pistonheads.com columnist Robert Farago had this to say:

I can hardly begrudge buyers a car they need like they need satellite-controlled headlights that swivel to follow the road. I'm more concerned about the Cayenne's effect on Porsche.... Is this really the same company that agonized for years about making a four-door 928? It's as if they decided to apply their motor sport heritage to designing brief cases. Oh wait, they have. (Farago, February 17, 2002, posted on http://www.pistonheads.com/truth/default.asp?storyId=3809)

Farago went on to lament about the brand dilution caused by the Cayenne and the domino effects it may have on other Porsche cars. As he noted, "Every man-hour Porsche spends on the Cayenne—designing, marketing, servicing, etc.—is one man-hour less for maintaining and extending their dominance in the sportscar market. In other words, the Cayenne is a waste of time."

4. First Test-Drives: "It Feels like a Porsche, but I'm Not Sure I Still Identify With Porsche"

In late 2002, anticipating the first test-drives in the Porsche Cayenne, Frederick Schwab, president of Porsche of North America, noted that "Mom will be comfortable driving it, and Dad will have a ball" (Ritzler, 2002a, p. 1D). These comments were meant to bring more people into the showroom and to increase the number of women driving the Cayenne, yet they also sent a signal that the Porsche was no longer an exclusive sportscar, suitable only for skilled drivers and race tracks. Despite comments by Porsche Chairman Wendelin Wiedeking that "the Cayenne looks like a Porsche, accelerates like a Porsche, drives like a Porsche, and feels like a Porsche" (quoted in Dowling, 2002, p. 6), first glimpses of the car, unveiled in October, 2002, at the Paris Auto Show, did little to calm the fears of Porsche traditionalists. As one writer noted to a colleague, "It's all wrong though, isn't it? Porsches are all about aspiration, about really wanting one—you won't feel that way about this thing, will you?" (quoted in Riley, 2002a, p. 39).

Fortunately for Porsche, the Cayenne was up to the challenge. Several early test drives produced rave reviews, even from the most skeptical of critics. Test drivers claimed that Porsche had "redefined the SUV" (Gallagher, 2002, p. 45), and that Cayenne was an engineering marvel (Dowling, 2002). Even hard-core Porsche traditionalist Robert Farago, who had called the Cayenne a "waste of time" a few months earlier, had this to say after his test drive:

> Sweet Mother of Porsche Traction Management, the Cayenne loves a loose surface! I was accelerating, cornering and stopping at fantastic speeds, without a hint of wheel spin or tail wagging. The formerly annoying spring suspension made the mixed gravel as comfortable as a feather mattress. A lake masquerading as a puddle couldn't impede our progress, or mute braking power. And the engine—Hell, we were waving at motorway traffic as we passed. (Farago, November 26, 2002, p. 1, posted on www://pistonheads.com/doc.asp?c=105&i=5868)

Despite its apt performance, however, many reviewers couldn't let go of the fact that the Cayenne was an SUV and not a sportscar. The common theme running through their criticism was the inconsistency between s potential owners of the Cayenne and the typical Porsche driver. This theme suggested that the Cayenne not only affected perceptions of Porsche's organizational identity but also threatened the identities of individual Porsche owners. That is, because the Porsche identity was so tightly linked to one kind of car (i.e., a highly exclusive sportscar), it also became linked to a specific set of owners (e.g., well-to-do, thrill-seekers and auto enthusiasts) who, in turn, were threatened when the set of Porsche owners was potentially expanded to include soccer moms and dads. As one commentator noted:

> Has Porsche forgotten what its most fervent, most dedicated customers told it not long ago, when the front-engined, V8-powered 928 was announced as the first of a new generation of Porsches? To them, the only real Porsche had a boxer engine behind the rear wheels of a sportscar. That package gave Porsches their characteristic sound, appearance and driving dynamics. (Will Hagon, ABC radio motoring commentator, quoted in Dowling, 2002, p. 6)

By the end of 2002, auto writer Robert Farago echoed the sentiments of many writers when he sadly accepted the fact that the old Porsche was no longer around. However, he and most others who test drove the Cayenne also appeared to embrace the Cayenne as worthy product. As he wrote, "Does the Cayenne signal last Orders for the Porsche brand? Yes and no. On the one hand, their SUV is a betrayal of the company's core values. It makes a mockery of their hard-earned sportscar street cred. On the other hand, I reckon the Cayenne is the fastest and most capable off-roader that money can buy. I want one, but not for the right reasons" (Farago, November 26, 2002, p. 2).

In the end, the effects of the Cayenne on the Porsche identity may also have been good and bad. Porsche had produced a product that was widely viewed as frame breaking and high performing (thus affirming its capabilities), yet this product also redefined the company focus and its customer base (i.e., a large part of its "identifiers"). As a result, it's likely that the Porsche identity will incur long-term changes associated with their production of the Cayenne.

7

Organizational Perception Management Following Acclaim Events

Although we most often hear about organizational crises or controversies that have negative implications for organizational images, identities, or reputations events that have positive implications for perceptions of organization (i.e., acclaim events) are actually more common. Positive financial performance, favorable product ratings, and recommendations from external review groups or organizations are commonly included in organizational press releases, advertising campaigns, and annual reports as routine forms of perception management (Fombrun, 1996). However, the ubiquity and ordinary nature of these events tends to undermine their effectiveness as the content of perception management because corporate audiences are more likely to attend to events that are unexpected and unusual (Fiske & Taylor, 1991). In other cases, the low impact of acclaim events is rooted in the objectified and indefinite nature of corporate communications, especially communications regarding financial performance (Aerts, 1994). For example, the very nature of the accounting model by which corporate performance is measured often makes it difficult for audiences to see positive economic performance as the result of superior decision making by organizational leaders. As Aerts (1994) noted,

> When specific actions and events are objectified by accounting explanations, they are generalized, disconnected from the personal impact or motives of the actor.... the assignation of responsibility becomes problematic or vague. As a result, the public is brought to appreciate the facts and performances

presented as the outcome of a rule-bound reality, governed by more general-ized organizational and societal norms. (p. 339)

Aerts also notes, "Accounting explanations ... never directly point to spe-cific actions, decisions or influences. They stop at intermediary causes or reasons; they never confront original motives or impulses. An important characteristic of accounting explanations seems to be that they do not impact on management's future behavior alternatives" (p. 340). Finally, because positive events can be as much the result of luck as good decision making, corporations may be hesitant to blow their horns too loudly, lest they set un-reasonable expectations for their future performance. Further, because it is widely held that highly capable firms need not protest their valor (Ashforth & Gibbs, 1990), organizations may be reluctant to bring too much attention to their successes.

For these reasons, capitalizing on the positive implications of acclaim events often proves to be a more daunting task than responding to the nega-tive implications of organizational controversies or crises. In this chapter, I discuss what makes acclaim events important opportunities for organiza-tional perception management and how organizational spokespersons can respond to them for maximum benefit. In short, this review suggests that, when it comes to perception management and acclaim events, less is more.

DEFINING ACCLAIM EVENTS

Organizational acclaim events come in two primary types, recognition by industry analysts or evaluators and achievement of organization goals. The first type occurs when external audiences perceive the organization in a positive light according to some externally designated criteria. By contrast, the second type happens when organizational insiders deem the perfor-mance of the organization as having met an internally set goal. Although acclaim events may follow from crisis events (i.e., a positive response to a crisis event, such as Odwalla's quick and thorough response to the e coli poisoning discussed in Chapter 4, in this chapter, I focus on acclaim events that occur independent of such crises or controversies.

Recognition by Industry Analysts or Evaluators

Organizational reputations of high quality and competence are often highly dependent on the evaluations of industry groups or review boards who or-ganize contests that rank firms or products based on some preset criteria (e.g., product performance, customer satisfaction; Fombrun, 1996; Rao,

1994). Such certification contests (Thompson, 1967) include well-known product rankings from sources such as *The Michelin Guide* (restaurants), *Consumer Reports* (consumer products from vacuum cleaners to speed boats), and the *Business Week* rankings of U.S. business schools (Rao, 1994). For example, as noted in Chapter 2 of this volume, Staw and Epstein (2000) found that corporations that employed popular management techniques such as teams, quality programs, and employee empowerment were rated in the survey of "most admired companies" conducted by *Fortune* as more innovative and higher status than similar firms who did not use these cutting-edge techniques. In a review of such corporate contests, Fombrun (1996) reported that there are now some 16,000 corporate awards given annually for outstanding performance in products, processes, social performance, environmentalism, and leadership.

When an organization receives praise or high ranking from an industry group, that commendation serves as credible evidence that the organization is capable of high performance and thus may be used by the organization to build reputations for quality and industry status. As Fombrun (1996) put it, "Mention the Pulitzer Prize, the Academy Award, or the Grammy Award, and most people know what you're talking about" (p. 169). As a result, positive reputations may be managed through the advertisement of an organization's "wins" in certification contests. As Rao (1994) explained, "[V]ictories in certification contests are small, fortuitous events that create a reputation that becomes magnified by positive feedback ..." (p. 32).

As a case in point, Rao (1994) described how early U.S. automobile manufacturers advertised their successes in competitions pitting cars against horses to build the legitimacy and status of the organization. As he noted,

> Winning firms reaped substantial publicity because of press coverage and proclaimed these victories in their advertising campaigns. After winning some hill-climbing contests, the Peerless Company advertised its car as a 'rapid and powerful hill climber.' Similarly, St. Louis Motor Carriage Company, after faring well in some endurance contests, touted its cars as 'rigs that run.' ... Buick, after winning several contests, proclaimed 'Tests tell—could you ask for more convincing evidence?' Thus, the advertising campaigns planned by automobile producers were mechanisms to inform the public of their winning record. (p. 35)

In other cases, firms may use the ranking group's press releases of top performers in certification contests to manage distinctive organizational images such as trustworthiness or high value. In this manner, Murrell (2001) described the benefits of being included in the annual press release from *Working Mothers* magazine regarding its ranking of the most family-friendly companies. This press release was covered by major U.S. newspapers (e.g., *The Wall Street Journal*), magazines, television stations, and radio networks. In turn, Murrell found that firms that made the list of most family friendly for the first time experienced significantly better stock returns than most firms in their industry.

Finally, in some cases, organizations may rely on the mere exposure gained by media attention to positive business activities when no certification contest is involved. In these cases, the image or reputation as an industry leader may be informally recognized by industry writers, who focus on cutting-edge technologies, products, operating procedures, or personnel at the organization. One such case involved a 425-pound college student and the Subway sandwich chain. In November, 1999, under the heading "Stupid Diets that Work," *Men's Health* reported that a 20-year-old Indiana University college student had lost 245 pounds in one year by eating only Subway sandwiches, twice a day (Swierczynski, 1999). Two nutritional experts—Anne Fletcher, M.S., R.D. and author of the "Thin for Life" book series, and Tina Ruggerio, M.S., R.D. a New York City dietician—praised the diet for its convenience, portion control, and high fiber content (Swierczynski, 1999). Although Subway had not known about the diet before the story broke, the publicity gained from its success, along with the apparent endorsement of the diet by widely known nutrition gurus, made the magazine story an unexpected acclaim event for the corporation. As I describe in more detail later in this chapter, Subway used perception management in response to this acclaim event to put a face to its product and to improve its reputation for quality substantially as a result.

Achieving Organizational Goals

A second type of organizational acclaim event is achieving or exceeding a desired organizational goal. Such events include betterment of financial performance forecasts (e.g., the announcement by eBay of increased quarterly earnings during the dot-com bust of the early 2000s), the successful launch of a new product (e.g., introduction of the Apple iPod), resolution of a customer problem (e.g., Northwest Airlines changing to all non-smoking flights in response to evidence of the dangers of secondhand smoke), or better meeting the needs of a set of existing or potential customers (e.g., the introduction of the impotence drug, Viagra by the pharmaceutical company Pfizer).

In some cases, organizational goals are advertised to audiences prior to any attempts at achieving them (e.g., the case of the Porsche Cayenne, SUV described in Chapter 6). In these cases, the organization may gain more from achieving its goals because of the added attention it has gained through this pre-event publicity. However, the organization also has more to lose by failing to meet stated goals in these cases as a result of this same attention. Accordingly, organizations typically advertise goals in specific situations, including when they are fairly certain that they can meet them (e.g., goals for the release date of a highly anticipated movie sequel by a Hollywood movie studio), when they expect that other groups or organizations will set goals for them if they do not do it themselves (e.g., the goals of the Atlanta Olympic Committee for upgrading city infrastructure prior to the 1996 Summer Olympic Games), or when they expect that the mere act of setting the goal will be beneficial, regardless of whether or not it is achieved (e.g., the goal set by a university to see a high percentage of its student-athletes graduate). For example, the ice cream company Ben & Jerry's set a goal of rewarding its highest paid employee with a salary no more than seven times the amount earned by its lowest paid employee (Theroux, 1991). The announcement of this goal alone received widespread acclaim by business writers who were increasingly appalled at the high salaries paid to company executives, even as the company profits tumbled and the lowest paid workers were required to supplement their income with welfare checks (Theroux, 1991). Further, the goal was relatively easy to achieve, as meeting it was completely in the hands of organizational decision makers.

Public goals set by organizations may be relatively nonspecific and open to interpretation, allowing corporate spokespersons to use perception management tactics to improve the chances that audiences view the organization as successful in achieving these goals. Tactics may involve using anticipatory impression management to set expectations prior to the event as well as to spin outcomes of the event positively. For example, Sutton and Kramer (1990) described how the presidential administration of Ronald Reagan used perception management to portray the 1986 Iceland Arms Control talks between Reagan and then-chairman of the Soviet Union Mikhail Gorbachev as a success. As they noted, prior to the talks, Reagan administration spokespersons attempted to set modest expectations regarding the extent to which the two superpowers would reduce their stocks of nuclear weapons. To this end, Reagan's spokespersons portrayed the fact that the talks would be held at all as a success and noted that, although the idea for the talks had come from Gorbachev, the Americans should be given credit for setting the dates for the talks. Then, after the talks, White House communications director Patrick Buchanan called the talks "Reagan's finest hour" (quoted in Sutton & Kramer,1990, p. 237), even though there had been no real agreement for arms reductions by either side. Instead of portraying the event as a failure, Reagan administration spokespersons portrayed it as an acclaim event because, as Buchanan noted, "The president made the most sweeping, far-reaching arms control proposal in history" but "Gorbachev said 'No'" (quoted in Sutton & Kramer, 1990, p. 239).

In other cases, organizations announce the existence of long-standing goals only after they have been achieved. In these cases, the goals are likely to have been difficult to achieve, such as the resolution of long-standing industry problems (i.e., reducing the size of computer components) or the development of technically superior products or processes (i.e., the introduction of allergy medications with few side effects). One such case involves the pharmaceutical firm Pfizer and its introduction of the impotence drug Viagra. Before Viagra, men wanting treatment for impotence had to rely on painful injections or implants as modes of treatment (Tran, 1998). Pfizer announced that it had gained FDA approval for an impotence drug that came in the form of an easy-to-take pill with few side effects; Viagra represented a major medical breakthrough that had implications for 30 to 40 million American men and countless others worldwide (Kolata, 1998). The fact that the medication was originally designed to treat heart disease made no difference to the public and to the health care community in terms of the magnitude of the discovery (Kolata, 1998). As I describe in more detail in the case study at the end of this chapter, the introduction of Viagra was a clear acclaim event.

ORGANIZATIONAL PERCEPTION MANAGEMENT STRATEGIES FOLLOWING ACCLAIM EVENTS

Effective perception management following acclaim events appears to be used most often for two specific purposes. First, perception management is used to show how the acclaim event reinforces the long-term reputation of an organization for high status or quality in a particular arena. In this manner, the acclaim event is framed as just one more example of the organization's fitness for categorization as high status or high quality in its area of expertise (e.g., the continued high quality ranking of an auto manufacturer by industry surveys can be touted as long-term evidence of a reputation for quality). Second, perception management is used to show how the acclaim event adds to the growing evidence that an organization is deserving of a distinctive identity. In this manner, acclaim events can be used to show how an organization is making progress toward a stated goal of changing its focus or its performance (e.g., a food manufacturer attracting new consumers who are on a heart-healthy diet provides evidence of an identity that is based on a health-conscious categorization) or is continuing to perform in ways consistent with its established identity (e.g., a highly rated, upscale restaurant chain opens a more moderately priced chain of restaurants that wins praise for providing same attention to detail and quality as its higher priced sibling).

Both of these perception management instances suggest that managers most often view acclaim events as providing incremental evidence in support of a long-term, organizational perception (i.e., reputation or identity) rather than big events that signal a radical change in a distinctive organizational image. The prevalence of such incremental strategies further suggests that organizational perception managers are particularly attuned to the pitfalls (described later in this chapter) of protesting too much and raising expectations in response to acclaim events. That is, effective organizational perception managers appear cautious about making too much of an acclaim event, for fear that such hoopla will be viewed as either evidence that the acclaim event was overblown or evidence that the organization is infallible in the area of acclaim (and thus vulnerable to backlash if they fall short in the future). I discuss the effective use of perception management strategies in both acclaim situations next.

Affirming Reputations for High Status and Quality Following Recognition Events

Affirmations of high status or high-quality reputations following recognition events typically involve actions designed to verify that the organization continues to pursue such status and quality goals. These actions include self-categorizations that affirm that the organization is in an exclusive and elite league of organizations as well as conspicuous affiliation with these same elite organizations.

Exclusive Self-Categorizations

Winning a certification contest, by definition, suggests that an organization is highly ranked compared to its peers. Over time, then, consistent recognition by industry evaluators, through high ratings or rankings, is an ideal opportunity for promoting organizational reputations for status. Although such reputations are valuable for all types of organizations, they appear especially important for organizations in service industries (e.g., financial services, consulting, education) because potential customers can't see the product before they purchase it and thus must rely on reputation to get an idea of its quality. As Fombrun (1996) noted,

> In the service sector, intangibles like reputation are even larger contributors to a company's economic performance. Businesses that rely on people skills, information, know-how, and other "credence goods"—companies involved in consulting, advertising, law, software development, and accounting—depend heavily on their reputations to attract customers and investors. (p. 238)

Given the importance of reputations in these industries, it's not surprising that firms belonging to them go to great pains to find and publicize top rankings in some category, even if that category is highly specialized and with few competitors (e.g., an award for the North American mining company with the best environmental programs). Being able to claim the #1 ranking in any area helps an organization to claim the categorization of high status legitimately. Thus, Fombrun (1996) reported,

> Most companies look hard to find a statistic—any statistic—that provides them with a number 1 ranking to use for self-promotion. For instance, the trade journal *Institutional Investor* regularly ranks investment banks by the total assets they manage, the volume of underwriting they do, and the quality of advice they give. Banks that come out on top in any of these categories are generally quick to take out ads in the business media to convey their prominence and remind existing and potential clients about their relative standing.

In a similar manner, Elsbach and Kramer (1996) found that business schools used selective and specialized categorizations to promote their high-status following the *Business Week* rankings of U.S. business schools. For example, although not ranked #1 overall, the University of California, Berkeley, touted its rank as the best value in MBA education and as one of the highest ranked public universities in the survey. Similarly, the University of Michigan was quick to bring attention to its high ranking in the area of executive MBA education and also noted its high ranking among public institutions. These achievements were publicized on school Web sites, in alumni magazines, and in monthly business school newsletters. In fact, if you look at the official Web site of almost any U.S. business school, you can find mention of some elite categorization to which they lay claim (e.g., the University of South Dakota Business School Web site mentions that it is "the only AACSB accredited business program in the state of South Dakota," and the Graduate School of Management at the University of California, Davis, consistently claims that it is "the youngest public MBA program ever to be nationally ranked").

Affiliation With Other High-Status or High-Quality Groups

Whereas organizations that have won certification contests use public self-categorizations as a verbal strategy of reputation affirmation, these organizations may also use behavioral strategies to demonstrate and affirm their high-status or high-quality reputations. One effective behavioral strategy is to affiliate consistently and conspicuously with other organizations that are viewed as prototypical members of high-status or high-quality groups. In fact, research on the economic benefits of high-status affiliations among wine producers has shown that wineries that are already high status gain the most (in terms of the prices they may command for their wine) from affiliating with other high-status organizations (Benjamin & Podolny, 1999). Benjamin and Podolny suggested that this result is due to the intransient nature of status hierarchies (i.e., status hierarchies tended to be reinforced over time, even if organizations have no incentive to do so). As a result, organizations that win their first status contests are wise to affiliate conspicuously with long-term, high-status organizations to increase the value of their reputations.

Affirming Distinctive Identities After Achieving Goals

Because many organizational goals are specific to the products, services, and cultures of that organization, the achievement of these goals presents opportunities for affirming enduring and distinctive identities. Identity affirmation following acclaim events most often occurs through public entitlings (e.g., claiming primary responsibility for an achievement through advertisements), symbolic behaviors (e.g., announcing new policies, procedures, or goals in light of the achievement), and the display of physical markers (e.g., changes in logos or advertisements that include recognition of the achievement).

All three of these tactics rely on the effects of "labeling" to help frame and interpret "the meaning and importance of events" (Ashforth & Humphrey, 1995, p. 53). Labeling theorists (Ashforth & Humphrey, 1995) define a label as "a signifier of a given object [that] typically activates a set of cognitions (and related affect) about the object" (p. 43). Further, they propose that a primary purpose of labeling is to facilitate social control (i.e., to impose some desired meaning onto an event or object). This definition distinguishes labeling from categorization, which is argued to be used primarily to facilitate accurate understanding of an event or object.

I argue that labeling is used most commonly following acclaim events because perception management following such events is likely to be deliberately and voluntarily chosen (in contrast to perception management following crises, which is almost demanded or required by critical audiences). Because labeling is the product of deliberate and strategic thinking by organizational leaders, it is best suited to situations in which perception management can be internally controlled (such as following acclaim events). Further, I propose that labeling is most likely to be used to affirm identities, rather than to manage images or reputations, because such perceptions are most likely to be internally defined and relevant. I discuss next how labeling may be carried out through entitlings, symbolic behaviors, and the display of physical markers.

Entitlings

As noted earlier, entitlings are claims of responsibility for an event. When an organization achieves a goal or milestone, it may affirm its identity by publicly naming those groups of organization members who were most responsible for the achievement. Such naming serves to label those groups as worthy and valued and affirms the organizational identity based on having such members. In some cases, entitlings are designed to preserve a historical or even mythical perception of the company and its leaders. For example, Rowlinson and Hassard (1993) described how the chocolate maker Cadbury, at the time of its 100th anniversary, commissioned the writing of two corporate histories to make public the entitlings of company founders and those founders' ideals. Rowlinson and Hassard's analysis of these corporate histories reveals that the authors attribute, inaccurately, much of Cadbury's innovative business practices (e.g., the construction of "Garden Cities" to house workers) to the company founders and their Quaker faith. As Rowlinson and Hassard noted, "The history of Cadbury based on Quakerism served the purpose of corporate cultures ... and all invented traditions ... by providing legitimacy.... In an increasingly secular society, the apparent conformity of Cadbury to a religious ideal gave the firm an identity which made it special, imbued with a morality probably perceived as lacking elsewhere" (p. 321).

Symbolic Behaviors

Organizations may also carry out strategic and symbolic behaviors to affirm their distinctive identities in the wake of achievements or successes. In this manner, organizations prime the situated identities of organizational members by using a shared event to remind members of the distinctive traits of the organization (e.g., safety or quality) and of their contribution to maintaining those traits. For example, Rousseau (1998) described how Southwest Airlines uses symbolic behaviors related to achieving high on-time ratings as an identity affirmation. As she noted,

> Southwest Airlines regularly sends its employees a bonus check (under US $50) each month when it receives an on-time rating in the top half of the airline industry. Co-workers who rally around a successful on-time record each month or discuss the failure to achieve a desirable rating share a common experience with each other and the firm. The cognitive effects of such activities are a shared focus of attention on performance, and a blurring of the boundaries among employees with different roles and functions, creating a sense of "one company." (p. 220).

In this manner, Southwest's bonus checks, and the celebration surrounding them, act to label employees as high performers with regard to on-time performance and to affirm the company identity as a customer service-oriented organization.

Physical Markers

In many cases, winning certification contests or being recognized by industry evaluators leads organizations to add the logo or name of the certifying organization to their letterheads, signage, or other identifying markers. For example, organizations that are identified as official sponsors of the Olympic Games often add the Olympic symbol (i.e., the five interlocking rings) to their letterheads and logos, along with the phrase "Official Sponsor of the [Year] Olympic Games." In this manner, physical markers are used to affirm the company identity as an industry leader or a company dedicated to the ideals espoused by the certifying organization (e.g., the ideals of the Olympic Games).

PITFALLS OF ORGANIZATIONAL PERCEPTION MANAGEMENT FOLLOWING ACCLAIM EVENTS

Because acclaims are more rare than accounts, there are fewer examples of acclaims going badly, yet one can image how acclaim events could backfire on organizations. For instance, it's not hard to imagine an acclaim event being viewed as hubris or arrogance or merely as protesting too much—which may explain why organizations are so reluctant to engage in acclaiming. However, there are other not so obvious pitfalls of acclaiming that may affect organizations. These pitfalls arise not from the acclaiming event itself but from what happens days, weeks, or years after the acclaim event. Specifically, acclaiming can set up organizations for a later fall by raising expectations of organizational audiences or by self-aggrandizing perceptions of the company by leaders and employees.

Raising Expectations

A first potential pitfall of organizational acclaiming is that organizations may raise, unrealistically, the expectations of organizational audiences for future organizational performance. Researchers have found that unrealistic expectations, more than actual experience, account for user satisfaction in a variety of contexts (van Dijk, Zeelenberg, & van der Pligt, 2003). Thus, those who have high expectations are more disappointed by the same poor outcomes than those who have low expectations (Zeelenberg, van den Bos, van Dijk, & Pieters, 2002). For example, a hotel chain that boasts of its sterling customer service ratings from executives staying in its top-priced executive suites may lead lower paying guests to believe that the organization will provide four-star service even in its two-star rooms. Customers who find the service to be less than stellar will be doubly disappointed because their expectations were raised.

Further, the negative effects of a single disappointment may grow over time due to the way that individuals deal with disappointment. Research on hindsight bias (i.e, a situation in which, post hoc, people exaggerate the a priori predictability of an uncertain event) has shown that when people are disappointed by an outcome, they are likely to have high levels of hindsight bias (or the "knew-it-all-along" effect). Specifically, researchers have shown that when a poor decision outcome leads to disappointment for those affected by the decision, those affected persons are likely to perceive that the decision makers "should have known" that the negative effect was going to happen (e.g., my stockbroker should have known that a fallen stock was a bad investment; the pharmaceutical company Merck should have known that its arthritis medication Vioxx would cause heart problems; Schkade & Kilbourne, 1991). As a result of this hindsight bias, audiences who are disappointed (because of unrealistically high expectations) are likely to perceive that the organization responsible for their disappointment is not just unlucky, but incompetent.

Self-Aggrandizement

A second, potentially negative outcome of organizational acclaims is that the organization itself may begin to believe in its own superiority and overestimate its own abilities or distinctive accomplishments in a self-aggrandizing manner (Brown, 1997). As Brown noted, "These claims to uniqueness often emphasize the prowess and accomplishments of the organization in ways that are palpably exhibitionistic and exaggerated.... For instance, at AT&T employees like to narrate the story of how they dealt with a major fire, which exaggerates their ability to cope with disasters (Kleinfield, 1981: 307)" (p. 659).

Self-aggrandizement may cause an organization to focus on the more celebrated dimensions of its identity, to the neglect of other dimensions. In these cases, self-aggrandizement can lead to an underappreciation for necessary contingency plans or preparations to deal with threatening environmental events, such as loss of market share to competitors, product failures, or accidents. For example, a corporation that is routinely recognized and complimented for its high ranking in a popular industry survey (e.g., *Fortune*'s most admired companies) may find that it becomes focused on improving only those dimensions of its business that are measured in the survey (e.g., stockholder wealth) while neglecting aspects of its business that are not measured (e.g., career development of managers).

In this manner, self-aggrandizement by CEOs has been blamed for "nonsensical acquisitions" by corporations during the 1980s—acquisitions that served primarily to affirm and boost executives' egos and need for power and prestige but eroded the profitability of corporations that knew nothing of the acquired firms' industries (Lamb, 1987). Similarly, the precipitous downfall of U.S. automakers and the subsequent wake of Japanese dominance in the industry during the 1970s and 1980s have been blamed, to a great degree, on the self-aggrandizement of U.S. auto manufacturers and the faulty belief that they could not be challenged by Asian automakers (Cole, 1990). Even in the late 1970s, when it was becoming clear that U.S. autos were inferior to the Japanese autos in terms of quality, U.S. auto manufacturers continued to portray their companies as firmly in command of the U.S. market (Cole, 1990). Further, when U.S. automakers did concede points to the Japanese, the concession was on minor issues such as appearance items. As Cole reported,

> In the late 1970s, U.S. automakers developed a "new" conventional wisdom for explaining the differences in quality between domestic and Japanese cars. In a November 1978 interview with the Detroit Free Press, Ford Chairman and CEO Philip Caldwell announced that Ford owners are happier

with the quality of their cars than with any other domestic producer. He made no mention of the foreign automobile competition. In a 1980 Associated Press story, John Manoogian, Ford's newly appointed Executive Director for Product Assurance, conceded that "the Japanese have a slight edge in quality delivered to the dealer." Later in that same year, Ford vice president Bidwell told the Detroit Free Press that "the high quality of Japanese cars is to some extent real, and to some extent perceived." In a November 1980 issue of GM's Tech Center News (an internal organ), GM's President-elect James McDonald first extolled GM's quality, but then resorted to the familiar fit-and-finish argument: "We think we have not always given enough attention to some appearance items." (p. 71)

CASE ILLUSTRATION: PFIZER INC. AND VIAGRA

In 1991, Pfizer Inc., a multinational pharmaceuticals company, began testing a drug for the relief of angina (i.e., the chest pains caused by the blocking of blood vessels that lead to the heart; Kolata, 1998). The results were not promising. After about a year, Dr. Ian Osterloh, a British scientist working for Pfizer Inc., was ready to abandon the trials when he was confronted with a number of odd requests by trial participants. Many of the men in the trials didn't want to return their unused samples (Lerner, 1998). It turned out that the drug—whose pharmaceutical name was sildenafil citrate—was alleviating impotence (i.e., the inability to achieve or sustain a penile erection) in these men. Further studies confirmed that the drug blocked an enzyme that interfered with penile erections but did not affect other parts of the body (Kolata, 1998). By 1997, Pfizer scientists had come up with a pill, called Viagra, that was effective for treating male impotence and had very few side effects. The drug was so effective and had so few side effects that the U.S. Food and Drug Administration (FDA) approved it in only 6 months, without consulting an advisory committee of outside experts (Kolata, 1998).

Following the FDA approval of Viagra but before the drug was made available to the public, a word-of-mouth campaign led to a virtual frenzy of requests for it (Kolata, 1998). The buzz about Viagra led some pharmaceutical industry analysts to predict that Viagra could be the most successful new prescription drug in history (Freudenheim, 1998). The drug had the potential to alleviate a problem afflicting 30 million men in the United States alone (Kolata, 1998). Pfizer executives, along with a number of top impotence-treating physicians, called the drug the "biggest advance in the treatment of sexual dysfunction in decades" (Lerner, 1998, p. 1A). Industry analysts called the potential upside for Pfizer "unbelievable" after the company stock achieved a 52-week high following the FDA announcement (Bloomberg News, 1998, p. B2). Finally, prior to the launch of Viagra, Pfizer sent a delegation to the Vatican committee on science to brief members on the use and effects of the drug (Tran, 1998). Pfizer spokesperson Andy McCormick later reported that the Vatican had no objections to the drug and noted, "They felt that because impotence can hurt relationships and couples, Viagra can help in improving marital relations" (Vatican: Viagra OK, 1998, p. A10).

Based on these events, the launch of Viagra, in March 1998, was a clear acclaim event for Pfizer. In response, it appears that Pfizer used cautious perception management aimed at protecting its reputation as a mainstream maker of medicine as well as separating it from the identity of a maker of lifestyle drugs (i.e., drugs that can help people who are not seriously ill improve their quality of life). Pfizer had recently launched a number of highly effective drugs for treating potentially serious medical problems, including the cholesterol drug Lipitor, and the antibiotic Zithromax. It also was working on a drug that would compete with the depression drug Prozac, which was widely viewed as lifestyle drug for people who were not clinically depressed (Bloomberg News, 1998, March 24; Cookson & Green, 1998). Like most mainstream pharmaceutical companies, Pfizer appeared averse to carrying the identity of a maker of lifestyle drugs. Such drugs were viewed as the products of less legitimate organizations, including the makers of herbal remedies and traditional ethnic healing products.

Given this stance, Pfizer's perception management tactics following the introduction of Viagra appeared designed to take credit for the drug cautiously and to provide support for the company reputation as maker of serious medicine while disidentifying the company from less legitimate "drug" makers. I illustrate Pfizer's use of these tactics next.

Initial Perception Management: Cautious Entitlings and Disidentification

Pfizer's initial public statements about Viagra focused on its use and effectiveness. These statements seemed typical of those accompanying new product introductions; that is, they focused on educating the public about proper and safe use of the drug and clarified definitions of its effectiveness. These accounts also appeared to be designed to portray Viagra as a medicine for treating serious illness rather than as a lifestyle drug (Cookson & Green, 1998). In this way, Pfizer sought to disidentify itself from makers of herbal aphrodisiacs and other unregulated "sex drugs." For example, one of the first public statements from Pfizer addressed pre-introduction rumors about the potential for use of Viagra by non-impotent men. As Pfizer senior vice president of medical and regulatory operations, Joe Feczko, noted, "Viagra is not an aphrodisiac. This drug should only be used by men who are suffering from erectile dysfunction. Men will need prescriptions from their doctors to use it" (quoted in Morrow, 1998c, p. D1). This message was repeated in numerous media accounts in the early days following the release of the drug (Gillis, 1998a; Weeks, 1998). Pfizer spokespersons also advertised a toll-free information number about Viagra and continued to note that the drug would not work without sexual stimulation (Morrow, 1998a).

However, as the unprecedented success of the drug became apparent during its first weeks on the market, Pfizer spokespersons began to make entitling statements (i.e., statements intended to show their responsibility for the positive events). For example, the first week after its launch, industry analysts noted that doctors had written 36,000 new prescriptions for Viagra, making it the most successful product launch in pharmaceutical history (Gillis, 1998a). In response to these reports, Pfizer appeared to take credit for recognizing the potential need for an effective impotence treatment. As spokesperson Andy McCormick noted, "We've been saying that erectile dysfunction is a major unmet medical need" (Gillis, 1998a, p. C1).

To legitimate these entitlings further, Pfizer backed up these statements with comments by physicians and scientists. For example, Pfizer featured the developer of the drug, Dr. Ian Osterloh, in most of its early press releases about the drug (Kolata, 1998). Further, Pfizer flew several impotence specialists to seminars on Viagra in the months before the drug was launched and included many specialists in the FDA trials for the drug (Lerner, 1998). These physicians then provided comments to the press about the effectiveness of the drug. For example, Dr. William Borkon, who directs of the Sexual Health Center in Minneapolis and tested Viagra on a dozen patients for Pfizer, exclaimed, "It's truly remarkable. If you told me five years ago we'll have a drug to help men with erections ... I would have laughed at you" (Lerner, 1998, p. 1A).

In the weeks that followed, prescribing doctors claimed that the demand for the new drug was like nothing they had seen before. As Dr. James B. Regan, head of the Georgetown University Hospital's Erectile Dysfunction Treatment Program, noted, "In the 20 years I've been involved in urology, I've never seen anything like it. If we were in the military, I think we would call in and say our position is being overrun" (Gillis, 1998b, p. A1).

On the downside, however, this extreme demand led to some questionable practices by those eager to profit from the popularity of the drug. Cut-rate distributors offered the drug over the Internet with little screening of patients. For example, one Web site, www.penispill.com, offered prescriptions for Viagra after a $50 telephone consultation. Further, herbal supplements with similar sounding names (e.g., Viagro, Vaegra) cropped up in attempts to take advantage of the Viagra craze (Russell, 1998b).

In response to these events, Pfizer attempted to disidentify itself from these questionable practices and from the perception that the drug was similar to herbal remedies and aphrodisiacs. As Pfizer spokesperson Mariann Caprino claimed, in regard to the sale of Viagra over the Internet, "A doctor doesn't buy from us. He buys through a wholesaler or supplier that is several steps away from us" (Lore, 1998, p. 3E). Pfizer was also quick to file trademark infringement lawsuits against copycat drugs, such as Viagro and Vaegra (Russell, 1998b). Finally, Pfizer pointed out that it had not foreseen the unusually high demand for the drug and did not, as some had suggested, hold back information on the drug from insurers to create patient interest in the drug before insurance companies could evaluate whether or not the drug should be covered (Stark, 1998). In one such defensive account, Pfizer spokesperson Andrew McCormick noted, "Viagra is a social phenomenon. We couldn't control public interest. It happened more quickly than even we thought it would" (Stark, 1998, p. E2).

Secondary Perception Management: Symbolic Behaviors to Affirm Identity and Reputation

Observing the initial frenzy over the launch of Viagra, one industry analyst quipped, "the company's name is no longer Pfizer, it's Viagra" (Freudenheim, 1998, p. D1). Although this perception may not have been predicted by Pfizer, their actions in the months following the introduction of Viagra suggest that such a link between the drug and the company was not unwelcome. In particular, as the popularity of the drug began to stir controversy about the proper use of health care benefits among insurance companies (Morrow, 1998b), Pfizer appeared more and more willing to market the drug actively at the corporate level (vs. through third-party physicians). Leaving behind an early reticence to make corporate statements that actively promoted use of the drug, Pfizer spokespersons began to actively push the prescription of the drug. As spokesperson Andrew McCormick reported, "Our position is that when a doctor is treating a medical condition and he prescribes Viagra, we hope that it would be broadly covered. We also hope that Viagra will be covered irrespective of the cause of erectile dysfunction, meaning psychological causes as well as medical" (Morrow, 1998b, p. A1).

Pfizer spokespersons also made recommendations about the number of pills patients should receive a month, noting that the six pills a month covered by many insurers was less than the number used in its clinical trials, based on the 1994 "Sex in America" study done at the University of Chicago (Morrow, 1998c). These symbolic behaviors portrayed Pfizer as an expert on the use of the drug and appeared designed to help support their reputation as a high-status and reputable pharmaceuticals firm.

Later Perception Management: Weathering Early Downturns Through Identity-Affirming Accounts and Behaviors

Given the huge number of new patients taking Viagra, it is not surprising that some experienced adverse effects. These effects began to appear in the second month after the launch. In late May, 1998, Pfizer reported to the FDA that six people had died after combining Viagra with nitrates used to combat heart disease (Associated Press, 1998). Then, in July of that year, a diabetic patient filed a lawsuit against Pfizer after suffering a heart attack that he claimed resulted from his recent use of Viagra (Bone, 1998). Finally, news writers questioned the safety of Pfizer's implied support of women taking Viagra after the company began drug trials including women in Europe (Elias, 1998).

Pfizer responded to these events in the same way it had engaged in perception management following the early success—with cautious accounts that identified the company as a serious drug maker and distanced it from less legitimate firms. In this manner, Pfizer spokespersons responded to concerns over the six deaths by claiming that the company reported all adverse effects of the drug to the FDA immediately and that, because Viagra was carefully tested, they were doubtful that properly used doses of Viagra were responsible for any deaths (Russell, 1998a). At this time, Pfizer also issued a warning to paramedics and emergency room physicians to not administer nitroglycerin to heart patients who were taking Viagra (Cornell, 1998). Viagra spokesperson Mariann Caprino noted that this warning had been given since the drug was first released and that it was not prompted by the recent deaths. Instead, she implied that the warning was just a reiteration of the initial warning and was given at this time because of the huge number of new prescriptions that had been issued. As she put it, "We hit around the million-prescription mark over the last week. We just wanted to set the record straight" (Cornell, 1998, p. 7).

In a similar vein, Pfizer responded to concerns about women using Viagra by staunchly opposing such actions. As spokesperson Mariann Caprino noted, "We never endorse off-label use of a drug.... It's never a good idea to take a medication when safety has not been proven" (Elias, 1998, p. 8D).

Because Pfizer had focused all its previous perception management on building and sustaining its reputation and identity as a legitimate and serious drug maker, these types of responses to negative events appeared consistent and credible, and the effects of these downturns appeared negligible. In fact, Pfizer's early perception management following the "blockbuster" introduction of Viagra helped the company weather all the early storms that accompany new but wildly popular products (i.e., the kind of products, like cell phones and diet pills, that get used in the wrong way by the wrong people and inevitably have negative effects). By responding to the early success of Viagra with actions and words that portrayed the company as a serious and legitimate drug maker, supported by credible physicians and the FDA, Pfizer was able to enhance its reputation as a high-status pharmaceutical firm while distancing its identity from less legitimate makers of unregulated aphrodisiacs.

By the end of 1998, Viagra had been approved for sale in Europe and Asia, and Pfizer had begun airing television commercials during prime-time viewing hours (Wells, 1998). During its introduction into Singapore, it was clear that Pfizer was staying on message. In talking about the drug to a group of physicians, Pfizer marketing director Michael Khor noted, "Viagra is a very serious drug, for a very serious illness. It is different from other drugs because it almost sells itself. So instead of selling, we have to see how we can educate people about it. We never had to hire a PR agency before. But for Viagra, we need a more educational, rather than marketing approach" (Ching, 1998).

III

Emerging Issues in Organizational Perception Management

8

Ethics and Organizational Perception Management: Emerging Insights on Leadership and Social Responsibility

The preceding chapters have outlined four of the most common perception management contexts for organizations (i.e., crisis events, evolving controversies, anticipated controversies, and acclaim events). In addition to these contexts, there are a number of emerging issues for organizations to consider as the audiences of organizational perception management become increasingly critical in their appraisal of organizational events and the expectations put on perception managers change with societal norms. Interestingly, most of these issues relate to the notion of corporate ethics and organizational ethicality. Examples include the extensive media attention given to ethical breaches by Enron Corporation (i.e., fraudulent practices in selling energy), Martha Stewart Living Inc. (i.e., lying to SEC officials), and Marsh & McLennan Companies Inc. (i.e., insurance industry kickbacks). However, anecdotal evidence shows no clear formula for effectively presenting an image of ethicality. In some cases, images of ethicality appear to be achieved by fighting allegations of unethical behavior. For example, Microsoft has been quite effective at fighting accusations of antitrust violations brought by the U.S. Justice Department. In other cases, however, readily accepting responsibility and punishment seems to be an effective response. For instance, Martha Stewart went to jail instead of appealing what many viewed as an excessive punishment for lying to officials about a stock sale. Her image was so improved by her jail stint that her company put together a deal for a new television series, starring Martha, even while she was incarcerated. These examples suggest that the effective management of corporate images of ethicality depends on, among other things, the nature of the ethical breach as well as the focus of blame.

To explore the management of corporate ethics more fully, in this chapter I examine emerging insights on the effective (and sometimes ineffective) portrayal of corporate ethicality in response two increasingly common events: scandals attributed to organizational leadership and controversy surrounding the enactment of non-normative, organizational social responsibility campaigns. I briefly describe these two events and present case illustrations that suggest effective strategies for dealing with each.

LEADERSHIP AND ORGANIZATIONAL PERCEPTION MANAGEMENT FOLLOWING SCANDAL

Because of common, romanticized notions of leadership (Meindl, Erlich, & Dukerich, 1985), organizational leaders are often held accountable for decisions that lead to organizational scandals (i.e., preventable events that are viewed as the result of immoral or unethical behavior; Marcus & Goodman, 1991; Sutton & Galunic, 1996). Such romanticized notions include a number of stereotypical traits that we ascribe to good leaders (Lord et al., 1986). These stereotypic traits include: control (i.e., the belief that leaders have the final say in important decisions and that they are in charge of what happens), competence and consistency (i.e., the beliefs that leaders will make the right decisions and will remain consistent in the thinking that guides those decisions over time), and absolute certainty (i.e., the belief that leaders are completely certain about the things they say and do).

At the same time, social psychological research suggests that maintaining such stereotypical images may require people to engage in behaviors that counter what we know about effective leadership (Cialdini, 1984; Greenberg, 1990). That is, our stereotypic conceptions of strong leadership may be inconsistent with what effective leaders actually do. These paradoxes or "stereotype traps" may mean that short-term gains in leadership images (and repair of organizational images) may, ultimately, give way to long-term ineffectiveness in leadership performance. Further, it appears that maintaining the first of these traits (i.e., control) may produce a cascading effect in which the other traits (i.e., competence, consistency, and certainty) must also be maintained.

Case Illustration: The Catholic Church Sex Abuse Scandal and Cardinal Bernard Law

To explore these stereotype traps more fully, I discuss each of the leadership stereotypes described previously and suggest how maintaining such stereotypes may undermine leadership effectiveness in the wake of an organizational scandal. I illustrate these stereotype traps with evidence from a case study of the 2001–2002 sex abuse scandal in the U.S. Catholic Church (i.e., the scandal arising from the revelation that priests known to be pedophiles were repeatedly reassigned to new parishes where their abuse continued).[1]

The Control Trap

Probably the most common trait we ascribe to strong leadership is control. We expect strong leaders to be in charge and running the show (Sutton & Galunic, 1996). Our image of a strong leader includes a mental picture of former U.S. President Harry Truman, with his famous "the buck stops here" sign on his desk. We want to know that, when all is said and done, the person at the top has the final say. Psychologists suggest that this need to have one person in control stems from our desires to reduce uncertainty and to have leaders fulfill our expectations about what strong leaders "look like" (Hogg, 2001). That is, as humans, we like to be able to predict the events that may affect our lives. If we perceive that one person is in charge of these events (vs. numerous people), and that person conforms to our prototype of a strong leader, then it is easier for us to predict what life-altering events may occur.

However, leaders who attempt to convince others that they have strong, central control over their organizations may also convince audiences (and themselves) that the views and input of others are neither important nor necessary for decision making. In turn, the expertise of advisors may eventually be withdrawn. Over time, leaders themselves may begin to believe their own perception management and fall prey to illusions of control (i.e., unrealistically high perceptions of their degree of control over the outcomes of events; Langer, 1975) and overconfidence (i.e., unrealistically high perceptions of their likelihood of obtaining desired outcomes; Oskamp, 1965). If such perceptions are contradictory to what the public perceives (i.e., the public perceives the leader to lack control based on a scandalous event), then continued expressions of control may be seen as both arrogance and hubris and may ultimately lead to loss of respect and trust for the leader.

---

[1] An earlier version of this case appears in Elsbach (2005).

Such mistaken confidence in one's own abilities can be seen over and over in responses to the sex-abuse issues in the Catholic Church presented by Cardinal Bernard Law of the Boston Archdiocese. Law was one of the most powerful and influential figures in the U.S. Catholic church, and thus, the person to whom most U.S. Catholics looked for leadership. However, in response to early complaints of sex abuse by priests in the 1980s, Cardinal Law, like many Church leaders, rejected advice based on scientific research. As Reverend Thomas P. Doyle, a Catholic Air Force chaplain who had written a 1985 report on the problem of clergy sexual abuse while working as a canon lawyer at the Vatican Embassy in Washington, reported, "The Catholic hierarchy has stonewalled any attempts to do any kind of study on this issue, and they've had offers to do it" (Paulson, 2002d, p. A1).

Later, following the publication of a *Boston Globe* opinion poll, which found that nearly half of all Boston-area Catholics wanted Cardinal Law to resign because of his poor handling of abusive priests, the Cardinal resolutely announced that he had no intention of stepping down (Paulson, 2002c, p. A1). Instead, he claimed that he, alone, would be the best person to guide the Church through the current crisis. As he stated in a homily given the day after the opinion poll was published:

> I believe that, with regard to the issue at hand, that by the experience of being here when all of this was taking place, I have the ability to do something as bishop to make things better for the future, and I think that it would not serve that cause of protecting children if I were, at this point, to submit my resignation to the Holy Father.... Beyond that, it's important to remember that a bishop is not a corporate executive, is not a politician ... the role of a bishop in relationship to the church he serves is something different. It's the role of a pastor, the role of a teacher, the role of a father. (Paulson, 2002c, p. A1)

These comments suggest overconfidence and illusions of control by the Cardinal, especially given the public sentiment at the time. As one priest noted, "For him to think that he can be of any value in this role is proof in itself that he doesn't understand that he's a culprit, that what he's done is in many ways as damaging as what the priests have done. The very fact that he doesn't get that makes him incapable of participating in the solution" (Pfeiffer, 2002, p. B4). An abuse victim echoed this sentiment: "This is like a criminal telling me, 'Listen, I am the best person to prevent break-ins because I've done them in the past.' This is a criminal activity, as far as I'm concerned. For him to have the audacity to stay—he's operating in the surreal" (Pfeiffer, 2002, p. B4).

This continued evidence of a "control" image presented by Cardinal Law and other top Church leaders is important not only because it reduced input by experts and appeared to support the Cardinal's overconfidence and illusions of control but also because it appeared to induce a cascade of related perception management. Specifically, in maintaining an image of control, the Cardinal also made it important that he be seen as competent, consistent, and certain as a leader—because these traits were important to justifying his control over the Boston Archdiocese. As I describe next, Cardinal Law may have further hampered his effective leadership by projecting these images.

The Competency and Consistency Traps

In addition to being in control, we like to think of our leaders as unfailingly competent at the jobs they do (Meindl & Ehrlich, 1987) as well as consistent in the ideals that guide their actions (Cialdini, 1984). We have chosen them, specifically, because we view them as competent decision makers and policy implementers (Lord et al., 1986). Further, we have chosen them because we feel confident that we understand their views and that those views will not change over time. Because we pick our leaders for the long-term (years vs. days), we tend to view leaders who change their minds often to be untrustworthy and weak-minded (Cialdini, 1984). If we cannot count on a leader to maintain a competent and consistent set of actions over this long-term period, we may be unwilling to support him or her in the first place.

Despite the apparent rationality of these perspectives, the requirement for competency and consistency in our leaders becomes troublesome when it causes those in leadership positions to view occasional human mistakes (e.g., misjudgments, biased information search, unscientific analysis)—what Hendry (2002) called "honest incompetence" (p. 100)—as unacceptable. In such cases, the need to appear unfailingly competent often causes leaders to deny making human mistakes and to defend previous actions that led to undesirable outcomes. When combined with the need to appear consistent over time, such a stance can lead to an escalating commitment to a failing course of action (Brockner, 1992; Staw, 1976).

When the first cases of child abuse began to be publicized in the 1980s, Catholic leaders stood firm on their approach of counseling and prayer within the church, rather than following the advice of emerging scientific research that suggested that pedophiles were rarely "cured" of their sexual preferences. As the sex-abuse cases mounted, Law and other Church leaders continued to defend their earlier stance, it appeared, as a means of maintaining the correctness of this stance and supporting their own images of competence. As Cardinal Law's lawyer put it, "[E]ach assignment of [an abusive priest], subsequent to the first complaint of sexual misconduct, was incident to an independent medical evaluation advising that such assignment was appropriate and safe" (Paulson, 2001, p. A1). Church leaders never reported , however, that these evaluations were largely performed by one institution, which later claimed that the Church had concealed past information about priests' behaviors and had largely ignored its recommendations regarding reassignment of priests to new parishes (Rich & Hamilton, 2002).

A second problem resulting from defending leadership competency and consistency is that, if obviously wrong and recurrent actions cannot be attributed to incompetence, then the most likely alternative explanation is that they are due to a lack of integrity. This is because incompetence and lack of integrity are the most common traits associated with untrustworthy behavior by leaders (Clark & Payne, 1997). If Cardinal Law did not commit the untrustworthy behavior of reassigning abusive priests because he was incompetent (i.e., he wrongly discounted the research on pedophilia because he didn't understand it), then he must have taken these wrong actions because he lacked integrity (e.g., he didn't want to bring attention to the problem and was protecting his own image at the cost of children). Thus, in explaining the reasons for an untrustworthy action, leaders may trade a violation of competency for a violation of integrity (Clark & Payne, 1997). Such a trade can be even more damaging to a leader's effectiveness than the original bad act because incompetence may be viewed as a trait that can be corrected (i.e., through training), whereas lack of integrity is typically viewed as a trait that is innate.

The Certainty Trap

Related to the stereotypic trait of leadership consistency is the trait of leadership certainty. Leaders are expected to speak in absolute terms with regard to their beliefs and intentions. This means that what they say can be trusted and what they propose to do will be done (Clark & Payne, 1997). However, certainty at one point in time may easily become uncertainty a few moments later. Information that was thought to be iron-clad can turn out to be incomplete or inaccurate. Data that was used to make predictions can be found to be unreliable or invalid due to the way they were collected or measured. Leaders who must backtrack on statements—especially statements made with expressions of certainty—may lose the trust of audiences regarding all future statements.

This need for absolute certainty caused problems for Cardinal Law in the wake of the sex-abuse scandal. After finally admitting that rehabilitation of priests through counseling and prayer was not an effective approach, the Cardinal moved to remove a large number of priests, who had been accused (but not convicted) of abuse, from contact with children. When asked if any priests who had committed sexual abuse of minors remained in active service, the Cardinal repeatedly claimed that he was certain that none remained. As he asserted in a press conference on January 25, 2002:

> There is no priest known to us to have been guilty of the sexual abuse of a minor holding any position in this archdiocese.

> We cannot and we do not put people into positions now who have been guilty of sexual abuse.

> I can tell you that there is no priest presently assigned anywhere who is, as far as we know, guilty of sexual abuse.

> As I have indicated, there is no priest, or former priest, working in this archdiocese in any assignment whom we know to have been responsible for sexual abuse. I hope you get that straight. (Rezendes & Robinson, 2002, p. A1)

Yet, only eight days after making these assertions, Cardinal Law's Archdiocese removed two more priests from Boston-area parishes, having discovered that both men had been accused of sexually abusing children in the past (Rezendes & Robinson, 2002). These events caused Church officials to admit that priests guilty of molesting children may still be working in parishes but they will be removed as evidence is uncovered (Rezendes & Robinson, 2002). Not surprisingly, these comments further weakened the trust parishioners held for the leadership of the Catholic Church, including Cardinal Law. As the *Boston Globe* reported:

> [Raymond L.] Flynn [former mayor of Boston and U.S. ambassador to the Vatican], like other Catholics interviewed in recent days, said he is increasingly making a distinction between his faith in God, which he said remains intact, and his attitude toward the church hierarchy. "I don't go to church because I pray to the priest or the bishop or the cardinal—I go to church because I pray to God to make me a better person," [Flynn] said. (Paulson, 2002, p. A1)

The combined effects of the events described here appeared to damage audiences' trust in Cardinal Law critically. Over time, it became apparent to Church leaders that this eroded trust could not be recovered with Law in his current position of leadership. On December 13, 2002, Cardinal Bernard F. Law resigned his post (Rezendes, 2002).

Effective Perception Management for Leaders Following Organizational Scandals: Resisting Strong Leader Stereotypes

In the wake of scandals, like the one described previously, effective perception management appears to require organizations and their leaders to resist inclinations to conform to stereotypes of strong leadership. Instead, the most effective words and deeds that organizations can use following scandals appear to run in the opposite direction, including admitting incompetence (at least in terms of human failings), ceding control (at least temporarily), and giving up traditional mantras in favor of new ideals.

First, it's important that leaders admit some incompetence in their initial accounts or explanations of a negative event (Pearson & Clair, 1998; Staw et al., 1983). Because scandals are typically shown to be the result of deliberate organizational actions, accounts that deny responsibility for them (e.g., excuses or denials) are not likely to be viewed as credible. Instead, apologies or justifications which admit responsibility for the scandalous actions are more likely to be accepted by audiences. Of these two types of accounts, apologies are often preferred following scandals that call into question the integrity of an organization because such scandals often involve actions, such as criminal activities, that are hard to justify at any level (Hearit, 1994).

Effective apologies combine both an admission of blameworthiness and an acknowledgment of human failings (e.g., "we were wrong"; "we made a human error") with a promise that the problem that led to the scandal has been isolated and resolved (e.g., "we won't let this happen again"; Hearit, 1994). In this way, apologies are designed to convince the audience that the undesirable event should not be considered a "fair representation" of what the organization is really like or will be like in the future (Schlenker, 1980, p. 154).

Second, organizational leaders must, at least temporarily, cede control in the remaking of the organization. One of the most effective means of "proving" that an organization is currently distinct from the organization that caused a scandal is to take reparative actions that alter core structures or procedures (e.g., changing leadership). Such actions demonstrate a concern for the welfare of harmed audiences, and provide "proof" of an organizational commitment to "righting the wrong" in situations where mere explanations and accounts would be met with suspicion (Marcus & Goodman, 1991).

Finally, reparative actions that involve changes to fundamental organizational structures and practices—such as changing the nature of evaluation and training programs—help audiences focus on the future of the organization, rather than on its past. Such a focus allows organizational leaders to give up old mantras that have lost their credibility and concentrate on re-establishing a history of credible behavior and re-earning a reputation for integrity.

SOCIAL RESPONSIBILITY CAMPAIGNS
AND ORGANIZATIONAL PERCEPTION MANAGEMENT

A second event that calls into question the ethicality of an organization is the introduction of a controversial social responsibility campaign. Social responsibility—a focus on improving the world for the good of society, rather than for economic benefit—has become an institutional norm in many industries, especially in first-world countries. Social responsibility programs in organizations include everything from minor recycling efforts in corporate offices to complete overhauls in manufacturing methods designed to reduce environmental pollution and increase human safety.

Although social responsibility efforts are largely viewed as having a positive effect on organizational images and reputations (e.g., social responsibility efforts are included in the *Fortune* rankings of the most admired companies), pursuing social responsibility goals is not cost-free for the organization, especially in terms of organizational identities. Stockholders, employees, and even customers may find that they must make sacrifices for a corporation's pursuit of idealistic social goals (e.g., research by an oil company into solar energy may reduce profits and stock value, at least temporarily, as money is poured into experimental ventures). Further, a company that is highly visible in pursuing a social responsibility goal that puts it at odds with most other firms in its industry may risk alienating industry insiders and lead competitors to portray the organization as radical in its identity. Thus, the effective use of perception management may be crucial to the success of social responsibility campaigns.

In the following sections I discuss how successfully pursuing social responsibility requires a balance between symbolic behaviors and self-categorizations that depict the identity of the organization as distinct but also legitimate. As I argue next, this balance requires that organizations and their spokespersons depict the social responsibility campaign as an action that provides the organization "optimal distinctiveness" in its industry (Brewer, 1991). I illustrate this type of organizational perception management with the case of British Petroleum and its campaign to reduce greenhouse gas emissions in its energy production businesses.

Case Illustration: British Petroleum

In May, 1997, British Petroleum (BP)—one of the largest energy companies in the world, with over $200 billion in sales of petrochemicals, gas, electricity, and solar energy—broke ranks with most of the oil industry by acknowledging its role in climate change. In a landmark speech at Stanford

University (Browne, 1997), CEO John Browne formally accepted the emerging consensus of the scientific community that greenhouse gases, most notably from the burning of petrochemicals, were largely responsible for ozone depletion and global warming. Further, Browne made public commitments to engage in a social responsibility campaign to reduce BP's contribution to global warming. In particular, Browne pledged to: reduce greenhouse gas emissions produced by BP during oil refining, join international efforts to reduce greenhouse gases worldwide, and focus on solar energy as one of the top business lines for BP (Lowe & Harris, 1998). This speech came on top of BP's 1996 departure from the Global Climate Coalition, a lobbying and public relations organization based in Washington, DC, that catered to the needs of big oil and utility companies and largely dismissed scientific reports about global warming (Reinhardt & Richman, 2001).

These actions put BP squarely in opposition to most of the oil producers in the world and threatened its image by distancing and delegitimating BP from the core of the oil industry. As one industry insider said, on the condition of anonymity, "He's out of the church" (Gertenzang, 1997, p. C6). U.S. Senate Majority Leader Trent Lott further denounced the stance as a "hippies' program from the '70s" (Gertenzang, 1997, p. C6). Even so, BP was able to maintain its legitimacy and emerged stronger than ever four years later (Reinhardt & Richman, 2001). How was BP able to maintain its legitimacy within the oil industry while pursuing a strategy that seemingly put the planet ahead of profits? As I explain next, it appears that BP used a strategy of using verbal accounts and symbolic behaviors to signal "optimal distinctiveness" (i.e., showing that it was distinct from others, but not so distinct to be illegitimate) from its peers (Brewer, 1991).

Effective Perception Management in Social Responsibility Campaigns: Optimal Distinctiveness

Brewer (1991) suggested that individuals strive for a sense of optimal distinctiveness in comparison with others to balance "a fundamental tension between human needs for validation and similarity to others (on the one hand) and a countervailing need for uniqueness and individuation (on the other hand)" (p. 477). As a result of this tension, Brewer posited that individuals seek out affiliations with groups that allow them to be both "the same and different [from others] at the same time" (p. 477). This notion explains the popularity of obscure hobbies, such as cigar collecting, that increase in popularity after they have been legitimated by a high-profile celebrity or public figure. The obscurity of the hobby gives those who affiliate with it a distinctive identity, but the association with a celebrity pastime also ensures that they aren't seen as so distinct that they're illegitimate.

The phenomenon of *optimal distinctiveness striving* has also been observed at the organizational level of analysis, especially when organizational leaders feel that distinctive features of the organization may be seen as illegitimate. For example, Elsbach and Kramer's (1996) study of business school responses to the *Business Week* rankings showed that faculty, staff, and students of business schools that were ranked lower than they would have liked often qualified their lower (but still respectable) rankings by highlighting leadership in distinctive areas not measured by the rankings (i.e., research orientation or collegial culture of their schools). This tactic was used to differentiate themselves from other schools and to suggest that they were able to maintain respectable rankings (and thus should be perceived as legitimate) despite their distinctive traits or pursuits.

British Petroleum used a similar strategy to protect its image of legitimacy as it changed its focus from manufacturing petrochemical fuels only to producing many energy sources, including solar and wind power sources, as a means of reducing greenhouse gas emissions. For example, when leaving the Global Climate Coalition, rather than widely publicizing its departure as a means of clearly separating from the rest of the oil industry, BP left quietly and without fanfare. This action was symbolic of their agreement with the uncertainty of the Coalition about the evidence for global warming. As one BP policy advisor noted, "We did not try to call attention to our departure from the coalition; we just didn't renew our membership. We felt, and still feel, that the scientific evidence on global climate change is inconclusive. But we felt that the coalition's public statements were inappropriately dismissive" (Reinhardt & Richman, 2001, p. 7).

Similarly, at the same time that he identified the company as a member of the global community whose customers included those concerned about the environment, Browne took pains to identify BP as business, first and foremost, with the same business concerns as other oil companies. As Browne (1997) put it in his Stanford speech:

> Real sustainability is about simultaneously being profitable and responding to the reality and concerns of the world in which you operate. We're not separate from the world. It's our world as well.... To be sustainable, companies need a sustainable world. That means a world where the environmental equilibrium is maintained but also a world whose population can all enjoy the heat, light, and mobility which we take for granted and which the oil industry helps provide.

In 2002, BP further demonstrated its commitment to being an environmentally conscientious but still profitable business by closing two solar energy projects in California because they were losing too much money (reported in the 2003 sustainability report).

In carrying out his promise to reduce greenhouse gas emissions, Browne also took pains not only to seek out ways to improve the viability of solar and wind power but also to reduce emissions from traditional energy sources such as oil and gas. As Browne pointed out when discussing solar energy in his 1997 Stanford speech, "But let me be clear. This [solar energy] is not instead of oil and gas. It is additional." These comments made it clear that BP was not abandoning its traditional energy sources and would continue to be concerned with the problems associated with oil and gas production even while it was pursuing alternative sources of energy. In a later interview, a BP spokesperson explained how the continued reliance on oil and gas as a viable business line had led the company to some innovative ways to reduce emissions. As he noted:

> What do we do to make more money for the company while protecting the environment? Let me give you [an example]. ... Reduced Gas Venting. Natural gas venting is also a huge opportunity for greenhouse gas reductions at low cost. Venting means that gas either leaks or is deliberately released into the atmosphere. And by the way, methane (natural gas) is twenty times more potent a greenhouse gas than carbon dioxide. As an example: one of our pipeline businesses replaced pneumatic valves with electronic valves on its pipeline, reducing venting to save about 500,000 tons of COZ equivalent in methane every year. And by selling that methane rather than venting it in the environment the project had a 67 percent return. (Bulkin, 2003, p. 7)

Finally, Browne continued to identify BP as an environmental yet still market-based business (in this way, affiliated with the other major oil companies) by choosing a market-based approach to reducing greenhouse gas emissions. Specifically, BP began using a system in which tradeable carbon dioxide allowances were given to each business unit in the company. These allowances were treated like cash flows, making it possible for a unit that did not use up all its allowances (because it lowered emissions) to trade those allowances for revenue (Reinhardt & Richman, 2001). Again, these tactics demonstrated that BP wasn't willing to throw profits out the window in pursuit of protecting the planet but rather that BP was a legitimate energy business that had found creative ways to make environmentalism profitable.

The case of BP illustrates a persistent problem in dealing with corporate ethics: Ethicality is socially constructed and changing over time. Organizational practices that were widely viewed as ethical 50 years ago, such as chemical companies dumping chemical waste into the Love Canal area of Michigan, would not be viewed as ethical today. Further, as ethical norms change, there are often differences in the extent to which various audiences believe the emerging ethical framework should be changed. For instance, when considering the rights of gay workers, some audiences believe that not providing medical and life insurance benefits for gay partners is unethical, whereas other audiences believe that those benefits should be provided only for the children of gay workers, not for their partners.

Thus, the task of conforming to changing social values in organizational policies and programs is complicated by divergence in time and across audiences. In such an environment, one of the only consistent (or relatively consistent) guideposts is the organizational identity. Effectively managing perceptions of organizational ethicality under the backdrop of social values, then, appears to require a clear understanding of the organizational identity and a matching of perception management tactics to that identity. For British Petroleum, the long-time identity as a profitable energy producer made it impossible for the company to dissociate itself completely from the oil industry as a business. At the same time, the CEO's own values were integral in shaping the company identity as an environmentally conscientious energy company and global citizen and dictated a shift in the identification with mainstream oil industry values. BP's strategy of optimal distinctiveness was the result of perception management efforts that sought to reconcile the existing and emerging identity of the company.

CONCLUDING THOUGHTS

As this chapter illustrates, perception management concerns are likely to be an ever-present and ever-evolving challenge for organizations. Understanding the most common types of perception management contexts and some responses to these contexts, as outlined in this volume, is only the beginning of the process of effective organizational perception management. As social norms, audience expectations, and organizational roles evolve, the nuances of perception management contexts and responses will also evolve. Keeping up with these changes may require organizational efforts that are not obvious in their economy. However, as the Catholic Church is now experiencing, the long-term effects of neglecting these efforts may be even more costly. As the philosopher Cicero noted, "to disregard what the world thinks of us is not only arrogant but utterly shameless."

References

Aerts, W. (1994). On the use of accounting logic as an explanatory category in narrative accounting disclosures. *Accounting, Organizations, and Society, 19,* 337–353.

Albert, S., & Whetten, D. A. (1985). Organizational identity. In B. M. Staw & L. L. Cummings (Eds.), *Research in Organizational Behavior* (Vol. 7, pp. 263–295). Greenwich, CT: JAI.

Allen, M. W., & Caillouet, R. H. (1994). Legitimation endeavors: Impression management strategies used by an organization in crisis. *Communication Monographs, 61,* 44–62.

America's all-male golfing society. (2002, November 18). *The New York Times,* p. A18.

Arkin, R. M., & Baumgardner, A. H. (1985). Self-handicapping. In J. H. Harvey, W. Ickes, & R. F. Kidd (Eds.), *New directions in attribution research* (Vol. 3, pp. 169–202). Hillsdale, NJ: Lawrence Erlbaum Associates.

Arndt, M., & Bigelow, B. (2000). Presenting structural innovation in an institutional environment: Hospitals' use of impression management. *Administrative Science Quarterly, 45,* 494–522.

Arnold, S. J., Handelman, J., & Tigert, D. J. (1996). Organizational legitimacy and retail store patronage. *Journal of Business Research, 35,* 229–239.

Aronson, J., Blanton, H., & Cooper, J. (1995). From dissonance to disidentification: Selectivity in the self-affirmation process. *Journal of Personality and Social Psychology, 68,* 986–996.

Ashforth, B. E., & Gibbs, B. W. (1990). The double-edge of organizational legitimation. *Organization Science, 1,* 177–194.

Ashforth, B. E., & Humphrey, R. E. (1995). Labeling processes in the organization: Constructing the individual. In L. L. Cummings & B. M. Staw (Eds.), *Research in organizational behavior* (Vol. 17, pp. 413–461). Greenwich, CT: JAI.

Associated Press. (1992, October 23). Sears posts 1st loss since 1933. *Los Angeles Times,* p. D1.

Associated Press. (1998, May 22). Viagra hard on heart, paramedics say. *The Toronto Star,* p. A2.

Balmer, J. M. T., & Greyser, S. A. (2002). Managing the multiple identities of the corporation. *California Management Review, 44,* 72–86.

Bansal, P., & Clelland, I. (2004). Talking trash: Legitimacy, impression management, and unsystematic risk in the context of the natural environment. *Academy of Management Journal, 47,* 93–103.

Barney, J. B., & Hansen, M. H. (1994). Trustworthiness as a source of competitive advantage. *Strategic Management Journal, 15,* 175–190.

Bartunek, J. (1988). The dynamics of personal and organizational reframing. In R. E. Quinn & K. S. Cameron (Eds.), *Paradox and transformation: Toward a theory of change in organization and management* (pp. 137–162). Cambridge, MA: Ballinger.

Benjamin, B. A., & Podolny, J. M. (1999). Status, quality, and social order in the California wine industry. *Administrative Science Quarterly, 44,* 563–589.

Benoit, W. L. (1999). Acclaiming, attacking, and defending in presidential nominating acceptance addresses, 1960–1996. *Quarterly Journal of Speech, 85,* 247–267.

Berglas, S., & Jones, E. E. (1978). Drug choice as a self-handicapping strategy in response to noncontingent success. *Journal of Personality and Social Psychology, 36,* 405–417.

Bettman, J. R., & Weitz, B. A. (1983). Attributions in the board room: Causal reasoning in corporate annual reports. *Administrative Science Quarterly, 28,* 165–183.

Bies, R. J., Shapiro, D. L., & Cummings, L. L. (1988). Causal accounts and managing organizational conflict: Is it enough to say it's not my fault? *Communications Research, 15,* 381–399.

Blaney, J. R., Benoit, W. L., & Brazeal, L. M. (2002). Blowout!: Firestone's image restoration campaign. *Public Relations Review, 28,* 379–392.

Bloomberg News. (1998, March 24). TV report helps boost Pfizer's shares. ABC's 20/20 highlighted firm's new pill that will help treat impotence. *The Milwaukee Journal Sentinel,* p. B2.

Bone, J. (1998, July 18). Heart attack victim sues Viagra firm for $80 M. *The London Times,* p. 1.

Borden, S. (2002, September 6). Women's group softens its stance. *New York Daily News,* p. 106.

Brazaitis, T. (1997, November 2). IRS is planning to shuck its surly image, become friendly. *Cleveland Plain Dealer,* p. 16A.

Brelis, M. (1997, November 16). IRS and taxpayers call truce to tackle problems; Agency hopes to soften hard-nosed image. *The Boston Globe,* p. B1.

Brennan, C. (2002, December 5). Augusta National's Hootie not making any points at all. *USA Today,* p. 3C.

Brewer, M. B. (1991). The social self: On being the same and different at the same time. *Personality and Social Psychology Bulletin, 15,* 475–482.

Brickson, S. (2000). The impact of identity orientation on individual and organizational outcomes in demographically diverse settings. *Academy of Management Review, 25,* 82–101.

Brockner, J. (1992). The escalation of commitment to a failing course of action: Toward theoretical progress. *Academy of Management Review, 17,* 39–61.

Brockner, J., Konovsky, M., Cooper-Schneider, R., Folger, R., Martin, C., & Bies, R. J. (1994). Interactive effects of procedural justice and outcome negativity on victims and survivors of job loss. *Academy of Management Journal, 37,* 379–409.

Brockner, J., & Siegel, P. (1996). Understanding the interaction between procedural and distributive justice: The role of trust. In R. M. Kramer & T. R. Tyler (Eds.), *Trust in organizations* (pp. 390–413). Thousand Oaks, CA: Sage.

Broder, J. M. (1996, October 31). NRA's still flexing its muscle as some question its influence. *Los Angeles Times,* p. A14.

Brown, A. D. (1997). Narcissism, identity, and legitimacy. *Academy of Management Review, 22,* 643–686.

Brown, C. (2002a, November 12). At club in Augusta, policy of chairman remains 'men only.' *The New York Times,* p. A1.

Brown, C. (2002b, July 10). Augusta answers critics on policy. *The New York Times,* p. D4.

Brown, A. D., & Jones, M. (2000). Honourable members and dishonourable deeds: Sensemaking, impression management and legitimation in the 'Arms to Iraq Affair.' *Human Relations, 53,* 655–689.

Browne, J. (1997, May 19). Where BP stands on global climate change. Address at Stanford University. Retrieved from http://www.bp.com/pressoffice/speeches/sp_970519.htm.

Buckley, S. (2002, December 15). Hootie, Martha and the Masters: The characters and the conflict. *St. Petersburg Times,* p. 1A.

Bulkin, B.J. (2003). BP = bringing profits: In a socially responsible way. *Mid-American Journal of Business, 18,* 7–11.

Burnett, J. J. (1998). A strategic approach to managing crises. *Public Relations Review, 24,* 475–488.

Butler, J. K., Jr. (1991). Towards understanding and measuring conditions of trust: Evolution of a conditions of trust inventory. *Journal of Management, 17,* 643–663.

Camerer, C., & Vepsalainen, A. (1988). The economic efficiency of corporate culture. *Strategic Management Journal, 9,* 115–126.

Cayenne: Porsche's SUV. (2000, July 12). *Businessworld,* p. 1.

Chaung, Y., & Baum, J. A. C. (2003). It's all in the name: Failure-induced learning by multi-unit chains. *Administrative Science Quarterly, 48,* 33–59.

Chen, C. C., & Meindl, J. R. (1991). The construction of leadership images in the popular press: The case of Donald Burr and People Express. *Administrative Science Quarterly, 36,* 521–551.

Cheney, G. (1991). *Rhetoric in an organizational society: Managing multiple identities.* Columbia, SC: University of South Carolina Press.

Ching, L. (1998, November 7). Viagra: Do take it seriously. *The Singapore Straits Times,* p. 65.

Cialdini, R. B. (1984). *Influence. The new psychology of modern persuasion.* New York: Quill.

Clark, M. C., & Payne, R. L. (1997). The nature and structure of workers' trust in management. *Journal of Organizational Behavior, 18,* 205–224.

Cole, R. (1990). U.S. quality improvement in the auto industry: Close but no cigar. *California Management Review, 32,* 71–85.

Conlon, D. E., & Murray, N. M. (1996). Customer perceptions of corporate responses to product complaints: The role of explanations. *Academy of Management Review, 39,* 1040–1056.

Cookson, C., & Green, D. (1998, May 7). Take one before bedtime: Clive Cookson and Daniel Green look behind the hype surrounding the world's fastest-selling drug ever. *The London Times,* p. 18.

Cornell, T. (1998, May 22). Nitro–Viagra combo deadly. *The Boston Herald,* p. 7.

Cowden, K., & Sellnow, T. L. (2002). Issues advertising as crisis communication: Northwest Airlines' use of image restoration strategies during the 1998 pilots' strike. *Journal of Business Communication, 39,* 193–219.

Crenshaw, A. B. (2001, July 1). Nowhere for tax cheats to hide; IRS tempers feel-good PR campaign with enforcement. *The Washington Post,* p. H2.

Crocker, J., & Gallo, L. (1985, August). *Prejudice against outgroups: The self-enhancing effects of downward social comparisons.* Paper presented at the Annual Convention of the American Psychological Association, Los Angeles, CA.

Curtin, D. (1999, April 10). Critics take aim at NRA courses. College will offer group's curriculum. *The Denver Post,* p. A1.

D'Aunno, T., & Sutton, R. I. (1992). The responses of drug abuse treatment organizations to financial adversity: A partial test of the threat-rigidity thesis. *Journal of Management, 18,* 117–132.

D'Aveni, R. A., & O'Neill, R. (1992). *Toward a multiple-constituency model of organizational scope and distinctive competence: A study of strategic positioning and groups among business schools.* Unpublished manuscript, Amos Tuck School of Business Administration, Dartmouth University.

Deutsche Welle Productions. (1999). *Porsche: Portrait of an industry leader.* Princeton, NJ: Films for the Humanities and Sciences.

Damage Control. (2000, October 8). *60 Minutes.*

Dirsmith, M. W., Jablonsky, S. F., & Luzi, A. D. (1980). Planning and control in the U.S. Federal Government: A critical analysis of PPB, MBO, and ZBB. *Strategic Management Journal, 1,* 303–329.

Donlon, J. P. (2000). Why John Chambers is the CEO of the future. *Chief Executive, 157,* 26–36.

Dowling, J. (2002, November 15). Cayenne and Able. *Sydney Morning Herald,* Motoring Section, p. 6.

Dukerich, J. M., & Carter, S. M. (2000). Distorted images and reputation repair. In M. Schultz, M. J. Hatch, & M. H. Larsen (Eds.), *The expressive organization. Linking identity, reputation, and the corporate brand* (pp. 97–114). New York: Oxford University Press.

Dutton, J. E., & Dukerich, J. M. (1991). Keeping an eye on the mirror: Image and identity in organizational adaptation. *Academy of Management Journal, 34,* 517–554.

Dutton, J. E., Dukerich, J. M., & Harquail, C. V. (1994). Organizational images and member identification. *Administrative Science Quarterly, 39,* 239–263.

Dutton, J. E., & Penner, W. J. (1993). The importance of organizational identity for strategic agenda building. In J. Hendry & G. Johnson (Eds.), *Strategic Thinking: Leadership and the Management of Change* (pp. 89–113). New York: Strategic Management Society, Wiley.

Editorial. (1991, August 22). *The New York Times,* p. A26.

Elias, M. (1998, July 16). Pill's possibilities excite women, but Viagra's effects on female bodies remain a medical mystery. *USA Today,* p. 8D.

Elsbach, K. D. (1994). Managing organizational legitimacy in the California cattle industry: The construction and effectiveness of verbal accounts. *Administrative Science Quarterly, 39,* 57–88.

Elsbach, K. D. (1999). An expanded model of organizational identification. In B. M. Staw & R. I. Sutton (Eds.), *Research in Organizational Behavior* (Vol. 21, pp. 163–200). Stamford, CT: JAI.

Elsbach, K. D. (2001a). The architecture of legitimacy: Constructing accounts of organizational controversies. In J. T. Jost & B. Major (Eds.), *The psychology of legitimacy: Emerging perspectives on ideology, justice, and intergroup relations* (pp. 391–415). Cambridge, UK: Cambridge University Press.

Elsbach, K. D. (2001b). Coping with hybrid organizational identities: Evidence from California Legislative Staff. In J. Wagner (Ed.), *Advances in Qualitative Organizational Research* (Vol. 3, pp. 59–90). Oxford, UK: Elsevier .

Elsbach, K. D. (2003a). Organizational perception management. In R. M. Kramer & B. M. Staw (Eds.), *Research in organizational behavior* (Vol. 25, pp. 297–332). Oxford, UK: Elsevier.

Elsbach, K. D. (2003b). Relating physical environment to self-categorizations: A study of identity threat and affirmation in a non-territorial office space. *Administrative Science Quarterly, 48,* 622–654.

Elsbach, K. D. (2004a). Interpreting workplace identities: The role of office decor. *Journal of Organizational Behavior, 25,* 99–128.

Elsbach, K. D. (2004b). Managing images of trustworthiness in organizations. In R. M. Kramer & K. Cook (Eds.), *Trust and distrust in organizations: Dilemmas and approaches* (pp. 275–292). New York: The Russell Sage Foundation.

Elsbach, K. D. (2005). Looking good vs. being good: Pitfalls of maintaining perceptions of strong leadership following organizational scandals. In J. Bartunek, M. A. Hensdale, & J. Keenan (Eds.), *Church ethics and its organizational context: Learning from the sec abuse scandal in the Catholic Church* (pp. 69–80). Lanham MD: Rowan & Littlefield.

Elsbach, K. D., & Bhattacharya, C. B. (2001). Defining who you are by what you're not: Organizational disidentification and the National Rifle Association. *Organization Science, 12,* 393–413.

Elsbach, K. D., & Elofson, G. (2000). How the "packaging" of decision explanations affects perceptions of trustworthiness. *Academy of Management Journal, 43,* 80–89.

Elsbach, K. D., & Kramer, R. M. (1996). Members' responses to organizational identity threats: Encountering and countering the *Business Week* rankings. *Administrative Science Quarterly, 41,* 442–476.

Elsbach, K. D., & Sutton, R. I. (1992). Acquiring organizational legitimacy through illegitimate actions: A marriage of institutional and impression management theories. *Academy of Management Journal, 35,* 699–738.

Elsbach, K. D., Sutton, R. I., & Principe, K. E. (1998). Averting expected controversies through anticipatory impression management: A study of hospital billing. *Organization Science, 9,* 68–86.

Erfle, S., McMillan, H., & Grafman, B. (1990). Regulation via threats. Politics, media coverage, and oil pricing decisions. *Public Opinion Quarterly, 54,* 48–63.

Farago, R. (2002). *On road and off.* Retrieved November 26 from www.pistonheads.com/coc.asp?c=105&i=5868.

Fisher, R., & Ury, W. (1991). *Getting to yes: Negotiating agreement without giving in.* New York: Penguin.

Fiske, S. T., & Taylor, S. E. (1991). *Social cognition* (2nd ed.). New York: McGraw-Hill.

Folger, R., & Cropanzano, R., 1998. *Organizational justice and human resource management.* Thousand Oaks, CA: Sage.

Fombrun, C. (1996). *Reputation.* Boston, MA: Harvard Business School Press.

Fombrun, C., & Rindova, V. P. (2000). The road to transparency: Reputation management at Royal Dutch/Shell. In M. Schultz, M. J. Hatch, & M. H. Larsen (Eds.), *The expressive organization. Linking identity, reputation, and the corporate brand* (pp. 77–96). New York: Oxford University Press.

Fombrun, C., & Shanley, M. (1990). What's in a name? Reputation building and corporate strategy. *Academy of Management Journal, 33,* 233–258.

Frankel, A. (2002, November 17). How brilliant, how pointless. *The London Times,* p. D4.

Freudhenheim, M. (1998, March 28). Impotence drug expected to be a popular pill. *The New York Times,* p. D1.

Gallagher, S. (2002, November 15). Porsche's Cayenne redefines the SUV. *The London Times,* p. 45.

Gellene, D. (1992a, June 12). New state probe of Sears could lead to suit. *Los Angeles Times,* p. D1.

Gellene, D. (1992b, June 16). Sears car repair shops come under fire in N.J. *Los Angeles Times,* p. D2.

Gellene, D. (1992c, June 11). State to seek to lift auto repair of Sears. *Los Angeles Times,* p. A1.

Gellene, D. (1995, March 24). Sears will get back into the lube business in just a Jiffy. *Los Angeles Times,* p. D2.

Gertenzang, J. (1997, May 24). Oil boss turns heretic on warming. BP executive's call for a corporate rethinking puts him 'out of the church.' *Toronto Star,* p. C6.

Getlin, J. (1998, June 9). Heston chosen to lead NRA back to mainstream. *Los Angeles Times,* p. A1.

Gillis, J. (1998a, April 21). Pfizer's stock soars on success of drug; New impotence pill boosts firm's value. *The Washington Post,* p. C1.

Gillis, J. (1998b). Impotence pill: Who will pay? Men besieging doctors for drug. *The Washington Post,* p. A1.

Ginzel, L. E., Kramer, R. M., & Sutton, R. I. (1993). Organizational impression management as a reciprocal influence process: The neglected role of the organizational audience. In L. L. Cummings & B. M. Staw (Eds.), *Research in organizational behavior* (Vol. 15, pp. 227–266). Greenwich, CT: JAI.

Gioia, D. A., & Thomas, J. B.,1(996). Institutional identity, image, and issue interpretation: Sensemaking during strategic change in academia. *Administrative Science Quarterly, 41,* 370–403.

Glynn, M. A., & Abzug, R. (2002). Institutionalizing identity: Symbolic isomorphism and organizational names. *Academy of Management Journal, 45,* 267–280.

Goldberg, R. A., & Vargas, I. (2003). ConAgra Foods. *Harvard Business School Case Series* (May 22). Boston, MA: Harvard Business School Publishing.

Golden-Biddle, K., & Rao, H. (1997). Breaches in the boardroom: Organizational identity and conflicts of commitment in a nonprofit organization. *Organization Science, 8,* 593–611.

Gotsi, M., & Wilson, A. (2001). Corporate reputation management: "Living the brand." *Management Decision, 39,* 99.

Greenberg, J. (1990). Looking fair vs. being fair: Managing impressions of organizational justice. In B. M. Staw & L. L. Cummings (Eds.), *Research in organizational behavior* (Vol. 12, pp. 111–157). Greenwich, CT: JAI.

Greenberg, J. (1994). Using socially fair treatment to promote acceptance of a work site smoking ban. *Journal of Applied Psychology, 79,* 288–297.

Greenberg, J., Bies, R. J., & Eskew, D. E. (1991). Establishing fairness in the eye of the beholder: Managing impressions of organizational justice. In R. A. Giacalone & P. Rosenfeld (Eds.),

Applied impression management in organizations. How image-making affects managerial decisions (pp. 111–132, Thousand Oaks, CA: Sage.

Greene, L. (2002, August 4). At Augusta, it's symbols that mean most. *The New York Times,* p. H11.

Haga, C. (1998, February 8). IRS putting on a friendly face; Folks at the Internal Revenue Service, tired of all the bashing, are taking steps to spruce up their image by declaring partial amnesties, softening language—and smiling. *Minneapolis Star Tribune,* p. 1B.

Harig, B. (2002, August 31). Keeping women out at all costs. *St. Petersberg Times,* p. 1A.

Hart, K. M., Capps, H. R., Cangemi, J. P., & Caillouet, L. M. (1986). Exploring organizational trust and its multiple dimensions: A case study of General Motors. *Organizational Development Journal, 4,* 31–39.

Hatch, M. J., & Schultz, M. (2000). Scaling the Tower of Babel: Relational differences between identity, image, and culture in organizations. In M. Schultz, M. J. Hatch, & M. H. Larsen (Eds.), *The expressive organization. Linking identity, reputation, and the corporate brand* (pp. 11–35). New York: Oxford University Press.

Healy, J. R. (2001, September 8). January memo revealed tire flaws. Firestone execs linked cost of defects, Decatur. *USA Today,* p. 3B.

Hearit, K. M. (1994). Apologies and public relations crisis at Chrysler, Toshiba, and Volvo. *Public Relations Review, 20,* 113–125.

Hein, R. (1996, March 30). Post office should cancel ad campaign, patrons say. *Chicago Sun-Times,* p. 3.

Hendry, J. (2002). The principal's other problems: Honest incompetence and the specification of objectives. *Academy of Management Review, 27,* 98–113.

Hensel, Jr. (2002, June 26). Southwest starts strictly enforcing seat policy today; Its rule on larger passengers generates dispute. *The Houston Chronicle,* p. B1.

Hewitt, J. P., & Stokes, R. (1975). Disclaimers. *American Sociological Review, 40,* 1–11.

Higgins, R. L., & Snyder, C., R. (1989). The business of excuses. In R. A. Gracalone & P. Rosenfeld (Eds.), *Impression management in the organization* (pp. 73–86). Hillsdale, NJ: Lawrence Erlbaum Associates.

Himmelstein, J. L. (1997). *Looking good and doing good: Corporate philanthropy and corporate power.* Bloomington, IN: University of Indiana Press.

Hiskey, M. (2002, July 11). Augusta National gender debate: Display of arrogance is par for the course. *The Atlanta Journal-Constitution,* p. 3D.

Hogg, M. A. (2001). A social identity theory of leadership. *Personality and Social Psychology Review, 5,* 184–200.

Hogg, M. A., & Abrams, D. (1988). *Social identification: A social psychology of intergroup relations and group processes.* London: Routledge.

Holusha, J. (1989, April 21). Exxon's public relations problem. *The New York Times,* p. D1.

Hopkins, J. (2002, December 4). Augusta member resigns as dispute escalates. *The London Times,* p. 40.

Humphreys, M., & Brown, A. D. (2002). Narratives of organizational identity and identification: A case study of hegemony and resistance. *Organization Studies, 23,* 421–447.

Ingram, P. (1996). Organizational form as a solution to the problem of credible commitment: The evolution of naming strategies among U.S. hotel chains, 1896–1980. *Strategic Management Journal, 17,* 85–98.

Janofsky, M. (1998, June 8). N.R.A. tries to improve image, with Charlton Heston in lead. *The New York Times,* p. A1.

Johnson, P. (2002, December 5). Spiked golf columns drive "Times" debate. *USA Today,* p. 3D.

Jones, E. E., & Pittman, T. S. (1982). Toward a general theory of strategic self-presentation. In J. Suls (Ed.), *Psychological perspectives on the self* (pp. 231–262). Hillsdale, NJ: Lawrence Erlbaum Associates.

Jost, J. T., & Elsbach, K. D. (2001). How status and power differences erode personal and social identities at work: A system justification critique of organizational applications of social identity theory. In M. A. Hogg & D. J. Terry (Eds.), *Social identity processes in organizational contexts* (pp. 181–196). Philadelphia, PA: Psychology Press/Taylor & Francis.

Justice, R. (2002, December 15). The players; Spat for the course; Female furor at Augusta National rages on. *The Houston Chronicle*, p. S1.

Kahneman, D., & Tversky, A. (1979). On the interpretation of intuitive probability: A reply to Jonathan Cohen. *Cognition, 7*, 409–411.

Kaplan, R. S., & Horvath, P. (1993). *Porsche AG* (Harvard Business School Case Series). Boston, MA: Harvard Business School Publishing.

Kauffman, J. (2001). A successful failure: NASA's crisis communications regarding Apollo 13. *Public Relations Review, 27*, 437–448.

Kaufman, L., & Atlas, R. D. (2002, April 28). In a race to the mall, J. Crew has lost its way. *The New York Times*, p. C1.

Kim, W. C., & Marborgne, R. A (1993). Procedural justice, attitudes, and subsidiary top management compliance with multinationals' corporate strategic decisions. *Academy of Management Journal, 36*, 502–526.

Kiszla, M.. (2002, July 11). Last haven for male bonding. *The Denver Post*, p. D1.

Kolata, G. (1998, March 28). U.S. approves sale of impotence pill; Huge market seen. *The New York Times*, p. A1.

Kramer, R. M. (1993). Cooperation and organizational identification. In J. K. Murnighan (Ed.), *Social Psychology In Organizations* (pp. 244–268). Englewood Cliffs, NJ: Prentice-Hall.

Kreps, D. M., & Wilson, R. (1982). Reputation and imperfect information. *Journal of Economic Theory, 27*, 253–279.

Lakamp, P. (1997, November 16). IRS devotes a day to helping taxpayers and its own image. *The Buffalo News*, p. 1A.

Lamb, R. B. (1987). *Running American business: CEOs rethink their major decisions*. New York: Basic Books.

Lamertz, K., & Baum, J. A. C. (1998). The legitimacy of organizational downsizing in Canada: An analysis of explanatory media accounts. *Canadian Journal of Administrative Sciences, 15*, 93–107.

Large-passenger policy prompts few protests. (2002, July 7). *The New York Times*, p. E3.

Langer, E. J. (1975). The illusion of control. *Journal of Personality and Social Psychology, 32*, 311–328.

Leary, M. R. (1996). *Self-presentation: Impression management and interpersonal behavior*. Oxford, England: Westview Press.

Lerner, M. (1998, March 28). First pill to treat impotence approved; Viagra, a failed heart drug, is touted as the most significant advance in the area of sexual dysfunction in decades. *The Minneapolis Star Tribune*, p. 1A.

Lind, E. A., Kanfer, R., & Early, C. (1990). Voice, control, and procedural justice: Instrumental and noninstrumental concerns in fairness judgments. *Journal of Personality and Social Psychology, 59*, 952–959.

Longman, J. (1994, March 15). NRA heeds Olympic call to end team affiliation. *The New York Times*, p. B14.

Lord, R. G., De Vader, C., & Alliger, G. (1986). A meta-analysis between personality traits and leadership perceptions: An application of validity generalization procedures. *Journal of Applied Psychology, 71*, 402–410.

Lore, D. (1998, April 23). Heath Watch; Viagra, Internet raise issues of medical ethics; Doctors prescribe drug without seeing patients. *The Atlanta Journal-Constitution*, p. 3E.

Lowe, E. A., & Harris, R. J. (1998). Taking climate change seriously: British Petroleum's business strategy. *Corporate Environmental Strategy, 5*(2), 22–31.

Magner, N., & Johnson, G. G. (1995). Municipal officials' reactions to justice in budgetary resource allocation. *Public Administration Quarterly, 18*, 439–457.

Majeta, J. (2000, August 11). Porsche serves up a dash of silliness: German automaker's Cayenne is new king of meaningless monikers. *The Ottawa Citizen*, p. C4.

Marcus, A. A., & Goodman, R. S. (1991). Victims and shareholders: The dilemmas of presenting corporate policy during a crisis. *Academy of Management Journal, 34,* 281–305.

Martin, S. (2000, June 10). Porsche adds bit of spice. *London Daily Telegraph,* p. 59.

Mayer, R. C., & Davis, J. H. (1999). The effect of the performance appraisal system on trust for management: A field quasi-experiment. *Journal of Applied Psychology, 84,* 123–136.

Mayer, R. C., Davis, J. H., & Schoorman, F. D. (1995). An integrative model of organizational trust. *Academy of Management Review, 20,* 709–734.

McAllister, B. (1994, June 8). Postal board outraged over declining service; Urban problems bring demand for accountability. *The Washington Post,* p. A21.

McCarthy, M. (2002, September 5). Group might ask public to pressure companies whose execs are members. *USA Today,* p. 12C.

McCarthy, M., & Brady, E. (2002, September 27). Privacy becomes public. *USA Today,* p. 1C.

McDonald, N. (1999, September 23). Porsche 4WD to fast track marque's sales. *The Australian,* p. 32.

Mcgavin, C. (2002, March 7). Porsche takes to the hills. *The Melbourne Age,* p. 3.

McMahon, B. (1999, October 2). Porsche adds zip to the sports utility market. *Queensland, Australia Courier Mail,* p. 39.

McNamara, G., Moon, H., & Bromiley, P. (2002). Banking on commitment: Intended and unintended consequences of an organization's attempt to attenuate escalation of commitment. *Academy of Management Journal, 45,* 443–452.

Meindl, J. R., & Ehrlich, S. B. (1987). The romance of leadership and the evaluation of organizational performance. *Academy of Management Journal, 30,* 91–109.

Meindl, J. R., Ehrlich, S. B., & Dukerich, J. M. (1985). The romance of leadership. *Administrative Science Quarterly, 30,* 78–102.

Mertl, S. (2000, October 20). Porsche hopes its Cayenne will be hot: Search for higher profits prompts radical foray into sport-utility market by sports car firm. *The Ottawa Citizen,* p. C16.

Meszaros, J. R. (1999). Preventive choices: Organization's heuristics, decision processes, and catastrophic risks. *Journal of Management Studies, 36,* 977–998.

Meyer, M. (1994, July 11). Culture club. *Business Week Magazine,* 38–42.

Meyer, J. W., & Rawon, B. R. (1977). Institutionalized organizations: Formal structure as myth and ceremony. *American Journal of Sociology, 83,* 340–363.

Miles, P. (2002, October 26). Passengers have right to be moved if crushed. *London Daily Telegraph,* p. 4.

Milgrom, P., & Roberts, J. (1982). Predation, reputation, and entry deterrence. *Journal of Economic Theory, 27,* 280–312.

Milgrom, P., & Roberts, J. (1986). Price and advertising signals of product quality. *Journal of Political Economy, 94,* 796–821.

Mitroff, I. I., Pearson, C. M., & Harrington, L. K. (1996). *The essential guide to managing corporate crises.* New York: Oxford University Press.

Mohamed, A. A., Orife, J. N., & Slack, F. J. (2001). Organizational reputation: A literature review and a model. *International Journal of Management, 18,* 261–269.

Molyneaux, D. (2002, July 7). Stuffing large bodies into tight plane seats. *The Plain Dealer,* p. K1.

Morrow, D. J. (1998a, April 21). Drug for impotence leads market. *The New York Times,* p. D1.

Morrow, D. J. (1998b, April 29). Insurers limiting payments for use of impotence pill. *The New York Times,* p. A1.

Morrow, D. J. (1998c, March 31). New means to make men feel younger. *The New York Times,* p. D1.

Moscoso, E. (2000, June 11). NRA flap: Eagle ruffles feathers. *The Atlanta Journal-Constitution,* p. 7F.

Moses, S. (1995, October 30). The road to bliss: We drive through hell in search of a curve, and a car's soul. *Adweek,* p. 18.

Mueller, C. W., Boyer, E. M., Price, J. L., & Iverson, R. D. (1994). Employee attachment and noncoercive conditions of work. The case of dental hygienists. *Work and Occupations, 21,* 179–212.

Murrell, A. (2001). Signaling positive corporate social performance. *Business & Society, 40,* 59–78.

Neff, E. (1996., June 20) Postal workers demonstrate nationwide. *Milwaukee Journal Sentinel,* p. 3.

Nelson, P. (1974). Advertising as information. *Journal of Political Economy, 81,* 729–754.

News Services. (2002a, July 10). Augusta National comes out swinging. *The Washington Post,* p. D2.

News Services. (2002b, September 1). CBS urged to dump Masters. *The Washington Post,* p.2.

NRA chief ties membership drive to renewal. (2001, June 24). *The Buffalo News,* p. C9.

O'Day, R. (1974). Intimidation rituals: Reactions to reform. *Journal of Applied Behavioral Science, 10,* 373–386.

Ohbuchi, K., & Kambara, T.,1(985). Attacker's intent and awareness of outcome, impression management, and retaliation. *Journal of Experimental Social Psychology, 21,* 321–330.

Olins, W. (1995). *Corporate identity: Making business strategy visible through design.* Boston: Harvard Business School Press

Ornstein, S. (1986). Organizational symbols: A study of their meanings and influences on perceived psychological climate. *Organizational Behavior and Human Decision Processes, 38,* 207–229.

Ornstein, S. (1992). First impressions of the symbolic meanings connoted by reception area design. *Environment and Behavior, 24,* 85–110.

Oskamp, S. (1965). Overconfidence in case study judgments. *Journal of Consulting Psychology, 29,* 261–265.

Pauchant, T. C., & Mitroff, I. I. (1992). *Transforming the crisis prone organization.* San Francisco: Jossey-Bass.

Paulson, M. (2001, July 27). Law defends his response in clergy sex abuse case. *The Boston Globe,* p. A1.

Paulson, M. (2002a, January 10). The Cardinal's apology; Actions follow an established course. *The Boston Globe,* p. A1.

Paulson, M. (2002b, February 4). Stung by sex-abuse cases, Catholics call for reform. *The Boston Globe,* p. A1.

Paulson, M. (2002c, February 11). A resolute Law repeats he won't go; vows to focus on protections for children. *The Boston Globe,* p. A1.

Paulson, M. (2002d, March 13). All faiths question handling of abuse. Debate over celibacy as factor rancorous. *The Boston Globe,* p. A1.

Pearce, J. L. (1993). Toward an organizational behavior of contract laborers: Their psychological involvement and effects on employee co-workers. *Academy of Management Journal, 36,* 1082–1096.

Pearce, J. L, Branyiczki, I., & Bakacsi, G. (1994). Person-based reward systems: A theory of organizational reward practices in reform-communist organizations. *Journal of Organizational Behavior, 15,* 261–282.

Pearson, C. M., & Clair, J. A. (1998). Reframing crisis management. *Academy of Management Review, 23,* 59–76.

Pennington, B., & Anderson, D. (2002, September 29). Some at Augusta National quietly seek a compromise. *The New York Times,* p. H1.

Perrow, C. (1984). *Normal accidents: Living with high-risk technologies.* New York: Basic Books.

Pfeffer, J. (1981). Management as symbolic action: The creation and maintenance of organizational paradigms. In L. L. Cummings & B. M. Staw (Eds.), *Research in organizational behavior* (Vol. 3, pp. 1–52). Greenwich, CT: JAI.

Pfeffer, J., & Sutton, R. I. (1999). *The knowing–doing gap: How smart companies turn knowledge into action.* Boston: Harvard Business School Press.

Pfeiffer, S. (2002). Law's decision to remain/Victims protest. Abuse victims decry Cardinal's letter as insult. *The Boston Globe,* p. B4.

Pollock, T. G., & Rindova, V. P. (2003). Media legitimation effects in the market for initial public offerings. *Academy of Management Journal, 46,* 631–642.

Porac, J. F., Wade, J. B., & Pollock, T. G. (1999). Industry categories and the politics of the comparable firm in CEO compensation. *Administrative Science Quarterly, 44,* 112–144.

Potter, J. (2002, July 10). Augusta resists pressure from women's group. *USA Today,* p. 1C.

Pratt, M. G., & Foreman, P. O. (2000). Classifying managerial responses to multiple organizational identities. *Academy of Management Review, 25,* 18–42.

Proudfoot, D. (1998, June 14). Porsche enters the sport utility market. *Toronto Sun,* p. D9.

Puchan, H. (2001). The Mercedes–Benz A-class crisis. *Corporate Communications, 6,* 42–46.

Rao, H. (1994). The social construction of reputation: Certification contests, legitimation, and the survival of organizations in the American automobile industry: 1895–1912. *Strategic Management Journal, 15,* 29–44.

Reger, R. K., Gustafson, L. T., DeMarie, S. M., & Mullane, J. V. (1994). Reframing the organization: Why implementing total quality is easier said than done. *Academy of Management Review, 19,* 565–584.

Reinhardt, F., & Richman, E. (2001). Global climate change and BP Amoco. *Harvard Business School Case Series,* Harvard Business School Publishing, Boston: MA. February 28, 1–24.

Reuters New Service. (2002, November 8). Policy on larger passengers working, Southwest says. *The Houston Chronicle,* p. 3.

Rezendes, M. (2002, December 13). Amid the pain, decision brings sorrow, relief. Lasting change seen as the key. *The Boston Globe,* p. A2.

Rezendes, M., & Robinson, W. V. (2002, February 3). Two priests ousted after abuse cited. DA to get data on Randolph, Quincy pastors. *The Boston Globe,* p. A1.

Rich, E., & Hamilton, E. (2002, March 24). Clinic says it was deceived by church; asserts information withheld on priests and past complaints. *The Boston Globe,* p. A33.

Ridoutt, B. G., Ball, R. D., & Killerby, S. K. (2002). First impressions of organizations and the qualities connoted by wood in interior design. *Forest Products Journal, 52,* 30–36.

Riley, C. 2002a, March 8). Absent Cayenne turns out to be red-hot topic. *The London Times,* p. 1.

Rindova, V. P., & Fombrun, C. J. (1999). Constructing competitive advantage: The role of firm–constituent interactions. *Strategic Management Journal, 20,* 691–710.

Rindova, V. P., Pollock, T. G., & Hayward, M. L. A. (2005). Celebrity firms: The social construction of market popularity. *Academy of Management Review,*

Rindova, V. P., Williamson, I. O., & Petkova, A. P. (2005). Being good or being known: An empirical examination of the dimensions, antecedents, and consequences of organizational reputation. *Academy of Management Journal.* Forthcoming.

Riordan, C. A., James, M. K., & Runzi, M. J. (1989). Explaining failures at work: An accounter's dilemma. *Journal of General Psychology, 116,* 197–205

Ritzler, K. (2002a, March 5). Porsche introduces an SUV. *Atlanta Journal-Constitution,* p. 1D.

Ritzler, K. (2002b, March 8). Porsche's spicy SUV; Sports car company hopes Cayenne red-hot. *Atlanta Journal-Constitution,* p. 1S.

Robinson, S. L., & Rousseau, D. M. (1994). Violating the psychological contract: Not the exception but the norm. *Journal of Organizational Behavior, 15,* 245–259.

Ross, J., & Staw, B. M. (1986). Expo 86: An escalation prototype. *Administrative Science Quarterly, 31,* 274–297.

Ross, J., & Staw, B. M. (1993). Organizational escalation and exit: Lessons from the Shoreham Nuclear Power Plant. *Academy of Management Journal, 36,* 701–732.

Rosseau, D. (1998). Why workers still identify with organizations. *Organization Science, 19,* 217–233.

Rowlinson, M., & Hassard, J. (1993). The invention of corporate culture: A history of the histories of Cadbury. *Human Relations, 46,* 299–326.

Russ, G. S. (1991). Symbolic communication and image management in organizations. In R. A. Giacalone & P. Rosenfeld (Eds.), *Applied impression management* (pp. 219–240). Newbury Park, CA: Sage.

Russell, S. (1998a, May 22). Deaths of six Viagra users reported by drugmaker. *The San Francisco Chronicle,* p. A18.

Russell, S. (1998b, April 30). Viagra: Big and getting bigger; Drug for impotence a resounding success story. *The San Francisco Chronicle,* p. A1.

Salancik, G. R., & Meindl, J. R. (1984). Corporate attributions as strategic illusions of management control. *Administrative Science Quarterly, 29,* 238–254.

Sandomir, R. (2002a, September 28). Group lobbies seven of Augusta's members. *The New York Times,* p. D3.

Sandomir, R. (2002b, July 18). Sponsors sidestep debate. *The New York Times,* p. D2.

Sandomir, R., & Elliott, S. (2002, August 31). In fight over women, Masters gives up ads. *The New York Times,* p. A1.

Sandoval, G. (2002, August 31). Augusta opts to go it alone; '03 Masters won't have commercials. *The Washington Post,* p. D1.

Schkade, D. A., & Kilbourne, L. M. (1991). Expectation–outcome consistency and hindsight bias. *Organizational Behavior and Human Decision Processes, 49,* 105–123.

Schlenker, B. R. (1980). *Impression management: The self-concept, social identity, and interpersonal relations.* Monterey, CA: Brooks/Cole.

Schmalensee, R. (1978). A model of advertising and product quality. *Journal of Political Economy, 86,* 485–503.

Schultz, M., Hatch, M. J., & Larsen, M. H. (Eds.). (2000). *The expressive organization. Linking identity, reputation, and the corporate brand.* New York: Oxford University Press.

Shapiro, D. L., & Bies, R. J. (1994). Threats, bluffs and disclaimers in negotiations. *Organizational Behavior and Human Decision Processes, 60,* 14–35.

Shapiro, D. L., & Brett, J. M. (1991). *Comparing the instrumental and value-expressive models of procedural justice under conditions of high and low decision control.* Paper presented at the meetings of the Academy of Management, Miami, FL. August.

Shapiro, D. L., Buttner, E. H., & Barry, B. (1994). Explanations for rejection decisions: What factors enhance their perceived adequacy and moderate their enhancement of justice perceptions? *Organizational Behavior and Human Decision Processes, 58,* 346–368.

Shapiro, L. (2002a, July 11). Augusta feels the heat. *The Washington Post,* p. D7.

Shapiro, L. (2002b, September 20). CBS will televise Masters; Network quickly responds to letter from NWCO. *The Washington Post,* p. D1.

Shapiro, L. (2002c, October 8). USOC chief urges reform; Augusta member joins fight against exclusion policy. *The Washington Post,* p. D7.

Shapiro, L. (2002d, November 22). Burk plans another round. *The Washington Post,* p. D1.

Sheeley, G. (2002, July 11). Augusta and the all-stars: Members: It's not our issue. *The Atlanta Journal-Constitution,* p. 1D.

Shrum, W., & Withnow, R. (1988). Reputational status of organizations in technical systems, *American Journal of Sociology, 93,* 882–912.

Sisario, B. (2002, November 18). The arts; The corporations behind the curtain: Six supporters of the arts. *The New York Times,* p. F13.

Sitkin, S. B., & Bies, R. J. (1993). Social accounts in conflict situations: Using explanations to manage conflict. *Human Relations, 46,* 349–370.

Sloan, J. (1998, February 12). Critics take wait-and-see position on IRS promise. *The Tampa Bay Tribune,* p. 12.

Small, W. J. (1991). Exxon Valdez: How to spend billions and still get a black eye. *Public Relations Review, 17,* 9–25.

Smith, E. A., & Malone, R. E. (2003). Altria means tobacco: Phillip Morris's identity crisis. *American Journal of Public Health, 93,* 553–556.

Smither, J. W., Reilly, R. R., Millsap, R. E., Pearlman, K., & Stoffey, R. W. (1993). Applicant reactions to selection procedures. *Personnel Psychology, 46,* 49–76.

Snyder, C. R., Higgins, R., & Stucky, R. J. (1983). *Excuses. Masquerades in Search of Grace.* New York: John Wiley & Sons.

St. John, K., & Zamora, J. H. (2002, June 20). Southwest to make overweight buy 2 seats; Advocates for obese blast airline's plan. *San Francisco Chronicle,* p. A17.

Stark, K. (1998, April 26). Insurance industry believes Pfizer guilty of creating demand for Viagra before; Full study possible. *Pittsburgh Post-Gazette*, p. E2.

Staw, B. M. (1976). Knee-deep in the Big Muddy—A study of escalating commitment to a chosen course of action. *Organizational Behavior & Human Performance, 16,* 27–44.

Staw, B. M., & Epstein, L. D. (2000). What bandwagons bring: Effects of popular management techniques on corporate performance, reputation, and CEO pay. *Administrative Science Quarterly, 45,* 523–556.

Staw, B. M., McKechnie, P. I., & Puffer, S. M. (1983). The justification of organizational performance. *Administrative Science Quarterly, 28,* 582–600.

Staw, B. M., & Ross, J. (1987). Behavior in escalation situations: Antecedents, prototypes, and solutions. In B. M. Staw & L. L. Cummings (Eds.), *Research in organizational behavior* (Vol. 9, pp. 39–78). Greenwich, CT: JAI.

Staw, B. M., Sandelands, L. E., & Dutton, J. E. (1981). Threat-rigidity effects in organizational behavior: A multilevel analysis. *Administrative Science Quarterly, 26,* 501–524.

Steele, C. M., Spencer, S. J., & Lynch, M. (1993). Self-image resilience and dissonance: The role of affirmational resources. *Journal of Personality and Social Psychology, 64,* 885–896.

Stoddard, S. (2000, September 11). Bridgestone president suggests tire defects not behind accidents. *Associated Press,* BC Cycle.

Stoffey, R. W., Millsap, R. E., Smither, J. W., & Reilly, R. R. (1991). *The influence of selection procedures on attitudes about organization and job pursuit intentions.* Paper presented at the Annual Conference of the Society for Industrial and Organizational Psychology, Saint Louis, MO. August.

Suchman, M. C. (1995). Managing legitimacy: Strategic and institutional approaches. *Academy of Management Review, 20,* 571–610.

Sundstrom, E., & Altman, I. (1989). Physical environments and work-group effectiveness. In L. L. Cummings & B. M. Staw (Eds.), *Research in organizational behavior* (Vol. 11, pp. 175–209). Greenwich, CT: JAI.

Sundstrom, E., & Sundstrom, M. G. (1986). *Work places: The psychology of the physical environment in offices and factories.* Cambridge, England: Cambridge University Press.

Sutton, R. I., & Callahan, A. L. (1987). The stigma of bankruptcy: Spoiled organizational image and its management. *Academy of Management Journal, 30,* 405–436.

Sutton, R. I., & Galunic, D. C. (1996). Consequences of public scrutiny for leaders and their organizations. In B. M. Staw & L. L. Cummings (Eds.), *Research in organizational behavior* (Vol. 18, pp. 201–250). Greenwich, CT: JAI.

Sutton, R. I., & Kramer, R. M. (1990). Transforming failure into success: Spin control in the Iceland Arms Control talks. In R. L. Kahn & M. W. Zald (Eds.), *International cooperation and conflict: Perspectives from organizational theory* (pp. 221–245). San Francisco: Jossey-Bass.

Swierczynski, D. (1999). Stupid diets that work! *Men's Health, 14,* 94–97.

Taylor, A., III. (2001, February 19). Can you believe Porsche is putting its badge on *this* car? *Fortune,* 168–172.

Taylor, S. E. (1983). Adjustment to threatening events: A theory of cognitive adaptation. *American Psychologist, 38,* 1161–1173.

Taylor, S. J., & Bogdan, R. (1980). Defending illusions: The institution's struggle for survival. *Human Organization, 39,* 209–218.

Taylor, S. M., Tracy, K. B., Renald, M. K., Harrison, J. K., & Carroll, S. J. (1995). Due process in performance appraisal: A quasi-experiment in procedural justice. *Administrative Science Quarterly, 40,* 495–523.

Tedeschi, J. T. (Ed.). (1981). *Impression management theory and social psychological research.* New York: Academic Press.

Terry, D. J., Carey, C. J., & Callan, V. J. (2001). Employee adjustment to an organizational merger: An intergroup perspective. *Personality and Social Psychology Bulletin, 27,* 267–280.

Theroux, J. (1991). Ben & Jerry's Homemade Ice Cream, Inc.: Keeping the mission(s) alive. *Harvard Business School Case Studies,* product number 9-392-025. Boston, MA: Harvard Business School Publishing.

Theus, K. T. (1993). Academic reputations: The process of formation and decay. *Public Relations Review, 19,* 277–291.

Thompson, J. D. (1967). *Organizations in action.* New York: McGraw-Hill.

Thomsen, S. R., & Rawson, B. (1998). Purifying a tainted corporate image: Odwalla's response to an E. Coli poisoning. *Public Relations Quarterly, 43,* 35–46.

Times staff. (1995, December 12). Retailing. *Los Angeles Times,* p. D-2.

Traeger, L. (1992, June 23). Sears admits pay system led to car repair over-billing. *San Francisco Examiner,* p. C1.

Tran, M. (1998, March 23). American notebook: Miracle drug taps into male psyche. *The London Guardian,* p. 18.

Tsui, A. S. (1990). A multiple-constituency model of effectiveness: An empirical examination at the human resource subunit level. *Administrative Science Quarterly, 35,* 458–483.

Turban, D. B., & Greening, D. W. (1997). Corporate social performance and organizational attractiveness to prospective employees. *Academy of Management Journal, 40,* 658–672.

Tyler, T. R. (1987). Conditions leading to value expressive effects in judgments of procedural justice: A test of four models. *Journal of Personality and Social Psychology, 57,* 850–863.

Tyler, T. R. (1990). *Why people obey the law: Procedural justice, legitimacy, and compliance.* New Haven, CT: Yale University Press.

Tyler, T. R., Boeckmann, R. J., Smith, H. J., & Yuen, J. H. (1997). *Social justice in a diverse society.* Boulder, CO: Westview Press.

Tyler, T. R., & Lind, E. A. (1992). A relational model of authority in groups. In M. Zanna (Ed.), *Advances in experimental social psychology* (Vol. 25, pp. 115–191). San Francisco: Jossey-Bass.

Union-Tribune News Services. (2002, November 14). It may take a U.N. resolution to avert protesters at the Masters. *The San Diego Tribune,* p. D4.

van Dijk, W. W., Zeelenberg, M., & van der Pligt, J. (2003). Blessed are those who expect nothing: Lowering expectations as a way of avoiding disappointment. *Journal of Economic Psychology, 24,* 505–516.

Vatican: Viagra OK. (1998, April 24). *Pittsburgh Post Gazette,* p. A-10.

VW and Porsche to make SUVs. (1998, June 5). *The Ottawa Citizen,* p. D8.

Walster, E., Walster, G. W., & Berscheid, E. (1978). *Equity.* Boston: Allyn & Bacon.

Weeks, L. (1998, April 26). Viagra debate vigorous; Drug sparks questions of sexual politics. *The Washington Post,* p. A1.

Weick, K. E. (1993). The collapse of sensemaking in organizations: The Mann-Gulch disaster. *Administrative Science Quarterly, 38,* 628–652.

Weigelt, K., & Camerer, C. (1988). Reputation and corporate strategy: A review of recent theory and applications. *Strategic Management Journal, 9,* 443–454.

Welch, D. (1999, August 16). Porsche readies debut of its SUV; Automaker hopes to double sales. *Chicago Sun Times,* Auto Times, p. 5.

Wells, M. (1998, October 26). Pfizer seeks Viagra revival with TV ads. *USA Today,* p. 1B.

Wernerfelt, B. (1984). A resource-based view of the firm. *Strategic Management Journal, 5,* 171–180.

White, G., & Maier, A. (1992, June 13). Firm begins effort to restore its image after fraud charges. *Los Angeles Times,* p. 1D.

Whitener, E. M., Brodt, S. E., Korsgaard, M. A., & Werner, J. M. (1998). Managers as initiators of trust: An exchange relationship framework for understanding managerial trustworthy behavior. *Academy of Management Review, 23,* 513–530.

Wiseman, P., Cauchon, D., Larrabee, J., Moore, M. T., O'Driscoll, P., & Sharp, D. (1997, November 17). Helpful IRS attracts thousands. Open houses in 33 cities called successful. *USA Today,* p. 3A.

Women at Augusta: The issue isn't golf. (2002, November 21). *The New York Times*, p. A36.

Wood, J. V. (1989). Theory and research concerning social comparisons of personal attributes. *Psychological Bulletin, 106,* 231–248.

Zbaracki, M. J. (1998). The rhetoric and reality of total quality management. *Administrative Science Quarterly, 43,* 602–636.

Zeelenberg, M., van den Bos, K., van Dijk, E, & Pieters, R. (2002). The inaction effect in the psychology of regret. *Journal of Personality and Social Psychology, 82,* 314–327.

Zelditch, M. (2001). Theories of legitimacy. In J. T. Jost & B. Major (Eds.), *The psychology of legitimacy: Emerging perspectives on ideology, justice, and intergroup relations* (pp. 33–53). Cambridge, England: Cambridge University Press.

Zremski, J. (1996, June 5). Debt, falling membership threaten NRA's firepower. *The Buffalo News*, p. 1A.

Author Index

Subject Index

A

Acclaim Events
    achieving organizational goals,
        136–138
    recognition by industry analysts or
        evaluators, 134–136
Accounts
    accommodative, 23–24
    anticipatory accounts, 6, 23, 115–119
    content, 25–26
    defensive, 23–24
    entitlings, 6, 141–142, 148
    form, 22–25
    medium, 26–27
    progressive accounts, 85, 88
Affiliation with high–status groups, 33,
    141
Anticipated Controversies
    identity changes, 111
        new identity statements, 61,
            114–115, 128
        new products, services, or modes of
            operation, 112, 113
    upcoming performance reviews or
        rankings, 6
Apologies and reparative action, 22,
    65–66
Audiences
    external, 39–40
    internal, 40

Augusta National Golf Club case illustra-
    tion, 97–110

B

British Petroleum, 7, 163–167

C

Cadbury, 142
Catholic Church Sex Abuse Scandal and
    Cardinal Bernard Law, 157
Chrysler, 25, 58, 63
Consideration of audience concerns, 64,
    86, 88
Crisis Events
    accidents, 2, 5, 37, 52, 57–58
    product failures, 59–60
    scandals, 58–59

D

Denials of wrongdoing, 24, 61
Distinctive categorization, 28, 139–140

E

Evolving Controversies
    contentious negotiations, 82–83
    controversial identity changes, 83–84
Exxon, 3, 64, 70, 87–88